AUDIENCE CRITICISM
AND
THE HISTORICAL JESUS

BOOKS BY J. ARTHUR BAIRD
Published by THE WESTMINSTER PRESS

Audience Criticism and the Historical Jesus
The Justice of God in the Teaching of Jesus

AUDIENCE CRITICISM AND THE HISTORICAL JESUS

By J. ARTHUR BAIRD

THE WESTMINSTER PRESS   *Philadelphia*

BS
2555.2
.B267

Published by The Westminster Press ®
Philadelphia, Pennsylvania

PRINTED IN THE UNITED STATES OF AMERICA

PREFACE

Synoptic studies in many ways have reached an impasse. The standard methods of analysis of Textual, Source, Form, and Literary Criticism have taken us seemingly as far as they can. Redaction Criticism has had a recent vogue, but its results have been so contradictory that the method appears intrinsically weak because of its extreme subjectivity. One of the results of this situation has been the turning of Synoptic studies to the historical assessment of its results, or the cataloging of the various opinions of countless exegetes. This has produced a significant dearth of truly creative contributions to Synoptic criticism.

What is needed is an entirely new approach to the Synoptics that will reveal untapped layers of evidence and provide new policies for breaking through the encrustations of outdated axioms and the encysting effects of old evidence and hoary arguments too oft repeated. This book is an attempt in that direction. It points the way to a totally new stance and approach to the Synoptics, and suggests several novel tools for that purpose.

The major thrust of these pages is to understand the origin, validity, use, and meaning of the Synoptic audience phenomenon. The two corollaries to this are the exploitation of this new method for hermeneutical and then for historical analysis. In general this book will present a new " scientific " method of Synoptic analysis that takes seriously the text as its own tool for exegesis, the historical Jesus as the primary source of that text, and the audience tradition as a critical tool for examining both text and history.

In many ways this is a radical book. It challenges some of the most cherished axioms of modern scholarship, not on conservative, but on radical, critical grounds, on the hypothesis that critics have not been critical enough, and so-called liberals not liberal enough. It suggests that Biblical Criticism has not yet come of age by entering into the twentieth century with a carefully developed scientific methodology. This book intends to be critical, but when it presents a new and more positive estimate of the Synoptic logia, it will sound to some as if it were precritical. It claims to be theological, but the reader will be surprised to find it at times highly statistical. It purports to be exegetical, but much of the methological is based on premises that are highly homiletical. It combines traditional techniques of Synoptic study with the use of IBM computers in ways that will seem unusual to say the least.

This book is a companion volume to an earlier work, *The Justice of God in the Teaching of Jesus* (The Westminster Press, 1963). As a sequel, it should really be a prolegomena, for the methodology used in that book is what is spelled out and defended in this one. The basic limitation of the present work is that it deals primarily, and almost exclusively, with the logia material. The narrative is discussed only as a framework for the teachings of Jesus. My defense is twofold: in the first place, the nature of the study, the interrelation between audience and logion, demands this kind of fixation. But there is a more practical reason. There is a greater possibility of talking seriously about the historical Jesus on the basis of the logia than the more clearly editorial narration. This does not discount the narrative blocks as history, but is rather the approach of one who wishes to begin the scientific analysis of a difficult question on the most feasible grounds.

A second limitation has to do with the very statistics that constitute so much of the book. Any statistic of this kind must be surrounded by so many relativities, so many prejudgments, that no one can be taken with absolute literalness. They are comparative, descriptive, and necessarily relative; and if one despairs at making all tables correspond mathematically, it would be well to remember this fact.

It only remains to thank the many who have been part of this project. The College of Wooster, through grant and research leave, has continued to demonstrate a great liberal tradition and dedication to scholarly research. The University of Pittsburgh Computer Center, with its farsighted concern to apply the computer to the humanities, has made possible the application of technical facilities to Synoptic studies in ways that a poor scholar could never have afforded on his own. Two theological seminaries, Pittsburgh and San Francisco, have shown again their commitment to research in the gracious extension of their hospitality so important in the community of learning. I must mention Robert Tobey, colleague and longtime friend, who first suggested, and then made possible, my entrance into the mysteries of computer analysis. Then there is Mary, who in typing manuscript, as in all things, is my beloved companion.

This book is dedicated to the late Thomas Walter Manson, a man ahead of his time.

J. A. B.

San Anselmo, California

CONTENTS

KEY TO ABBREVIATIONS

I. SPEAKER

In the text where the simple D, DG, GO, and O are used, this refers to the *audience* to which a logion is directed (cf. Ch. II). Where the audience designator is preceded by the letter A, this refers to the *logion* addressed to that audience. All A designations indicate Jesus as speaker.

A	The logia tradition generally
AA	Audience is ambiguous
AD	Logion to the twelve disciples
ADG(AL)	Logion to the larger crowd of disciples
AGO	Logion to the opponent crowd
AO	Logion to the hard-core opponents
AN	Logion addressed to no special audience
A1	Logion addressed to the D plus DG
A2	Logion addressed to the D plus GO
A3	Logion addressed to the D plus O
A4	Logion addressed to the D plus DG plus GO
A5	Logion addressed to the D plus DG plus O
A6	Logion addressed to the D plus DG plus GO plus O
A7	Logion addressed to the DG plus O
A8	Logion addressed to the DG plus GO
A9	Logion addressed to the GO plus O
AX	Logion addressed to the GO plus O
AY	Logion addressed to the D plus GO plus O
E	The editorial tradition generally

EA	Speaker in the audience is ambiguous
ET	Editor of Matthew is the narrator
ER	Editor of Mark is the narrator
EK	Editor of Luke is the narrator
ED	One of the twelve disciples is speaking
EDG	One of the crowd of disciples is speaking
EGO	One of the crowd of opponents is speaking
EO	One of the hard core of opponents is speaking
EJ	John the Baptist is speaking
EQ	Quotation, primarily from the Old Testament

II. HISTORICAL SEQUENCE

These divisions are based on those found in the *Synopsis of the First Three Gospels,* by Albert Huck, Ninth Edition (Oxford: Basil Blackwell & Mott, Ltd., 1949).

H1	Infancy narratives
H2	Galilean period (HL, 1–136)
H3	Lucan travel narrative (HL, 137–186)
H4	Journey to Jerusalem (HL, 187–195)
H5	Days in Jerusalem (HL, 196–213)
H6	Synoptic Apocalypse (HL, 214–230)
H7	Passion Narrative (HL, 231–253)
H8	Postresurrection narratives (HL, 254–259)

III. SOURCE

The following is based primarily on the source analysis of Burnett Hillman Streeter, *The Four Gospels: A Study of Origins* (London: Macmillan & Co., Ltd., 1951). Some judgments, however, are necessarily my own.

S1	The Marcan source, whether in Mark, Matthew, or Luke
S2	The Q source: where Matthew and Luke are parallel
S3	The M source: Matthew's special material
S4	The L source: Luke's special material
S5	Matthew and Luke follow Mark, add material from Q
S6	Matthew follows Mark, adds from M

S7	Luke follows Mark, adds from L
S8	Matthew and Luke follow Q; Matthew adds from M
S9	Matthew and Luke follow Q; Luke adds from L

IV. FORM

These categories represent a somewhat arbitrary combination of those of Rudolf Bultmann, Martin Dibelius, and Vincent Taylor. Generally speaking, the judgments as to form are derived from Bultmann, *Die Geschichte der synoptischen Tradition* (Göttingen: Vandenhoeck & Ruprecht, 1957), although some are my own.

FA	Apothegm (paradigm, pronouncement story)
FS	Saying
FP	Parable
FM	Miracle Story
FL	Legend (novellen, tale, historical story)
FN	No Form

V. MISCELLANEOUS

AP	Anti-Pattern (Cf. Ch. VI)
MP	Metaphor Pattern (Cf. Ch. V)
PP	Praxis Pattern (Cf. Ch. V)
TP	Theological Pattern (Cf. Ch. VI)
WP	Word Pattern (Cf. Ch. V)

(a), (b), (c) Pattern quality categories

#1, #2, #3 Agreement-disagreement categories

Types of Comparison (last number in the Agreement sequence, Appendix A)

Type 1 Matthew vs. Luke
Type 2 Matthew and Mark vs. Luke
Type 3 Mark vs. Luke
Type 4 Matthew and Luke vs. Mark
Type 5 Luke vs. Mark
Type 6 Mark and Luke vs. Matthew
Type 7 Matthew vs. Mark vs. Luke
Type 8 Matthew vs. Mark

La	Literary agreement in logia sequence

Ha	Historical agreement (Cf. Ch. III)
Ga	Geographical agreement
Aa	Audience agreement
Wa	Wording agreement
JGTJ	*The Justice of God in the Teaching of Jesus,* by J. Arthur Baird (The Westminster Press, 1963)

Chapter I

A NEW PROBLEM OF SYNOPTIC CRITICISM

THE AUDIENCE PHENOMENON

The Synoptic Jesus was a skillful preacher and teacher. The common people heard him gladly, and the intellectuals gave him their highest compliment by challenging him to debate. It should be no surprise, therefore, to discover that he is pictured adapting his words to his audience. Such has been the hallmark of great preachers and teachers through the ages. Indeed one cannot escape the abundant reference to Jesus as a selective teacher. The words, " He who has ears to hear, let him hear," weave like a dominant theme throughout the Gospels (Matt. 11:15; 13:9, 15-16, 43; Mark 4:9, 23; 7:16; 8:18; Luke 8:8; 9:44; 14:35).

> "With many such parables he spoke the word to them, as they were able to hear it . . . but privately to his own disciples he explained everything." (Mark 4:33-34; cf. Matt. 13:34-35.)

> "To you has been given the secret of the kingdom of God, but for those outside everything is in parables." (Mark 4:11; cf. Matt. 13:13; Luke 8:10.)

" Not all men can receive this precept, but only those to whom it is given." (Matt. 19:11.)

" I thank thee, Father, Lord of heaven and earth, that thou hast hidden these things from the wise and understanding and revealed them to babes, . . . for such was thy gracious will." (Matt. 11:25-26; Luke 10:21.)

"Lord, are you telling this parable for us or for all? " (Luke 12:41.) " What I say to you I say to all: Watch." (Mark 13:37.)

" They perceived that he had told the parable *against* them." (Mark 12:12, italics mine.)

Jesus, his disciples, and the Gospel editors are all pictured as being conscious of the importance of the audience to which a particular saying was directed. Yet critical scholarship has not really taken the Gospels seriously at this point. The context of the Synoptic sayings of Jesus is regularly assumed to be undependable, and the audience as part of that context has been pretty much disregarded. At the beginning of this century, K. L. Schmidt convinced an entire critical generation of the undependability of the topography and chronology of the Synoptics.[1] Joachim Jeremias has insisted more recently that the audience of the parables is one of the most unstable of contextual elements, and this is now the common assumption.[2] Being trained in this critical tradition, I have been considerably surprised to discover that, in fact, one of the most stable elements in the Synoptics is a part of this very context, the audience tradition, which preserves the image of Jesus as a skillful preacher and teacher who adapts his teaching to his audience.

This image of Jesus as a selective teacher is nothing new to Synoptic scholarship, and has indeed produced through the years a storm of objection to the picture of a Jesus who would be so selective.[3] What constitutes a new problem is one clear fact emerging from my research. The Synoptic Gospels are replete with a curious fixation on the audience to which Jesus' logia are given, and this audience tradition is preserved by all Evangelists and all sources with an agreement and continuity so high as to raise many critical questions and open many " incredible " possibilities.

In this study I do not intend to examine the theological implications of this selectivity phenomenon, nor shall I raise the question at this point as to whether or not the historic Jesus actually said these things. The one question I have already discussed at length in my book *The Justice of God in the Teaching of Jesus*. The other will be dealt with in the last chapter. For the moment I am suggesting that we take the Evangelists at face value and entertain the hypothesis that Jesus did indeed adapt his teaching selectively to his audience. Then, with this hypothesis in mind, let us examine the Synoptics exhaustively to see to what extent they support or deny this image and what use, if any, can be made of the phenomenon. I shall attempt to penetrate as far back into the primitive history of the Synoptics as possible, beginning on the rather superficial level of what the editor obviously wants us to know about the audience. We shall then go deeper, into the use to which the various sources put the audience. Next we shall attempt to go below this level to that of the early church and its concern for the audience. At that point we shall examine the possibility of using Audience Criticism as a new tool for breaking through the faith of the church into the bedrock history of the actual words of Jesus. Whether or not this is possible, it will hopefully become apparent that in Audience Criticism we have a useful tool for throwing new light on all kinds of old questions, both hermeneutical and historical.

HISTORY OF AUDIENCE CRITICISM

This approach to the Synoptic material by way of audience classification is relatively untried. K. L. Schmidt, in his classic study of the Synoptic context, distinguishes within the audience the *Gegner, Volk, Anhänger,* and *Zwölf,* and even goes so far as to organize Luke's travel narrative according to audience classifications. But the only use he really makes of this is to note the differing audiences and to argue from this that the history and geography of the narrative do not describe " *eine bestimmte Situation.*" " *Dass*

. . . *zeigt, dass in der Überlieferung die verschiedenen Jesussprüche eine verschiedene Addressierung erfahren haben.*" [4] There is no real sense here of the audience as a critical tool, and its occurrence seems for Schmidt mostly the choice of the redactor.[5] Bultmann does go into the audience question briefly in *The History of the Synoptic Tradition,* but he is mostly concerned to point this out as a redactor's device. For him, the logia circulated essentially without audience reference: " a mixture of tradition and editing." [6]

It was not until 1931 that what I am calling Audience Criticism really made its entrance with the work of T. W. Manson. In his book, *The Teaching of Jesus,* he clearly stated the basic insight of this new approach: " Both as to matter and method the teaching of Jesus is conditioned by the nature of the audience." Manson identified " three distinct and readily distinguishable streams " of audience tradition: the polemical utterances directed mostly to scribes and Pharisees (P), those addressed to the disciples (D), and those spoken to the general public (G).[7] He then went on to give illustrations of certain characteristics of Jesus' teaching where, for example, Jesus " rarely if ever spoke directly of God as Father except to his disciples and . . . in this way only after Peter's Confession," or where he speaks of God as his Father only to the disciples, or observes that Jesus only spoke of the Kingdom of God as something into which men enter when talking to his disciples.[8] Manson thus uses the audience as a tool for deciding hermeneutic as well as historical questions.

In three appendixes he then went on to isolate certain words and phrases that appear only when Jesus is addressing a certain audience. In this pioneering work, Manson only gave what he called " a prima facie case for a detailed examination of the teaching with particular reference to the nature of the audience." What he really did was to point the way to the kind of consistent and exhaustive analysis that this present study attempts to be.

Since Manson's work, nothing of any consequence has been done with this audience phenomenon. Jeremias, in his book *Die Gleichnisse Jesu,* deals inevitably with the audience, but is more concerned to point out the constant changing of the audience, and concludes *"der Rahmen der Geschichte Jesu weithin sekundär ist."* [9] Perhaps the most sympathetic to this approach in recent years have been John Wick Bowman [10] and Oscar Cullmann, [11] but these scholars give more the impression of being informed and sympathetic regarding Manson's thesis than that of using the method themselves. W. L. Knox, in *The Sources of the Synoptic Gospels* (1953), uses Myer's concept of "The Twelve Sources" as a rubric under which to gather logia given to the disciples, but the only use he makes of this is to identify another written source behind Mark. Since then, to my knowledge, nothing has been done on this approach. In 1949, while working for my doctorate in Edinburgh, I came across further evidence for the usefulness of this method, and through the intervening years in research, as in correspondence with Professor Manson, I have been encouraged by the mounting evidence that here indeed is a " solid," demonstrable, and usable phenomenon. There is an unusually high percentage of agreement and continuity in the manner in which the Evangelists identify the audience to which Jesus addressed his teaching. This is an intensely curious phenomenon, and one that needs careful examination. It may be that this is mere coincidence. Or it may well be that this phenomenon reveals something significant about the Synoptics, about those who preserved them, and even about Jesus himself. The question now is, How does one get at such problems?

TOOLS OF SYNOPTIC RESEARCH

The criticism of the Synoptic Gospels has advanced today to the point of sophistication where there are many approaches one may take in Gospel analysis: Textual, Source, Form, Historical, and what I would call Literary Criticism have all contributed enormously to our understanding of the Synoptics. Although there is much overlapping, each approach concentrates on one particular type of data within the material. But underlying the different data, interests, and techniques, there seem to be four basic, logical tools common to all critical disciplines: the phenomena of agreement, disagreement, continuity, and discontinuity. These have been the logical cutting edges for laying bare the theology of the Synoptics as well as for breaking through to the history of Gospel formation and the early church. These four have been both hermeneutic and historical tools for all critical disciplines, usually without being consciously identified as such.

For example, textual critics for years have been using the tools of agreement and disagreement between the MSS. to get at the primitive text of the Gospels. The continuity within certain groups of MSS. has pointed to the probable existence of " families " of texts. Literary Criticism has also long used the principle of continuity to get at the theology of the Synoptics. The word study technique is based on this discovery of " patterns " of continuity running throughout the material in its use of words and ideas. Source Criticism, furthermore, is based on the observation of agreement and disagreement between the three Gospels as a means of identifying such underlying sources as the hypothetical Q. All of Streeter's criteria for the priority of Mark involve the application of the concepts of agreement and continuity. Mark's internal continuity in the use of primitive words and rough Greek, the agreement of Matthew and Luke with Mark on wording or sequence of events, all have been used as tools for establishing the historical priority of Mark. The continuity within these collections called Q, M, and L has served to " solidify " them as separate collections, to locate them, and to identify the types of persons responsible for their existence. Form Criticism has used the principle of continuity of form to get through the editorial level back to the early church that produced the Gospels, in effect saying that continuity of " form " reveals something about the early history of Gospel formation. Finally, the post-Bultmannian school of Redaction Criticism has pulled back from Bultmann's radical use of form to reveal the early *church* in action, and has concentrated on the early *editor,* using the principle of continuity to identify the mind and practice of the Evangelist. All these disciplines have consciously or unconsciously made use of these four basic logical tools: agreement, disagreement, continuity, and discontinuity.

THE METHOD OF THIS STUDY

In one sense, then, there is little new in the methodology used in this study. In another sense, however, we are exploring uncharted regions, and new methods must be devised. For this reason we must be somewhat more self-conscious about our methodology than would otherwise be the case. In a very real sense this entire analysis is a discourse on method. The relation of these methods to the question of history will be reserved for Chaper VII. Here we prefer to use other terms and let our philosophy of history emerge naturally out of our methodology. This is the reverse of the usual procedure, but is, in our opinion, a much more viable approach.

Scientific Biblical Criticism. The theoretical basis of this study lies in the author's conviction that the application of the scientific method to Biblical scholarship in a self-conscious and consistent way is long overdue. Despite one hundred years of supposedly scientific Biblical study, in many ways Biblical Criticism is still operating in a nineteenth-century atmosphere of deductive thinking, larded with a prioris, impatient of evidence, and unwilling to be tied down to the drudgery of a truly scientific discipline. More than a generation ago Wrede railed against exegetical subjectivity, against what he called " psychology " in interpretation, and called for an exegetical method that allowed for such psychology only between *" feste Punkte "* when one can control the possibilities and necessities.[12] Whatever be one's views on these matters, it would seem justified when setting off into uncharted waters to make careful use of a method that is as little dependent on the " psychology " of the explorer as possible. To this end I offer all that follows as an attempt to apply the scientific method to Synoptic Criticism.

As science is being defined today, there are two aspects to scientific study. The first is method, the second is what James Conant calls " policy." [13] The " scientific method " is generally considered to consist of empirical observation; controlled experiment; inductive reasoning, which is really a kind of " club sandwich " of in-

duction and deduction;[14] and the constant testing and retesting of
theory. This much is well known. The second aspect of the scientific approach, that of " policy," is perhaps less well understood.
As Conant explains it, science is a dynamic undertaking aimed at
" lowering the degree of empiricism." [15] This means that the construction of theories that take isolated phenomena and relate them
to the whole in some coherent way are also important aspects of
what can be called the scientific task. Furthermore, science as policy emerges to the extent " that new concepts arise from experiments and observations and these new concepts in turn lead to
further experiments and observation." The test of a truly " scientific " theory is its ability to suggest, stimulate, and direct experiment.[16] A truly " scientific " theory, therefore, would represent
a door, a breakthrough into new areas of research. This study is
concerned to use both scientific method and policy in attempting to
analyze the audience question.

The " Neutral Sense." It has been common among those who
exegete the Bible to begin with one of two presuppositions: either
the Bible is true until proven false or it is suspect until proven
valid. The first is the approach of the conservative fundamen-
talist whose motives may be worthy, but whose approach tends
to put him on the critical defensive, and make him too gullible
in favor of his initial presuppositions. The other represents the
unspoken stance of many so-called " liberal " critics, especially
of the last fifty years. They begin with the laudable ambition of
being free from the cloying restraints of conservative fundamen-
talism, but often tend to become fundamentalists themselves,
liberal fundamentalists, with a different set of presuppositions,
though equally gullible, equally on the defensive, and often much
more aggressive. In either case, this is deductive method, and the
results tend to be so colored by presuppositions that one can pretty
much tell what an exegete is going to conclude merely by knowing
where he went to school.

One of the most common sources of this kind of error is the
practice of atomistically analyzing individual passages according to

certain presubscribed canons of Source, Form, or Redaction Criticism before one then pulls them all together into any large conclusions under the misapprehension that whatever conclusions one draws will have been refined and corrected by technical analysis. On the surface this seems valid and is the usual way of approaching the Synoptic material today; but the problem is that this produces circular scholarship. One brings to the material a whole set of a priori judgments which he superimposes upon the text before ever allowing it to speak, as Wrede has said, " *aus ihrem eigenen Geiste,*" what the narrator himself wants his readers to know.[17] We tend to know ahead of time so much better what Jesus meant to say than what we find the text telling us he actually said. As Robert Funk charges, Historical Criticism has tended to become channeled into the service of its own presuppositions.[18] So the material is judged in advance on the basis of external axioms and one's conclusion merely illustrates the a priori. The exegete has programmed the text to talk his own language. This is the opposite of scientific induction. Instead, I propose that as we begin our exegesis, we take the Synoptics at their word and in a " neutral " sense. They are neither true nor false until out of an exhaustive, empirical observation of the total text, certain probabilities emerge, which then must be checked against every existing canon of criticism. This neutral sense must be the constant guide of any truly scientific exegesis.

This means that we must be extremely cautious about propounding axiomatic canons of Biblical Criticism. Who is not guilty at that point? It means that every critical axiom is on trial every time we approach the text in a scientific way. It is this constant review of basic axioms which is as typical of the scientific spirit and as productive of creative advance as any element in this method. One has only to remember how long the phlogiston theory, considered axiomatic by an entire scientific generation, held back the modern understanding of the composition of matter. Circular critical logic is the bane of Biblical studies, and perhaps more than anything prevents us from the kinds of scientific breakthroughs that are needed. The fact that so many of our best modern minds are spending their time writing histories of exegesis instead of doing creative exegesis themselves, are consolidating and assessing the supposed gains of the last fifty years instead of challenging and rechallenging every critical axiom, is the chief illustration in our time of the stalling of exegesis in its own axioms, and the need for a scientific revolution to clear the way for further advance.

" Horizontal " Analysis. Traditionally the Synoptics have been examined in what might be called " vertical " fashion, in terms of large, more or less self-contained units such as a particular manuscript, a source, a particular Gospel with its redactional characteristics, comparing each to the other, and drawing conclusions as to the meaning and history of the material from patterns revealed in such parallel comparison. This kind of analysis has been extremely fruitful since the days of Tatian's diatessaron, and in any scientific exegetical method it must continue. What I am suggesting is that such analysis must be augmented by a more " horizontal " type of study that cuts across the various Gospel sources and manuscripts according to certain other standards of comparison. The Q hypothesis illustrates this in Source Criticism, for here was a source that presumably cut across Matthew and Luke, and perhaps Mark as well. In its own way this was a breakthrough. The Form Critics introduced a new analysis factor in the matter of form that cut horizontally across all sources in terms of this new standard. The result was the breakup of the large blocks of material into *Einzelstücke,* along the lines pioneered by Wellhausen, Schmidt, and others, and this has proved to be another breakthrough in Biblical study. Whatever scholars think of the conclusions to which various Form Critics came, it would seem pretty well agreed among critical minds that this *Einzelstücke* insight is essentially sound. In the study that follows, I shall act upon the hypothesis that this is a valid method and treat the logia as a collection of originally independent sayings attributed to Jesus, brought together in various ways and included in various sources (cf. Appendix A). Another use of this horizontal type of analysis will be that of the category of audience, cutting as it does across all sources and Gospels, from

a horizontal angle. It would seem that any method that attempts to be truly empirical must examine the Synoptics both vertically and horizontally in terms of all the available criteria. What I am proposing is a new horizontal criterion.

Exhaustive Analysis. But there is a great danger in the modern " atomistic " approach to the Synoptics. When one studies the Gospels in terms of individual units, one is liable to get a lopsided view, or to miss some important insight because of the narrowness of his study. What I am proposing is an exhaustive, comprehensive principle of exegesis that begins its study with a total survey of every bit of possible evidence bearing on a particular problem. This reveals phenomena that can only be discovered in this massive way. Neither history nor persons operate like a mathematical formula, always producing in each instance the same results. But statistical averages of a large sampling of material do reveal the subtleties of phenomena that occur " usually " or always in " most " situations; or that always occur, but in the vicissitudes of transmission and study only turn up " most " of the time. Such insights are much more likely to be historical or true to persons than ones based solely on an intensive study of isolated passages. This only works, of course, if there are enough examples to give one a fair cross section, and in the case of the Gospels the built-in problem of their status as selections places a special burden on the exegete for an exhaustive coverage of every word and passage possibly bearing on any particular problem. This means that any a priori selectivity on my part of what would or would not be applicable represents selectivity twice confounded. Inevitably in any historical-literary analysis there is a built-in factor of subjectivity and error, and the Biblical exegete need make no special apologies. All we can do is hope to reduce the angle of error and indeterminacy, and it would seem that the broadest of sampling is a sound application of the scientific principle of empiricism.

" Pattern " Analysis. The refinement of the exhaustive approach to Synoptic exegesis leads us to the " pattern " concept. It is at this

point that empiricism and scientific policy unite to identify objective reality, for this is what we are after: to so reduce the angle of subjective error that there will be a reasonable probability of our discovering what the Evangelists said about the audience, what the sources said, what the early church believed, and finally what Jesus himself probably said and did with this audience factor. For something to have this kind of objective identity, there are at least three qualities it must possess: it must be *unique* in that it is distinguishable from other aspects of reality; it must demonstrate a *regularity* in the impression it gives the viewer; and it must be sufficiently *permanent* to make it probable that it will be there when sought. The "pattern" is the phenomenon resulting from the uniqueness, regularity, and permanence that identify a focal point of reality. Thus Darwin through exhaustive observation identified certain laws, statistical averages, or patterns of the biological world. Thus the chemist identifies the existence of a new element, the astronomer a new star, or the historian the believable character and activity of a figure of history. Presumably things that exist act according to a certain regularity that is the basic clue to their identity and very existence. It is this which enables the scientist to manipulate them in repeatable experiments. The pattern is a device that transfers isolated empirical observations into scientific "policy" and leads to the probability of historical reality. The pattern sets the standard for determining what is authentic or not. Anything contrary to a scientifically induced pattern becomes suspect as nonauthentic. This principle, I take it, is what Bultmann was using when he argued from some "typical expression" of Jesus for or against its authenticity.[19] Or this is what Harvey refers to as the "unintentional data" which emerges between the lines as some of the most valuable of historical evidence.[20]

The principle we are enunciating is that of working from the known, observable, empirical data back to the unknown, and thus through the empirical trying to eliminate empiricism by finding a pattern, a law, a principle that explains the phenomena. That is, we are proceeding from science as empirical method to science as policy. But now we must go farther. For the pattern to be used as a scientific tool, it must be thoroughly disciplined lest it become just another device prostituted to the " psychology " of the researcher. I would suggest to that end the following principles:

1. The pattern by its very nature must emerge from the testimony of more than one witness.
2. The witnesses must not be dependent on each other.
3. The pattern must be readily observable by all observers, whatever their presuppositions, and must be the result of a minimum of interpretation.
4. The pattern must be repeatable and capable of manipulation and verification by any competent observer.
5. The pattern is most defensible when it cuts across all the available sources of information, especially when they are known to diverge from one another at various points.
6. The pattern is most defensible when it emerges inadvertently as " unconscious data."
7. The pattern is most defensible when it involves ideas or practices too subtle or complex to have been understood and consciously reproduced by the original reporter.
8. The pattern is most defensible when it is discontinuous with the known beliefs of the reporter.
9. The pattern will be most correctly interpreted when the number of viable alternatives are at an absolute minimum.

What we have been saying is that for these patterns to have meaning there must be enough limiting factors to provide the bounds for a controlled experiment, and a disciplined conclusion. These bounds must make sense in terms of the data sought: that is, the controls must be of such a nature as to permit the emergence of *meaningful* uniqueness, permanence, and regularity within what Toulmin might call the particular " field of argument " peculiar to that data.[21] For example, for a certain word to appear fifty times in the New Testament says little except that it is a term common to the first century, unless this term occurs only in the New Testament, in which case this would tell us that it was peculiar to the Christian church — but no more, unless the word or idea occurred only in the Synoptics, which would then tell us that it was probably in some way restricted to the kind of language coming out of the particular environment producing the Synoptics. If the word were further controlled by being limited to the words of Jesus, and further to his teaching to a particular audience, and further to his teaching to a particular audience about a particular subject, then the narrowing of the controls would restrict the possible field of meaning of this phenomenon, and one could say with an increasing degree of probability that this word represented an authentic word of some historic figure who operated in these ways. If the pattern occurred throughout the Gospels, that would more likely point either to the entire church or to the historical Jesus than to editorial activity. If the pattern occurred in all sources and contradicted the obvious beliefs of those sources, then this would more likely be the reflection of someone other than the source or editor. That is, if it became more difficult to believe that this pattern was the reflection of editor or community than of an authentic individual, we would be driven behind the editorial, ecclesiastical situation to bedrock in the mind and person of the historic Jesus. Thus it is in the scientific application of this " pattern " principle, based on exhaustive analysis of the individual units of the Synoptics as they exhibit the characteristics of agreement, disagreement, continuity, and discontinuity that we shall seek for the meaning, use, and authentic history of this audience phenomenon.

Computer Analysis. The Synoptic application of this scientific method demands some new tools, especially when it comes to the kind of exhaustive study I have been describing. After spending one whole summer on such an exhaustive audience analysis of *basileia tou theou,* it became painfully apparent that there were not enough years for any man to follow such a method. As a result, I was forced to seek mechanical aid, in this case a 7070 computer. As far as I know, this is the first time anyone has ever applied the computer to " content analysis " of the Bible.[22] The work of Andrew Q. Morton and James McLeman is well known, and when Morton sticks to his scientific method in researching the authorship of the Pauline corpus, his statistics come as welcome relief into a discussion long befogged with the mists of debate, homiletics, and special pleading.[23] It is unfortunate, however, that this first significant use of the computer for New Testament study was marred by Morton's own special pleading for a Biblical skepticism that had nothing to do with the evidence of his scientific study.[24]

My use of the computer has involved the editing of the Synoptic text for history, source, form, and audience, and the placing of the transliterated Greek text on computer tape. This was then run through the 7070 computer and three print-outs obtained, which arranged this information in various ways.[25] The basic method of this study has of course been eighteen years of slow research along traditional lines, such as Manson outlined and demonstrated in *The Teaching of Jesus* (pp. 20–21). It is only within the last year that this computer technique has been available to me. This has meant that within the last six months I have done more detailed Synoptic research than in the previous seventeen years. The basic tool that has given wings to my study is a concordancelike print-out where every word of the text, every time it is used, is arranged alphabetically; and opposite each usage in parallel columns are listed the reference, the speaker-audience relationship, the historic point, the source, and the form appropriate for that word. As a result, patterns of various kinds have become immediately apparent: patterns, I might add, that are the result of such an exhaustive cross section that they would not be observable in any other way. With this tool, the Synoptics have become a new world for one who thought he knew something about them. With this new technique, there is a possibility of Synoptic analysis achieving a measure of scientific accuracy. The work to follow in this book has been thoroughly informed by this computerized synopsis.

Probability Analysis. A final word must be said here for a new concept to appear in Biblical exegesis. If we are going to try to get exegesis on some scientific basis, and especially if we are to engage in exhaustive analysis with the aid of computers, we come up inevitably against a mathematical problem. Even as Wittgenstein saw the inevitable mathematical basis for logic, so must the scientific exegete take into account the mathematical nature of whatever judgments he makes on the basis of his study. One assumption that appears in all works on this subject is that all the scientist can talk about is the " probability " that some conclusion is accurate. For one to be absolutely certain about a conclusion, one would have to know all the phenomena possible of being known, and this, to put it scientifically, is " improbable." To see how far New Testament exegesis is from this ideal, one has only to pick up almost any commentary and read at random: " without a doubt," " there can be no question," " it is obvious that," " it is absolutely certain." There is no field of human thought farther from scientific discipline, at the moment, than that of Biblical exegesis. Here questions are begged with blithe innocence. Assertion replaces evidence and the student of exegesis is either turned into an eclectic, building " Rube Goldberg " theology from unrelated conclusions, or he retreats to the history of exegetical opinions or to a plaintive relativism, because exegetes simply won't spell out their evidence and give him something to use in making up his own mind. There are, of course, notable exceptions; but for all its bright, creative promise, critical exegesis has not gone very far in *method* beyond the first faint stirrings of the Cartesian revolution. Prooftexting continues, only now used perhaps most aggressively by militant liberals in defense of " critical orthodoxy." Deductive logic still abounds, undisciplined by empirical analysis. Declamation replaces solid creative and responsible work, and towering critical superstructures are built on foundations that one has not built himself, or tested himself, or recognized sufficiently as experimental and provisional. *Probability,* the " law " that is recognized to be only a *statistical average,* is all that the scientific method will permit.

Now probability is a thoroughly mathematical concept. Harvey defines it as " a way of talking about the degree of force a conclusion is believed to have by virtue of the given data and warrants." [26] The philosophical discussion over probabilities is beyond the scope of this book, nor is it necessary. For our practical purposes, it will be sufficient to quote two statements that have had a determinative effect on the modern use of probability. The first is by J. Venn, to the effect that probabilities that are based on statistical frequencies are alone capable of accurate measurement.[27] The second is the so-called Bernoulli-Laplace rule: " The probability of the occurrence of a set of mutually exclusive, yet ' equiprobable ' possible events is the ratio of the number of favorable possibilities (f) to the total number of all possibilities (f + u). The determination of an event's ' equiprobability ' proceeds by way of a priori considerations, indeed prescriptions, concerning the phenomena in question." [28] This simply means that with a well-made six-sided die, the probability of rolling any number is one in six. This simple rule of thumb will be used where appropriate in the following pages as we now turn to the demonstration of the above methods for analyzing a " new problem " of Synoptic Criticism.

Chapter II

THE IDENTIFICATION OF JESUS' AUDIENCE

One fact is inescapable. The Evangelists were intensely concerned to identify the audience that surrounded Jesus at any given moment. From the account of Jesus' entrance into Galilee until his ascension, Huck-Lietzmann's Synopsis divides the Synoptics into 422 separate units.[1] In 395, or 94 percent, of these the audience is clearly designated by the editor. Within these units there are approximately 352 individual logia of Jesus, of which 98 percent are clearly identified as to audience.[2] The general picture is one of an audience that is constantly shifting, often multilayered, with one audience sometimes blended into another, but where the Evangelist rarely allows the reader to lose sight of the particular groups present, and especially the specific audience to which a saying of Jesus is immediately directed. It is as if attached to each logion as it came to the Gospel writer, whether in oral or written form, was some indication of audience that was peculiarly important in the reporting of the tradition.

There are two basic types of audience identification: the one clearly by the Evangelist in narrative or editorial comment. We shall deal with these in the present chapter. The other type comes in the logia of Jesus, and these will be discussed later. Within both narrative and logia there are four basic audiences consistently described: the Twelve, the " crowd " of disciples, the opponent crowd, and the opponents. These represent concentric circles of Jesus' listeners, in terms of their closeness to, their understanding of, their sympathy for, him. In the general narrative sections the audience is usually many-faceted and one gets the impression that the editor is merely trying to be very exact in his historical description. At those points where the audience provides the setting for a logion, the audience is usually single and seems to have not only historical but hermeneutic significance for the editor. With a few exceptions (e.g., the temptation) one can probably assume that the editors believe that some of the Twelve were always present,[3] and the crowds or the larger group of disciples are often seen vaguely in the background. Whatever the complexity of the context, the Evangelists are usually careful to single out one of these four groups as the recipient of Jesus' teaching.

THE TWELVE DISCIPLES (D)

The most significant audience is that of the twelve disciples which we shall call D.[4] The Evangelists seem especially concerned to distinguish this from that larger group surrounding Jesus. They are the ones who formed the core of his missionary activity. To them he gave authority (Matt. 18:18). To them he explained his parables (Mark 4:33-34). It was for them that he reserved " the secret of the kingdom of God " (Mark 4:10-12). This theme so clearly enunciated by all of the Gospel writers comes to sharpest focus in the Lucan version of the call to the Twelve: " And when it was day, he called his disciples, and chose from them twelve, whom he named apostles " (Luke 6:13; cf. Mark 3:13-14, Matt. 10:1). There is a question often raised as to whether or not this represents authentic history. Actually there are two questions, and they should be decided separately. The one has to do with Jesus' use of a term translated, " disciple " or " apostle," and the other with whether or not

Jesus actually did select some such group as an inner circle.[5] One could perhaps agree that the abundant and restrictive use of *apostolos* was peculiar to the later period without necessarily denying that Jesus entertained some such *concept,* or separated out some such *group.*

Actually at this place in our discussion these questions are irrelevant. The point I am making is that the *Evangelists* want us to know, what *they* presumably believed, that Jesus did select a special inner circle. Later I shall attempt to show that the most convincing evidence for his actually doing so comes not from the occurrence of particular words like *apostolos,* but from the results of a massive study of audience, theology, vocabulary, and praxis patterns in the logia of Jesus. Then we shall see a difference between the Evangelists' more authoritarian concept of the Twelve and that of Jesus. The key to this approach lies in distinguishing what the Evangelists wrote in the clearly editorial material and what they quote Jesus as saying in the logia material. Failure to make this distinction causes much confusion in Synoptic study (cf. Chapter V).

The testimony of the Evangelists to this D group is seen in the following evidence. The abundance of it would seem to witness to their concern that we be aware of this distinction.

mathetai (Matt. 8:21; 13:10; 14:15, 19, 22, 26; 15:12, 23, 32, 33; 16:5, 13, 20; 17:6, 10, 13, 19; 18:1; 19:10, 13, 23, 25; 21:1, 6, 20; 24:3; 26:8, 17, 18, 19, 26, 35, 36, 40, 45, 56; Mark 4:34; 6:1, 41; 8:1; 9:14; 10:10, 13, 24; 14:16; Luke 9:16, 18, 54; 10:22, 23; 16:1; 17:22; 18:15; 19:29; 20:45; 22:39, 45)

mathetai autou (Matt. 8:23; 9:10, 11, 19, 37; 12:1, 49; 13:36; 23:1; 24:1; 26:1; Mark 2:15, 16; 3:7, 9; 6:35, 45; 7:2, 17; 8:4, 6, 10, 27, 33; 9:29, 31; 10:23, 46; 11:1, 14; 12:43; 13:1; 14:4, 12, 13, 32; 16:7; Luke 7:11, 19; 8:9, 22; 9:14, 43; 11:1; 12:1; 17:1)

dodeka matheton (Matt. 26:20)

dodeka mathetas autou (Matt. 10:1; 11:1; 16:21, 24)

dodeka (Matt. 10:5; 20:17; 26:14, 47; Mark 3:14, 16; 4:10; 6:7; 8:19; 9:35; 10:32; 11:11; 14:10, 17, 20, 43; Luke 2:42; 6:13; 8:1; 9:1, 12; 18:31; 22:3, 47)

dodeka apostolon (Matt. 10:2)
dodeka hous kai apostolous onomasen (Luke 6:13)
apostoloi (Mark 6:30; Luke 9:10; 17:5; 22:14; 24:10)
hendeka (Mark 16:14; Luke 24:9, 33)
hendeka mathetai (Matt. 28:16)
deka (Matt. 20:24; Mark 10:41)
heis ton meta Iesou (Matt. 26:51)

Mark 3:16-19 [6]	Matt. 10:2-4	Luke 6:14-16
Simon Petros	*Simon ho legomenos*	*Simona hon kai*
Iakobos	*Petros*	*onomasen Petron*
Ioanes	*Andreas*	*Andreas*
Andreas	*Iakobos*	*Iakobos*
Philippos	*Ioanes*	*Ioanes*
Bartholomaios	*Philippos*	*Philippos*
Matthaios	*Bartholomaios*	*Bartholomaios*
Thomas	*Thomas*	*Matthaios*
Iakobon ton tou	*Matthaios ho telones*	*Thomas*
Halphaiou	*Iakobos ho tou*	*Iakobon Halphaiou*
Thaddaios	*Halphaiou*	*Simona ton kalou-*
Simona ton	*Thaddaios*	*menon Zeloten*
Kananaion	*Simon ho Kananaios*	*Ioudas Iakobou*
Ioudas Iskarioth	*Ioudas ho Iskariotes*	*Ioudas Iskarioth*

The terms above serve the Evangelists to separate this inner circle from those other groups which extend out from Jesus in decreasing sympathy or increasing opposition. There appears to be no sharp distinction one can draw between the general terms, and their interchangeability is neatly illustrated at one point where the Marcan material seems to have been slightly modified by the other Evangelists.[7]

Matt. 26:20	Mark 14:17	Luke 22:14
dodeka matheton	*dodeka*	*apostoloi*

For the Gospel writers these various terms represent a type of person, one specially set apart, to whom Jesus spoke in particular ways. The Evangelists are more concerned to identify them as a

group than as individuals by name, although, of course, at times
this does occur. This concern becomes even clearer when we discover the editors giving us a character study of these disciples that
contains several patterns of clear continuity. There are thirty-five
units of editorial material containing sayings of the D, either in
direct or indirect address. Almost all of them come in dialogue
where the D are alone with Jesus. There are three terms peculiar
to this stratum: *diasaphisan, epistates,* and *potapos.* These words
pretty well epitomize the four basic patterns characterizing this
group: (1) their lack of understanding,[8] (2) their sense of wonder,[9]
(3) their persistent disbelief,[10] (4) their opposition to Jesus.[11] All
three Gospels and most of the sources converge at these four points.
Generally speaking, this is not a complimentary picture. The most
consistent image is their lack of understanding of most of the major
elements of Jesus' mission and message: his meaning and use of
parables, the nature of the Kingdom of God, his concept of the
eschaton, his death and resurrection, his self-conscious identity.
They are narrowly Judaistic. They lack faith in him, or in what he
teaches, and are constantly amazed, surprised, and afraid of his
powers. They do not seem to appreciate him. They are nervously
concerned over what the officials are thinking about Jesus and are
afraid to antagonize them. They are more interested in the rewards
of the Kingdom than in its demands. They are vain, weak, vengeful,
constantly at odds with Jesus, either through lack of understanding
or downright opposition to his own concept of mission and message. The image of Jesus which the D most willingly accepts is that
of " Lord " (*kurios*), " teacher " and " prophet," rejecting his role
as sufferer, radical critic, healer, and miracle worker. The Evangelists all give us a picture of an inner circle that was a constant
source of disappointment to Jesus, and we can see a kind of summary response to them in Mark 9:19: " O faithless generation, . . .
how long am I to bear with you? " [12] The decidedly negative picture of the D contained in this stratum suggests a surprisingly
candid and even unsympathetic view of the Twelve by those who
preserved this material.

THE "CROWD" OF DISCIPLES (DG)

The clarity of the D as a separate audience category comes to even sharper focus when it is distinguished from a larger group of disciples who, as Mark says, were " about him with the twelve " (4:10). These are identifiable when we find Jesus surrounded by a large crowd of sympathetic listeners who seem to rely on him for healing, instruction, and leadership, who defer to him as " teacher " and " master " and from whom he recruits not only the Twelve (Luke 6:13), but the Seventy (Luke 10:1 ff.) and others who serve him in various capacities. We shall call this the DG audience. The Evangelists are as concerned to identify them as they are the Twelve, so much so that their efforts often appear strained and awkward. There are ten types of persons the Gospel writers seem to place in this category.

1. Those who were with the Twelve.

mathetai

Matt. 8:21, *heteros de ton matheton* describes a man who offered to follow Jesus, but who first had to go bury his father and who presumably did not become one of the inner circle. Did Jesus have some refusals in his recruiting of the D? Luke calls this man simply *heteron*.

Mark 4:34, *tois idiois mathetais* concludes the section which Mark has introduced with *hoi peri auton sun tois dodeka*. This is one place where those to whom he explained his parables seem to be in this larger DG audience. This illustrates the difficulty the editor had at times in distinguishing D from DG.

Matt. 12:49, *mathetas autou* is defined by Jesus as " whoever does the will of my Father " and Mark identifies them as *ochlos* (3:32).

Mark 8:34 is an illustration of the difficulty the Evangelists had in distinguishing D and DG. Mark identifies the audience as *ton ochlon sun tois mathetais autou*, Matthew calls them *mathetas autou*, and Luke, *pantas*. The sympathetic nature of the crowd identifies them as DG.

Matt. 5:1; Luke 6:20 are both illustrations of where a series of connected logia are bounded on the left by *hoi mathetai autou* and on the right by *ochlos (laos)*. Matthew tries to mitigate the confusion by adding *ochlos* (5:1). Again, the sympathetic nature of this audience argues for their being DG: "You are the salt of the earth" (5:13).

allon hoi esan met auton
Mark 1:36 pictures Simon and others disturbing Jesus' prayer in a lonely place. Luke calls them *hoi ochloi* (4:42). This is presumably too early in the ministry for the D to have a clear identity.

Mark 2:15 gives us a picture of Jesus sitting at table, and the editor is concerned to distinguish between the "many who followed him," identified as tax collectors and sinners, and *tois mathetais autou*, clearly DG distinguished from D.

heterous hebdomekonta. The disciple character of these whose "names are written in heaven" is clear (Luke 10:1, 17).

hoi peri auton sun tois dodeka (Mark 4:10, 34). Here Mark clearly wants to include these as *mathetais*, but distinguish them from the Twelve.

hendeka kai tous sun autois. The postresurrection group hiding in Jerusalem includes DG (Luke 24:33).

plethos ton matheton (Luke 19:37). Luke's description of a multitude of disciples (DG) is supported by Mark's *polloi* (11:8) and Matthew's *ochloi* (21:9).

tois hendeka kai pasin tois loipois. Luke 24:9 makes this neat distinction between D and DG while Matt. 28:8 simply calls them *mathetais autou*.

2. Certain women "of our company." The orientation toward the L source is striking.

gunaikes, tines ex hemon (Luke 24:22).

Thugateres Ierousalem (Luke 23:28). Their obvious sympathy puts them in the category of DG.

Maria, Martha (Luke 10:38-42).

gune ek tou ochlou (Luke 11:27), " Blessed is the womb that bore you."

gunaikes hai sunakolouthousai auto (Luke 23:49; Mark 15:40-41; Matt. 27:55-56). Mark adds a significant detail, *kai diekonoun auto.* This appears to be a large company of women who probably had much more to do with the DG than is generally believed. (Cf. also Luke 23:26-32; 7:36-50; 7:11-17.)

3. Those saved by Jesus who became followers. The importance of this group is seen by the sharp detail surrounding certain classic examples such as Zacchaeus (Luke 19:1-10) and Bartimaeus (Mark 10:46-52).

4. Certain ones following Jesus who almost followed him " wherever you go " (Luke 9:57). This whole section in Luke and its parallel in Mark gives a picture of three such men who called Jesus " Lord " and " teacher " and are described as genuinely interested in his challenge to discipleship. There must have been many such, for example, the rich young ruler (Matt., ch. 19), and these we are calling DG, for the editors seem to wish to identify them, yet keep them separate from the D.

5. Those following Jesus in the crowd.

to akolouthounti auto ochlo (Luke 7:9). The RSV translates this " the multitude that followed him."

ochlos polus (Luke 7:11). Here the " crowd [who] went with him " are distinguished from the *mathetai,* and also from the *ochlos tes poleos* who came out with the bereaved widow. The same distinction seems to be made in Matt. 21:10, where *pasa he polis* ask, " Who is this? " and are answered by *hoi de ochloi* to the effect that he is " the prophet Jesus from Nazareth of Galilee " (v. 11). Their knowledge of him and the word " prophet " identifies them as DG.

ochlos polus matheton autou (Luke 6:17) is distinguished from *plethos polu tou laou.* Both of these can be called DG according to our definition. Luke's distinction seems to be geographic.

ochlos. The most common use of this term in all the Synoptics is to refer to those who show the basic sympathy and receptivity to Jesus which identifies them as DG. This is not always clear, for as we shall see, *ochlos* is also used for another type of audience. This is the crowd the opponents fear because of its sympathy for Jesus (Mark 12:12; Luke 20:16; Matt. 21:45).

laos. Only Luke uses this term to refer to DG (6:17, 20 to 7:29; 20:9, 19).

6. Friends or parents of the sick or demented who are credited with "faith." The centurion (Luke 7:1-10), Jairus (Mark 5:21-43), the man with the epileptic son (Mark 9:14-29), the Syrophoenician woman (Mark 7:24-30), all seem to be persons with faith not only in God, but in Jesus' power to heal: "Truly, . . . not even in Israel have I found such faith" (Matt. 8:10).

7. The sick or demented who are healed where there is a record of "faith" as part of the healing. Examples are the woman with the flow of blood (Matt. 9:20-22), the Samaritan leper (Luke 17:11-19), the Gerasene demoniac (Mark 5:1-20), and Bartimaeus who clearly followed him (Mark 10:46-52).

8. Certain godly individuals whose religious experience made them receptive to Jesus.

hekatontarches (Luke 7:2). Here is one described as *axios* (v. 5), whom Jesus then compliments for *tosauten pistin.*

Iaeiros (Mark 5:21-43) was an *archisunagogos* whom Jesus characterizes as a "man of faith" (v. 36).

huios eirenes (Luke 10:6). This characterizes the receptive home where the gospel will be received, and where the disciple's peace will descend. Matthew calls this *he oikia axia* (10:13).

matheteutheis te basileia (Matt. 13:52). This little parable very possibly describes the experience of godly scribes who responded to Jesus' message but did not wish to let go "what is old."

en prosdechomenos ten basileian tou theou (Mark 15:43). Here is Joseph of Arimathea whose devotion outshone Peter's at this moment of crisis.

tines ton grammateon (Luke 20:39). Here is a scribe who is impressed with Jesus. For other evidence of scribes " not far from the kingdom," Mark 12:34; cf. 15:43; Matt. 8:19-20; 13:52; Mark 9:14.

pas ho laos akousas kai hoi telonai edikaiosan ton theon, baptisthentes to baptisma Ioanou (Luke 7:29). These are contrasted sharply with the Pharisees and lawyers in terms of their acceptance of the purpose of God.

presbuterous ton Ioudaion (Luke 7:3). These elders appear to have faith in Jesus' healing power.

Simon ho Pharisaios (Luke 7:36-50). Simon is sympathetic enough to invite Jesus to dinner. There must have been much in common between Jesus and the Pharisees despite his violent denunciations.[18]

9. Certain religiously despised individuals for whom Jesus seems to have had great sympathy, and from whose numbers he recruited some for the Kingdom.

telonai kai hamartoloi (Luke 15:1). Here Luke identifies the sympathetic audience as one of religious outcasts. This situation occurs in all sources, either as editorial material (Matt. 21:32) or in the logia of Jesus (Mark 2:15; Luke 7:34; 5:32; 15:7; 18:10; 19:2; Matt. 21:31). This refinement of the DG audience is especially prominent in the Lucan source and in logia to the opponent audience.

10. The John the Baptist contingent (Mark 1:1-6; 3:11-12; Luke 3:7-9, 10-14; 7:18-23). There is a real question as to where to put this group. At times they seem almost like opponents (Mark 2:18; Luke 7:28), but the record of Jesus' approval (Luke 7:24 f.) suggests a basic sympathy. A continuing contact between Jesus and John's disciples after John's death is suggested by Matt. 14:12.

The listing above suggests a rather large group of those on whom Jesus could count for support and a sympathetic hearing, and the Evangelists are concerned to delineate them carefully as a type of disciple. These would be the crowds which, along with the Twelve, he taught on the mountain or fed beside the sea. This category covers a spectrum all the way from active discipleship to active criticism, but all with one thing in common: a basic receptivity to Jesus without being one of the Twelve. This whole human stratum represents an important facet of the early church, what one might call a kind of primitive laity.

The importance of this category for the Evangelists is supported by forty-two dialogue units where the words of the DG are reproduced in direct discourse. Out of this material certain patterns emerge that identify a kind of " collective type " of disciple. Two predominant patterns are present: (1) these are men and women of faith; (2) they have a high regard for Jesus. Curiously enough the Synoptic editorial material gives a much more complimentary picture of the DG than it does of the D. These are humble, worthy lovers of Israel, God-fearing, repentant men who do the will of God, whose names are written in heaven, while the D are called *oligopistoi* (Matt. 14:31) and are constantly pictured under the cloud of a contrasting negative. The sinners, the demon-possessed, the sick, the corrupt, the Samaritans, the Greeks, the soldiers, and even certain Jewish officials are much more receptive to Jesus' healing mission than are the Twelve. The Seventy seem to be more successful at healing than the Twelve (Luke 10:17-20; Mark 9:18). While the D and the DG call Jesus " teacher " and " prophet," the DG also refer to him as the " one who is to come," the " Holy One of God," the " Son of God," the " Christ," " God visiting his people." Some, of course, were reluctant to follow him (Luke 9:59), but the fact remains that the picture the Evangelists all want us to have is of men and women of deep religious sensitivity and experience, with education, ability, wealth, and power who responded to Jesus with amazing insight and served him faithfully, even to the end. When viewed against the contrasting picture of the D, this is an extremely curious fact.

That the later church was aware of such a larger group of disciples is clear from Eusebius, who has a paragraph on " the Apostles and the Seventy Disciples." [14] " And upon examination you will find that there were evidently disciples of the Savior over and above the 70, if you take the testimony of Paul, who said that after rising from the dead he appeared first to Cephas, afterwards to the Twelve, and after them to above five hundred brethren at once. . . . There were very many apostles." He knows of no extant list of the *hebdomekonta,* but finds evidence in the Bible, Clement, and certain legendary material for naming Barnabas, Sosthenes, Matthias, and Thaddaeus. There is a tradition in the Gospel of Matthias, quoted by Clement, that Zacchaeus was the Matthias referred to in Acts 1:23. Beyond these, and those listed above, one might mention Nicodemus (John, ch. 3), Prochorus, Nicanor, Timon, Parmenas (Acts 6:5), and Joseph called Barsabbas (Acts 1:23) as possible candidates. However this may be, it is apparent from the Synoptics that the DG were a large, capable, at times deeply committed and important part of the earliest Christian fellowship, and the Evangelists go out of their way to identify them as a distinct group.

THE OPPONENT CROWD (GO)

The audience takes on a decidedly different cast in this third type, which is the least clearly defined. Following Manson, for some time I considered this group as a kind of undifferentiated audience that was generally neutral, curious, but not attached in any serious fashion to Jesus, although at times certain positive or negative overtones developed within it.[15] More exacting study has forced me to correct this picture. I am still retaining the category, but many of those passages formerly assigned to what Manson called a G audience, I have reassigned to the DG category. The reason for this is a general insight to the effect that there really were no neutral persons pictured in Jesus' audiences. They were either for him or against him (Matt. 12:30), and the Evangelists were not greatly concerned to distinguish between those DG who were vitally committed and those more casually so, although Luke does in the word *hebdomekonta*. Even a seemingly neutral term such as *ochlos* reveals this, for it is used to refer to everything from those who followed him to the cross to those who merely came to hear or be healed. All of these are to be called DG. But now we come to the other side of that body of material which I formerly designated as G. These are the unsympathetic multitudes, and will be called GO and assigned to a separate opposition category because this seems truer to the practice of the Evangelists. This same negative reference carries over into the Gospel of John, where he lists the multitudes as simply " the Jews," and regularly shows them to be unsympathetic to Jesus.

This audience ranges from a vague astonishment bordering on suspicion (Mark 1:21-28) to the full-scale opposition of the mob that cried for his blood before Pilate. The Evangelists do not seem to be able to work out a unique set of categories by which to distinguish this audience, although at times they seem to be trying to do so (Mark 5:21, 38; Luke 7:12). The GO is an extension of what we shall describe as the hard-core opponent audience, but for their own reasons the editors wish to keep the two groups separate. The difficulty in differentiating exactly DG from GO depends, of course, not only on the lack of carefulness of the editors but also on the fact that any such set of categories as I am proposing has a certain artificiality when it comes to analyzing literary material not created like a scholarly dissertation. The Evangelists simply are not always consistent, and that is their privilege, as it is not the privilege of the critical scholar. The following terms identify the GO. It is striking to note their vague and general nature in comparison with the terms identifying the DG.

ochlos (Matt. 9:23, 25). The laughter identifies the opposition.

ochloi. In Luke 12:54, *ochlois* is defined by *hupokritai* (v. 56). In Luke 11:14 the *ochloi* seem composed of several smaller groups, some of whom charged him with being in league with Beelzebul, and others sought to " test " him, all of which brings a strong rejection from Jesus. The *ochloi* of Luke 11:29 could be DG or

GO. Luke is unclear. The fact that the Matthew version of this Q saying directs it against Scribes and Pharisees, and Luke follows this section immediately with several logia to an opponent audience, suggests GO.

ochlos tes poleos (Luke 7:12). Later (vs. 16-17) some of these might be called DG, but Luke is unclear.

muriadon tou ochlou (Luke 12:1). This seems to refer back to the opposition situation described in the preceding verses, although it is unclear.

polloi (Mark 6:2). The negative nature of this audience is echoed in the logion that follows where Jesus calls himself a prophet without honor in his own country.

pantas (Luke 4:36; Mark 1:27). The astonishment of the people in the Capernaum synagogue has a vaguely negative quality, but this is a borderline case.

tines (Luke 13:1-9). Jesus' reply in the logion that follows, " you will all likewise perish," identifies this as GO.

plethos (Luke 23:27). This multitude following him to the cross no doubt contained many sympathizers, like the " daughters of Jerusalem "; but subsequent narration suggests that for the E it was primarily GO.

tinas tous pepoithotas eph heautois hoti eisin dikaioi (Luke 18:9). The proud Pharisee reflects the GO.

The preponderance of Lucan references above agrees with the general polemical quality of Luke's Gospel. But now we can go a little farther in identifying this audience, for there are seven passages where the editors quote or paraphrase the GO.

Mark 6:2-3, " ' Where did this man get all this? What is the wisdom given to him? What mighty works are wrought by his hands! Is not this the carpenter, the son of Mary and brother of James and Joses and Judas and Simon, and are not his sisters here with us? ' And they took offense at him."

Mark 1:27, "And they were all amazed, so that they questioned among themselves, saying, 'What is this? A new teaching! With authority he commands even the unclean spirits, and they obey him.'"

Luke 9:53, "But the people would not receive him, because his face was set toward Jerusalem."

Luke 18:9, "Some who thought they were righteous . . ."

Luke 23:18, 21, "Away with this man, and release to us Barabbas. . . . "Crucify, crucify him!"

Mark 15:29-30, "Aha! You who would destroy the temple and build it in three days, save yourself, and come down from the cross!"

Mark 15:35, 36, "And some of the bystanders hearing it said, 'Behold, he is calling Elijah. . . . Wait, let us see whether Elijah will come to take him down.'"

Amazement, rejection, lack of understanding, these are the hallmarks of the general opposition found among the GO in this small body of material. Perhaps the most striking observation is the scarcity of evidence for a general opposition to Jesus. The Evangelists tell us, consciously or inadvertently, that the crowds were almost wholly receptive to Jesus, and the opposition centered not in the crowds but in a small group that stood as what one might call antidisciples, a category that matches the D, but at the opposite end of the spectrum.

OPPONENTS (O)

It is here, in this group removed the farthest from Jesus in sympathy, receptivity, and understanding, that the hard-core opposition is to be found. Here is the distilled essence of what killed Jesus, the crux of the antipathy between him and the religious establishment. The strength of concern to distinguish this group is revealed by the number and clarity of the terms used by all editors and all sources.

hoi antikeimenoi auto (Luke 13:17). This clearly refers to the *archisunagogos*, but the plural also would seem to include the "*ochlos*" (GO) (v. 14).

Pharisaioi. The attempts by many [16] to point out the high religious devotion of the Pharisees is no doubt warranted. The fact remains that the Synoptics are unanimous in centering the opposition to Jesus at this point (Matt. 9:9-13; 12:1-8, 9-14, 24-37, 38-42; 15:1-20; 19:1-12; 22:34-41; Mark 2:13-17, 18-22, 23-28; 3:1-6; 7:1-23; 10:1-12; Luke 5:17-26, 27-32, 33-39; 6:1-5, 6-11; 7:36-50; 13:31-33; 15:1-10; 16:14-15; 19:39-40).

grammateis (Matt. 9:1-8; 12:38-42, 43-45; 15:1-20; 21:15-17; 26:57-75; Mark 2:3-12, 13-17; 3:22-30; 7:1-23; 11:18, 27; 12:28, 32, 35; 14:53-72; Luke 5:18-26, 27-32; 6:6-11; 15:1-10; 19:47; 20:1, 39; 22:54-71).

nomikoi (Matt. 22:34-40).

Saddoukaioi (Mark 12:18-27; Matt. 22:23-33; Luke 20:27-40).

nomodidaskaloi (Luke 5:17).

archiereis (Matt. 21:15-17, 23-27; 26:47-56, 57-75; Mark 11:18, 27-33; 14:43-52, 53-57; Luke 19:47; 20:1-8; 22:47-53, 54-71).

archonton Pharisaion (Luke 14:1-6). This is possibly DG. Cf. Luke 7:36-50.

archisunagogos (Luke 13:14). Luke identifies him as *antikeimenos* (v. 17).

presbuteroi (Matt. 26:47, 57-75; Mark 11:27; 14:53-72; Luke 20:1; 22:54-71; *tou laou,* Matt. 21:23; 26:47).

strategous tou hierou (Luke 22:52).

holon to sunedrion (Mark 15:1; Luke 22:66).

protoi tou laou (Luke 19:47).

tous mathetas (of the Pharisees) *meta ton Herodianon* (Matt. 22:15-16; Mark 12:13).

tous polountas kai agorazontas en to hiero (Matt. 21:12-13; Mark 11:15-19; Luke 19:47-48).

heteroi de peirazontes semeion (Luke 11:16).

ho de thelon dikaiosai (Luke 10:29-37).

This clearly delineated group would seem to center around the Pharisees, but to include their immediate disciples, and a general cross section of Jewish religious officialdom. The stress on those tending toward a Biblical legalism (Pharisees, scribes, lawyers) rather than on the priestly, Sadducaic, sacerdotal element is comparable to the theological antipathy of Jesus found in the logia (cf. Chs. VI, VII). Again in this body of material we are presented with a *group* rather than certain individual types. The fact that the editors often agree that the audience is O, but disagree as to its exact composition, is clear evidence for this.[17] These were the ones, whatever they were called, who stood in most direct opposition to Jesus, and this is the fact the Evangelists wish to preserve.

If one pursues this farther, he discovers twenty-eight dialogue units where someone in this group is speaking (EO) and where the nature of the O audience is clearly detailed. There are seven Greek words peculiar to this stratum, again giving to it a kind of unity: *aletheia, exestin, apostasion, diastriphonta, didasko, enteuthen, Kaisar*. These terms serve to crystallize the four patterns of concern running throughout this material: (1) concern for Judaistic institutions and ideas, (2) interest in civic matters, (3) curiosity concerning John the Baptist, (4) a certain rational, didactic orientation. Mark gives us a fine sketch of this group (7:3-4): " For the Pharisees, and all the Jews, do not eat unless they wash their hands, observing the tradition of the elders; and when they come from the market place, they do not eat unless they purify themselves; and there are many other traditions which they observe, the washing of cups and pots and vessels of bronze." Here is official Judaism with strong ties to the Old Testament in its belief in God as the forgiver of sins (Mark 2:7) whose way (Mark 12:13-17) demands first of all love of God and man (Mark 12:32-33). They are concerned for the commandments of Moses (Mark 12:18-27; 12:28-34) and what is " permitted " in his law regarding such matters as divorce (Mark 10:1-12) and levirate marriage (Mark 12:18-27). They show their debt to that later development of Judaism reflected in the Apocrypha by their concern for demons (Matt. 9:32-34; Mark 3:20-22), for resurrection (Mark 12:18-

27), and for signs of the end (Mark 12:18-22). Mostly these dialogue sections reflect a concern for what is permitted in the "tradition of the elders " in matters such as Sabbath observance (Mark 2:23-28; 3:1-6; Luke 13:10-17), fasting (Mark 2:18-22), tribute to Caesar (Mark 12:13-17), sacrifice, offerings, and temple concerns (Mark 12:32-33; 14:1-2, 56-64), but especially for the tradition concerning ritual purity, for eating with sinners (Luke 15:1-10), and for the proper washing of hands (Mark 7:1-23). They reject John as a prophet (Mark 11:27-33) and their opposition to Jesus as Messiah (Matt. 21:15-16; Luke 19:39-44; 23:2) revolves around the question of his authority (*exousia*) to do what he does (Mark 11:27-33). They are nervously concerned for the approval of the political structure (Luke 23:2; 12:31-33; Matt. 28:11-15) and appear anxious to justify religiously the ways in which they are forced to pay tribute to Caesar (Mark 12:13-17; Luke 23:2). Their well-known rational orientation comes out not only in their attempts to trap Jesus polemically, or to interpret the Torah " rabbinically," but in their concern for *aletheia* (Mark 12:14, 32; Matt. 22:16; Luke 20:21). They are pictured as self-righteous (Luke 10:29-37), proud (Luke 11:45), lovers of money (Luke 16:14-15) by the Lucan tradition, which seems especially to give them a " bad press." In general it would seem that the Evangelists are agreed in giving a negative picture of the O and in characterizing them as the focal point of opposition to Jesus. As we shall see later, the logia picture Jesus in aggressive opposition to the O on almost every one of the above matters. Their opposition to him is a reflection of his opposition to them.

SIGNIFICANT CARE IN AUDIENCE IDENTIFICATION

We have pointed to the care with which the Evangelists identify the audience in the fact that 98 percent of all the Synoptic logia and 94 percent of all the Huck-Lietzmann units contain audience identifiers. We have seen this care in the terms used to designate the four types of audience, in certain words restricted to them, and in the dialogue units that reflect their character. Beyond this, there are a number of passages where the exact manner in which the editors work out their concern for the audience context becomes most awkwardly visible. There are, for example, many places where the audience is multilayered, and the Evangelists go to great lengths to spell this out. In Mark 2:13-17 (Matt. 9:9-13; Luke 5:27-32) within the space of four verses the editor identifies the following: *ochlos, Leui, telonai, hamartoloi, mathetais, grammateis, Pharisaion.* In one verse, Mark (14:43; Matt. 26:47; Luke 22:47) lists five elements in his audience, *Ioudas, ochlos, archiereon, grammateon, presbuteron* (cf. Mark 15:1). In Luke 24:10 the editor names the three women *kai hai loipai sun autais,* and sends them off to tell *tois hendeka kai pasin tois loipois;* and not wanting us to have any doubt, clarifies this with *pros tous apostolous.* In Luke 23:13, the O audience (*archiereis kai tous archontas*) is clearly set apart from the GO (*ton laon*), and in Mark 15:1-8 and Luke 23:4 the same is true where a highly complex O (*archiereis, presbuteron, grammateon, holon to sunedrion*) is distinguished from the GO.

The multilayered audience is treated in another fashion when we see the editor shifting from one audience to another in the midst of an extended discourse. In Matt. 19:1-9, Jesus directs his message about divorce to an O audience, and then in v. 10 shifts to the D. Mark observes the same audience shift, but curiously begins it one verse earlier (Mark 10:1-12). At times this concern to keep a multiple audience straight becomes quite complicated. For example, in Luke 12:1 the editor shows Jesus surrounded by his disciples and *ton muriadon tou ochlou* (GO, plus DG?). Then between verses 1 and 59, seemingly a single occasion for Luke, Jesus turns first to the D, then to the DG (vs. 13-21), then back to the D, and finally again to the GO (vs. 54-56). The same thing is true in Mark 7:1-23, where in a multiple audience he first directs his remarks to *hoi Pharisaioi kai tines ton grammateon* (v. 1), then turns to the DG (*ton ochlon,* v. 14), and ends this section with Jesus taking the D, *eis oikon apo tou ochlou,* and explaining the parable to them privately.

This shifting to a private scene, especially to explain a parable to the disciples, is characteristic of all the Evangelists, and repre-

sents one of the most defensible illustrations of audience carefulness. In Matt. 13:36, for example, Jesus leaves the crowd and goes
into a house to explain the parable of the tares to the D alone. The
same thing essentially occurs a few verses earlier (Matt. 13:10 ff.)
with a curious and inadvertent corroboration by Luke. Matthew
13:16 and Luke 10:23-24 both record the same logion about seeing " what you see." The literary, historical, and geographical contexts are quite different, but there is one contextual element that is
the same: they both have Jesus directing this logion to the D in a
private discourse. Luke makes this especially plain: *kai strapheis
pros tous mathetas kat'idian.*

At times the carefulness with which the audience is identified
contrasts sharply with vagueness in other contextual elements. Luke
in his travel narrative is extremely obscure regarding his topography, but surprisingly careful in observing changes in audience.
For example, one clear element that identifies a break or shift in
scene is a change not in geography but in audience (Luke 13:31).
In 11:1 (*en topo tini*) and 17:11 f. (*eis tina komen*) Luke's topo-
graphical references are hopelessly vague, but he is still careful to
identify those in the audience, in the one case, *matheton autou,* and
in the other, *deka leproi.*

There is a clear illustration of Luke's carefulness of audience in
a parenthetical remark in 7:29-30. In v. 24 Jesus continues *pros
tous ochlous,* which Luke apparently feels is too vague. So in a
parenthesis he characterizes the DG as tax collectors and others
(*laos*) who justify God and have been baptized with the baptism
of John. These he sharply distinguishes from the Pharisees and the
scribes who reject both God's purpose and John's baptism. One
can perhaps understand this concern for clarification when one sees
the unclear audience in the Matthew parallel.[18] The parenthetical
nature of this remark suggests that the logion came to Luke in Q
with some indication of audience (*ochlois,* Matt. 11:7; Luke 7:24),
but not certain enough in his opinion. Rather than rewrite his
source, he merely added his own parenthesis.

In Matt. 23:1-39 we see a rather good example of the editor
conflating into a single discourse material which he probably ob-

tained from Mark, Q, and his M source. In the case of each source the audience is single, being either DG (Mark 12:37 f.), D (Luke 20:45 f.), or O (Luke 11:39 f.; 13:34-35). In Matthew's conflated version, however, we find a three-layered audience consisting of DG (*ochlois*), D (*Mathetais autou*), and O (*grammateis kai Pharisaioi*). It would seem that Matthew is especially careful to avoid omitting any of the audience tradition.

In other places we see this precision in a characterization of the audience as " some who trusted in themselves that they were righteous " (Luke 18:9), or as one who wished to justify himself (Luke 10:29). In a saying attributed to John the Baptist, the editor carefully distinguishes John's teaching to the multitude from that to the tax collectors and the soldiers (Luke 3:10-19). At times (e.g., Mark 14:32-34) one Evangelist seems more anxious to specify the audience than another, but generally all Gospels and all sources show about the same concern to keep us informed concerning the audience at all times.

AUDIENCE OBSCURITY

There are a few illustrations of obscurity in audience identification, but the striking thing is their scarcity. Mark 1:14-15 introduces Jesus in Galilee preaching the nearness of the Kingdom of God to no one in particular; but this is a kind of summary of his entire message, and no audience is called for. Luke 9:23-27 is obscurely directed *pros pantas,* whereas the parallels in Matthew 16:24-28 and Mark 8:34 to 9:1 are clearly directed to the D and the D plus DG respectively; but it is probable that the Evangelist assumed that the statement " the Disciples were with him " (Luke 9:18), took care of the audience in 9:23-27. Matthew 11:20-30 is addressed vaguely to *tas poleis,* but the force of *tois ochlois* (11:7) (DG) was probably assumed to carry over to the woes against the cities, being directed against the cities, but given to the DG. The only passage where the audience is hopelessly obscure is Luke 13:23-30 where *eipen de tis* or *eipen pros autous* doesn't give us much to go on. It is noteworthy that this section is in Luke's geographically obscure travel narrative, and contains four logia that have " pseudo " parallels in various portions of Matthew, where in each instance the audience is clearly presented. Beyond these there are several places where it is difficult for the modern exegete to decide on the audience, but where the Evangelist himself seems to have thought it was clear. In Matt. 23:13-39 it is not certain whether Jesus is speaking directly to the O or to the D plus DG *about* the O. In Mark 1:21-22 the editorial introduction is unclear, but the paradigm which follows serves to clarify the audience. Beyond these few examples, I find nothing but an almost embarrassingly solicitous concern on the part of the editors to make sure that the reader knows not only the audience to which any particular logion is being addressed, but the exact complexity of the multiple audiences in his narration.

Chapter III

THE CORRELATION OF AUDIENCE

In beginning the use of the audience as a critical tool, we will first need to define exactly the details of the major audience phenomena. We are concerned to get an exhaustive overview of every logion in each of its audience correlations to discover as much as we can about the use of the audience by the editors and in the earliest tradition. Do the Evangelists exhibit certain characteristics in their use of the audience? Do their sources show particular patterns? Does the form of a logion say anything about the audience? How do the various editors, sources, and forms agree or disagree on the audience to which any particular logion is directed? We are looking for whatever pattern-induced probabilities emerge from a massive study of audience correlation with source, form, and redactor.

AUDIENCE–SOURCE CORRELATION DATA

In the Synoptics there are 352 separate logia,[1] occurring a total of 595 times in all three Gospels (cf. Appendix A). These are directed to eleven different audience situations [2] in nine source combinations.[3] When these twenty situations are correlated, certain patterns emerge that are important for Audience, Source, and Redaction Criticism, as the following series of charts will demonstrate.

CHART I. *General Audience-Source Summary*

This chart gives the number of times any logion occurs in a particular source situation and directed to any one of the audience possibilities.

	S1	S2	S3	S4	S5	S6	S7	S8	S9	Totals
AA	2	3	1	2			3			11
AD	132	51	37	20	2	7	3	3		255
ADG	25	22	4	13					2	66
AGO	4	4	4	8	1	1	2			24
AO	66	21	14	9	3				2	115
AN		2								2
A1	27	40	28	5			3	5		108
A5		3						8		11
A6				1						1
A7		1								1
A9				1						1
Totals	256	147	88	59	6	8	11	16	4	595

CHART II. *Audience-Source Correlation*

This chart gives the percentage of times each audience situation occurs to a particular source situation, in terms of the total number of examples of that audience situation. For example, AD occurs in S1 51 percent of the total 255 times this AD situation occurs.[4]

	S1	S2	S3	S4	S8	Total Logia
AD	51	12	14	8	0	255
ADG	38	33	6	20	0	66
AGO	17	17	17	34	0	24
AO	57	19	12	8	0	115
A1	25	37	26	5	5	108
A5	0	27	0	0	73	11

CHART III. *Logion-Audience Correlation*

This chart gives the percentage of total logia by audience.

AA	2	AO	20
AD	43	A1	18
ADG	11	A5	2
AGO	4		

CHART IV. *Source-Audience Correlation*

This chart gives the percentage of times logia occur in a particular source situation and to a certain audience combination. This is in terms of the total number of examples of that source situation. For example, out of the 256 S1 situations, 51 percent place the logia in an AD context.

	AD	ADG	AGO	AO	A1	A5	Total Logia
S1	51	10	2	25	11	0	256
S2	35	15	3	14	27	2	147
S3	42	5	5	16	37	0	88
S4	34	22	13	15	8	0	59
S6	88	0	22	0	0	0	8
S7	27	0	18	0	27	0	11
S8	19	0	0	0	31	50	16

CHART V. *Percentage of Total Logia by Source*

S1	43	S5	1
S2	25	S6	1.5
S3	15	S7	2
S4	10	S8	3

CHART VI. *Miscellaneous Audience Correlations*

This chart gives the percentage of all logia represented by a particular audience situation.

Single audience (AD, ADG, AGO, AO)	76
Multiple audience (A1, A5, A6, A7, A9)	22
All situations containing D and/or DG	74
All situations containing GO and/or O	25
All situations containing DG	31

In general these six charts reveal Synoptic logia given chiefly to a disciple audience (D and/or DG), with that to the Twelve over-whelmingly predominant. The recorded tradition contains three times as much material directed to sympathetic audiences as to those who were unsympathetic (Chart VI). Either Jesus most often spoke to those who appreciated him, or it is these who were most concerned to record the tradition, or for some other reason the Evangelists inadvertently preserve this fact. There is high agree-ment in directing the logia principally to a single audience. Where they are given to multiple audiences, these audiences are far less complex than in the narrative situations, being chiefly A1. Thus within highly complex narrative audience contexts, the Evangelists almost always specify one or at the most two audience groups as the immediate targets for the logia. The audience context of a logion is therefore much simpler than that of the narration. Later we shall see such distinctions between narration and logia emerging as a major factor in this study (Chapter IV).

An even finer measure of exactly what we have in the charts above comes when the percentage occurrence of any source to a particular audience (Chart IV) is placed in a ratio with the total number of logia (Chart III). When this is done, certain patterns emerge; that is, statistical ratios which stand out as above or below the average. The figures in Chart VII reveal the degree to which any percentage occurrence is above or below what one would expect it to be. For example, when we see that the AD situation occurs in 43 percent of all logia, this becomes a kind of control, and theoreti-cally we could expect AD to occur in 43 percent of any source if the sources all displayed the same interests, history, and character-istics. The degree to which the percentage occurrence of AD in any

CHART VII. *Audience-Source Ratio*

	AD	ADG	AGO	AO	A1	A5
S1	51/43	10/11	2/4	25/20	11/18	0/2
S2	35/43	15/11	3/4	14/20	27/18	2/2
S3	42/43	5/11	5/4	16/20	37/18	0/2
S4	34/43	22/11	13/4	15/20	8/18	0/2

given source differs from the control reveals as a pattern the characteristic interest of that source.

In the chart above, Mark shows a special knowledge of and interest in logia to the D and the O. The Q source reflects a strong concern for Jesus' teaching to the DG and in the A1 situation. Matthew's special source has a fairly high orientation toward the disciples. The Lucan source is especially filled with logia to the larger crowds, both of disciples and opponents. One can't help noting the movement from Mark to Q to M to L as that from a chief concern with the inner circle of disciples or opponents to that for the widening circle of DG and GO.

AGREEMENT–DISAGREEMENT DEFINED

One of the most important critical problems is that of the agreement or disagreement between the sources over the matter of audience. In order to get this in proper perspective, we shall focus attention upon audience agreement-disagreement in relation to all elements of the Synoptic text and context that can be legitimately compared. There are at least five such points of comparison: (1) the position of the logion in the literary sequence (La); (2) the historical location in the life of Jesus (Ha); (3) the geographical background for the logion (Ga); (4) the audience to which the logion is specifically directed or that generally in the background of the logion (Aa); (5) the exact wording of the Greek text of any logion repeated in more than one place (Wa). It is in the correlation of these elements that certain probabilities will emerge for the understanding of the audience tradition, as well as the history of the Synoptic formation.

Much work, of course, has been done on these matters in the study of Source, Form, and Historical Criticism. The names of K. L. Schmidt, Rudolf Bultmann, John C. Hawkins, and B. H. Streeter stand out, and I shall not attempt either to duplicate or even to summarize their work. Our concern is for audience agreement and its relation to agreement in other areas, and since such correlation has not been done before, this present study must stand on its own merits. As we shall see, there is some help, though minimal, from the studies of T. W. Manson; and others, like Joachim Jeremias, have made such comparisons in individual cases, and we shall refer to these at a later time. No general study such as the one contemplated here, however, has yet been made.

Before we go into this matter, one further tool is needed. When we compare these five elements, it is not enough merely to say that they agree or disagree. We must define what this means, and set up some categories delineating the quality of agreement. For this end the following three agreement-disagreement categories are suggested.

Category #1. Exact Agreement. For history and geography, this designates the same incident or sequence of events. For the literary progression, the logia must be within one or two verses of each other in sequence. For the audience, this has to be an exact duplicate of one of the eleven possibilities listed in the Key to Abbreviations. This does not mean that, for example, each O audience must contain exactly the same terms designating the O. As we pointed out in Chapter II, the important thing for the Evangelists was the audience as a group or type, not the specific term used. For the wording of the logion, Category #1 means exact reproduction of the Greek text. Where there are different words, there must be the possibility of the same Aramaic original underneath.

Category #2. General Agreement. For history and geography, this category designates logia placed in the same general region, for example in or near Jerusalem, and in the same one of the eight historical periods into which Huck-Lietzmann's Synopsis divides the narrative.[5] For literary position this could be several verses off, but must be in the same chapter and in the same general sequence. For audience, all the Evangelists must agree on at least one type of audience present. If one editor has A1 and the other AD, this would be agreement category #2, since both audiences contain the D. With the wording, this category signifies two versions that are recognizable as the same logion, and with some verbatim agreement.

Category #3. Disagreement. This category means that the historical position lies in different Huck-Lietzmann units, the geographical location is significantly different, the literary position is entirely different, the audience is similar in no way, and the wording reproduces apparently the same logion but with little general agreement.

SOURCE–AUDIENCE AGREEMENT–DISAGREEMENT

In the Synoptics there are 178 individual logia that can be compared between Evangelists. The following charts are based on an

CHART VIII.   *Audience Agreement-Disagreement*

The following chart shows the types of agreement-disagreement that occur relative to audience in this body of 178 logia. Numerators give percentages of the total 178. Denominators give the percentage of total logia.

AD (#1 and #2)	40/43	AD/ADG	(#2)	4 logia
ADG (#1)	7/11	AO/AGO	(#2)	2 logia
AGO (#1)	1/4	A5/AO	(#2)	4 logia
AO (#1)	14/20	A1/AGO	(#3)	3 logia
A1 (#1 and #2)	12/18	A1/AO	(#3)	2 logia
A1/AD (#2) [6]	9 logia	AO/AD	(#3)	2 logia

CHART IX.   *Percentage Source Agreement*

This chart shows the relative agreement of Matthew and Luke when following the Marcan and Q sources. Figures give the percentage of agreement on all five points of comparison and in terms of the three agreement categories. The Q percentages are in terms of the 79 logia, the Marcan in terms of the 99 logia and the Mark plus Q percentages in terms of the total 178 logia that can be so compared.

	Category	La	Ha	Ga	Aa	Wa
	#1	24	11.5	6	47	26
Q	#2	13	10	16	36	60
	#3	63	78.5	78	17	14
	#1	85	85	88	84	33
MARK	#2	3	2	0	14	57
	#3	12	13	12	2	10
TOTAL	#1	58	52	52	67	30
MARK	#2	8	6	8	24	58
PLUS Q	#3	34	42	40	9	12

CHART X. *Percentage Source Agreement Ratios*

The figures in Chart IX are here arranged so as to sharpen the agree-ment-disagreement distinction. Numerators give the combined Category #1 and #2 percentages. Denominators give Category #3 percentages.

	La	Ha	Ga	Aa	Wa
Q	37/63	22/78	22/78	83/17	86/14
MARK	88/12	87/13	88/12	98/2	90/10
Q PLUS MARK	66/34	58/42	60/40	91/9	88/12

exhaustive correlation of the five elements of comparison as they occur in the three Gospels and according to the above three cate-gories of agreement.

In Charts VIII–X one observation immediately stands out. The 91 percent general audience agreement is consistently higher than any other point of comparison. This kind of exhaustive analysis clearly shows the inadequacy of Jeremias' impression that the " fre-quently occurring change of audience " in the parables is norma-tive for the Synoptics.[7] Just the reverse is true. More than wording, and dramatically more than history, geography, or literary sequence, the Marcan and Q sections agree on audience. We note also (Chart VIII) that agreement on audience tends to follow almost exactly the percentage of total logia by audience (Chart III). In other words, no one audience tends to find a relatively higher agree-ment among the sources than another. All audience situations have this high percentage of agreement.

Another pattern indicates that audience agreement and wording agreement tend to parallel each other and to differ sharply from La, Ha, and Ga (Chart X). While these latter, more exclusively editorial elements tend to agree or disagree in concert, those two factors most intimately tied to the logia (Aa, Wa) follow each other against the other three. This is most apparent in Matthew and Luke's use of the Q source. The ratios between Wa/Aa and La/Ha/Ga are almost exactly the reverse. There seems to be an intimate correlation between wording and audience. One must probably say that audience was an important part of the wording of a particular logion; that is, wording and audience were equally important to the editors, and far more important than historical, literary, or geographical factors. There also seems to be some kind of distinction one must make between those elements most peculiar to the editorial narration and those tied more to the logia. Here again we see a distinction emerging between pure narration and logia.

Commenting on the patterns characterizing Mark and Q, we note that whereas the agreement on more purely narrative elements in Q (La, Ha, Ga) is fairly low, that in Mark is quite high. This, of course, reflects the probability that Q was a sayings source with little narration while Mark contained much narration which Matthew and Luke followed about as closely as they did Mark's wording of the logia. If the Evangelists had to supply their own narration for the Q collection, this high disagreement could be expected. Curiously the audience agreement within the Marcan material averages about 10 percent higher than agreement on the other four elements. This careful following of Mark on all matters reveals itself in Chart X and is contrasted clearly with Q where we see the relative independence of Matthew and Luke in using this hypothetical source.

In summary, this source-audience agreement analysis has revealed three general patterns: (1) The audience factor consistently shows the highest agreement with all three Evangelists. (2) A clear distinction has emerged between the material in the narration (La, Ha, Ga) and that in the logia (Wa, Aa). (3) In Mark and Q the Evangelists tend to agree about equally on audience and wording; but Matthew and Luke differ sharply in their agreement over the narrative elements in Q.

FORM–AUDIENCE AGREEMENT–DISAGREEMENT

Form Criticism emphasizes the way in which the early church as a community was a creative factor in shaping the Synoptic tradition. It was the use to which the material was put in the early church that determined the creation or the molding of the form of the many logia. If this is so, then it would seem that the category of form would be a necessary one to correlate with the audience for a correct assessment of the audience phenomenon. To this end we offer the following analysis of the audience tradition according to the five categories of form, using terms supplied by Dibelius, Bultmann, and Vincent Taylor somewhat arbitrarily, and with the following symbols: (FA) apothegm (paradigm, pronouncement story); (FS) saying; (FP) parable; (FM) miracle story; (FL) legend (novellen, tale, historical story).

CHART XI. *Form-Audience Percentage Ratios*

This chart gives the total number of logia showing the various forms, and compares their percentage placement ratios in the various audience contexts. The numerators give the percentage of the total occurrence of that form to that audience. The denominators give the percentage of total logia directed to that audience.

	Total Logia	AD	ADG	AGO	AO	A1
FA	50	37/43	17/11	13/4	29/20	0/18
FP	71	37/43	0/11	16/4	21/20	25/18
FS	185	47/43	6/11	7/4	15/20	24/18
FM	26	25/43	50/11	0/4	13/20	8/18
FL	30	65/43	13/11	9/4	7/20	0/18

In the chart above, the didactic emphasis is clearly seen in the high proportion of FS. Next comes the parable, more a homiletic form used in hortatory preaching. Then comes the apothegm which reflects the debate-polemic situation. Finally the legend and miracle story are reflective more of the narrative-oriented logia. It would seem that the historic situations reflected in their order of importance for producing logia are as follows: first teaching, then preaching, then debate, and finally historical event.

We note the high percentage of FA in the AO and AGO, indicating the polemical character of these opposition situations. Note-worthy also is the high percentage of FM to the DG, which merely puts into statistical language our definition of the DG as that group for which Jesus was effective as a miracle worker. A very suggestive figure is that which shows a high ratio of FL to the D and DG. If we say that these two audiences represented the early developing church, then the thorough orientation of this legendary material toward the church is apparent. Another curious fact is that there is not one parable recorded to the DG by themselves. Rather, the most striking ratio pattern shows Jesus directing the parable form relatively more often to the A1 situation (D plus DG). This, coupled with the high ratio of FS to this same audience combina-tion suggests that the most typical preaching-teaching situation was that of the Twelve surrounded by large crowds of sympathetic hearers. This is the Sermon on the Mount situation and argues that Matthew has given us a somewhat stylized, " model " teaching-preaching collation. This was the kind of audience that was typi-

CHART XII. *Form and Source Agreement-Disagreement*

In this chart the logia are distinguished according to form and then in the 178 comparison situations the relative agreement on La, Ha, Ga, Aa, Wa is compared between Mark and Q. All figures are percentages of the total number of logia of a particular form as found in Mark or Q. Each figure represents a combination of both agreement categories #1 and #2.

		La	Ha	Ga	Aa	Wa
FL	MARK	100	100	100	100	100
	Q	100	100	100	100	100
FM	MARK	100	100	100	100	100
	Q	0	33	33	66	66
FA	MARK	75	75	80	100	96
	Q	50	50	50	83	83
FP	MARK	87	73	73	93	93
	Q	33	8	8	59	92
FS	MARK	90	90	90	94	83
	Q	40	22	26	86	84

cal of Jesus' style combining teaching and preaching. Then when we see the high ratio of FS to AD, we can see that even as the hortatory, parable form typifies Jesus' approach to both the sympathetic and unsympathetic multitudes, so does a more intimate, didactic form predominate in his logia to the Twelve. The absence of miracle stories to the GO clearly documents the generalization that because of their unbelief, Jesus could do no mighty works among them (Mark 6:5-6).

In the chart above, we see the same distinction between Mark and Q that we have noted before. Mark is high on all categories of agreement. Q is high on Aa and Wa but relatively low on La, Ha, Ga. The surprisingly high literary agreement in FP and FS suggests that certain blocks of parables and sayings were joined together at a very primitive period, arguing for " Proto-Source " collections. It is also noteworthy that the distinction seen earlier between Aa/Wa and La/Ha/Ga stands out with equal clarity in Chart XII. Audience and wording reveal an approximately equal high level of agreement no matter how you examine the Synoptic material. From this it would seem clear that audience and wording are the most stable elements in those portions of the Synoptics that can be compared, and tend to be closely related.

Perhaps the most striking fact about this chart is the high agreement on most points of comparison with legends, apothegms, and the Marcan miracle stories. Furthermore, as the charts above do not show, almost every FM and FL logion agrees with a #1 quality of agreement. We also note that eighteen out of twenty-two FM and twenty-four out of twenty-nine FL are AD or ADG. This suggests that FL, FM, and FA are very intimately connected with the life of the early church and give us stories well rehearsed and brought into some kind of standardized form long before they were included in Mark and Q. The close agreement on wording would suggest early written narratives, and would support the common belief that such things as the Passion Legend were written and widely distributed prior to the final editing of our three Gospels.

THE CHARACTER OF AUDIENCE AGREEMENT–
DISAGREEMENT

Exact Agreement (Category #1). It should be sufficiently clear by now that the 91 percent general agreement (Chart X) and the 67 percent exact agreement (Chart IX) on audience constitutes a clearly demonstrable and usable Synoptic phenomenon. Before leaving this subject we should get the clearest possible picture of the nature of this agreement. At the risk of stylizing what shouldn't be stylized, one might divide the 67 percent of the logia showing exact audience agreement into three main types. The first shows the Gospels agreeing on audience, but disagreeing on literary, historical, or geographical contexts. For example, Jesus' saying about offenses against those who believe in him (Matt. 18:6-7; Mark 9:42) is given to the D in a Galilean context not long after the transfiguration and immediately following the discussion of the man who cast out demons in Jesus' name. Luke's version of this, however, occurs in his long travel narrative some time later in the region across the Jordan and immediately following the parable of the rich man and Lazarus, but *to the same audience*. The audience agreement stands out like a beacon. There are many examples of this. The same thing happens in Luke 22:24-27 and again in Luke 10:25-28, where Luke disagrees with Matthew and Mark on literary, historical, and geographical contexts but agrees on the audience.

A second significant type of agreement occurs when one or the other of the Evangelists has conflated several sources, and where one clear principle of conflation has been the agreement of the sources on audience. Each of the editors has examples of this. Matthew in his Sermon on the Mount is a notorious collator of material from many sources. The important thing is that between Matt. 5:1 and 7:27 there are thirteen separate logia where Luke agrees generally on audience but disagrees on almost every other element of the context. Furthermore, in this section there is an even more curious way in which Luke and Matthew agree on a multiple D plus DG audience in that material within the same literary context (Matt., chs. 5 to 7; Luke, ch. 6); but when Luke includes some of the Matthew material at other points in his sermon the audience becomes *either* D, DG, or GO, whereas Matthew continues the D plus DG multiple audience throughout. If Matthew's version is more original, then Luke has made the audience more specific. But if Matthew's version is a compilation, as seems the case, then he has given to the logia a general A1 context that covers all the cases. That is, the Sermon on the Mount is a kind of composite of the audiences of particular logia which Luke identifies more specifically at other points. As we have suggested, however, there is evidence that this kind of A1 situation was typical of Jesus' technique where teaching and preaching went together. In the woes against the Pharisees (Matt. 23:1-36) Matthew seems to have collated his audience again; for where Mark 12:37b-40 has a DG audience and Luke 11:11, 39-52; 13:34 is to the GO, Matthew's version has a multiple DG plus D plus O audience. He begins the section to A1 and then the context becomes A5.

Luke also shows a concern in his conflations to preserve the audience of his sources. We have already seen this in Luke 17:1-2. Elsewhere, in his description of the day of the Son of Man (17:22-37), he includes five logia found in Matthew where all the elements of the context are different, but where the D audience is the same. This is also true in the conflations found in Luke 12:1-12 and 16:14-31. The audience seems to be one of the major unifying factors.

Mark, too, shows this same propensity. This is more problematic because of the difficulties surrounding the formation of Mark. The fact remains that Mark, ch. 13, and its parallels differ seven times on literary, historical, or geographical context but always agree on audience. Along with the eschatological theme, audience is clearly one principle of collation for the editor of the " Little Apocalypse."

A third unusually clear type of agreement occurs in a complex multilayered audience situation where the Evangelist shows great care in directing the logia to one or the other specific group within the audience complex. A classic illustration occurs between Mark 10:1 and 12:37 outlined below.

Matthew	Mark	Luke
19:2 (*ochloi polloi*	10:1 (*ochlos*)	————————
19:3 (*Pharisaioi*)	10:2 (*Pharisaioi*)	————————
19:4-9 (O)	10:3-9 (O)	————————
19:10-14 (D) (18:3 (D))	10:10-15 (D)	18:15-17 (D)
19:16-21 (DG)	10:17-21 (DG)	18:18-22 (DG)
19:23-30 (D)	10:23-31 (D)	18:24-30 (D)
20:1-16 (D)	————————	————————
20:17-19 (D)	10:32-34 (D)	18:31-34 (D)
20:20-28 (D)	10:35-45 (D)	(22:24-27 (D))
20:29-34 (DG)	10:46-52 (DG)	18:35-43 (DG)
		19:1-10 (DG)
————————	————————	19:11-27 (Al)
(25:14-30 (D))		19:28-38 (D)
21:1-9 (D)	11:1-10 (D)	
21:18-19 (D)	11:12-14 (D)	————————
21:12-13 (O)	11:15-19 (O)	19:45-47 (O)

In the chart above we note the slavish following of Mark's audience by Matthew and Luke. They are even careful to continue Mark's audience in material they insert in this context from another source, or in another context from this Marcan source. Another less imposing illustration occurs in the change from D to DG and back to D in Mark 9:1-29 (Matt. 17:9-20; Luke 9:37-43; 17:6).

General Agreement (*Category #2*). A second group of logia contains thirty-nine examples of what we have called general agreement. Although they do not exactly agree, the audience situations lie within the same sympathetic or unsympathetic orientation, and so the differences are not significant. These fall into the following categories.

One illustration from this group will perhaps suffice to indicate their general character. In Luke 10:1-16, we seem to find an occa-

CHART XIII.   *General Agreement, Category #2*

The following list details those logia whose comparison reveals the following "general" agreement.

A1/AD   (log. 44, 47, 49, 50, 51, 52, 53, 54, 58, 141, 143, 144, 145, 146, 269, 327)
AD/ADG   (log. 10, 84, 86, 87, 90, 91, 102)
AO/AGO   (log. 135, 136, 137, 170)
A5/AO   (log. 215, 216, 229, 293, 295, 299, 301)
A1/ADG   (log. 289)
AD/A1/AA   (log. 176, 177, 178)
A1/AD/ADG   (log. 21)

sion where the distinction between the D and the DG audience caused Luke to preserve two traditions of Jesus' instructions to the disciples. This is a very complicated picture, with all three Gospels recording directions to the disciples, Matthew and Mark only to the D, but Luke to both the D (9:1 f.) and the DG (*hebdome-konta,* 10:1-16). The point is that Luke's instruction to the DG in 10:1-16 is at times in different terms, but at times in exactly the same terms as Matthew's and Mark's instruction to the D. There also seems to be an effort on Luke's part not to repeat the detail and wording of the incident of instruction to the D, thus keeping the occasions separate. What he puts in this continuous DG narra-tive is found scattered throughout Matthew and Mark, where all except Matt. 11:21-23 (GO) is to a D audience. There is at points therefore a definite audience contradiction, reflecting some confu-sion as to which type of disciple audience these instructions were given to (D or DG), but also reflecting Luke's concern to keep them separate. Here is a case where the concept of the larger group of disciples (DG) seems to have operated as an organizing prin-ciple for Luke. The problem appears to have been the concern of the Evangelist to maintain a sharp distinction between two types of audience (D and DG) which in the earliest tradition and in the mind of Jesus were perhaps not so clearly distinguished. The greater number of contradictions in this second group illustrates the lack of sharp distinction at times between these audiences within a general audience of unsympathetic orientation. This seems to have led the Evangelists to be willing to make such audience changes.

Audience Disagreement (*Category #3*). There are fifteen logia showing what might be called hard-core disagreement, where there is a conflict between one of the sympathetic audiences and one of those showing a lack of sympathy for Jesus.[8] These fall into the following five types.

CHART XIV.   *Category #3 Disagreements*

AO/AD	(log. 130, 197, 255)
ADG/AO	(log. 109)
A1/AO	(log. 26, 34, 65)
ADG/AA	(log. 70, 111, 112)
A1/AGO	(log. 23, 31, 48, 49, 150)

Several illustrations from this group will be needed to demonstrate some of the issues involved in these contradictions. To begin with, there are cases where it would appear that similarity to another logion caused an editor to locate a saying improperly. For example, the word of Jesus in Luke 12:10 about blaspheming against the Holy Spirit is given to a D audience. The same logion in Matt. 12:32 and Mark 3:29 is given to the O. The internal logic of this logion demands its thrust against those blaspheming against the Holy Spirit, or most probably an O audience, which suggests that Matthew and Mark have the correct context. The similarity of this idea to Luke 12:9 might possibly explain why Luke tore it from its Marcan context and included it at 12:10.

The dilemma presented by two traditions of the same or similar logion but with different audiences seems to be illustrated in the dual contradiction between Matt. 19:9 (AO)/Mark 10:11-12 (AD) and Matt. 5:32 (A1)/Luke 16:18 (AO). Since Mark, ch. 10, and Matt., ch. 19, obviously follow each other, we can assume that Matthew is copying Mark at this point; so Matt. 19:9 and Mark 10:11-12 are the same logion. But Luke 16:18 seems to represent a Q tradition of a saying so similar as probably to be the same logion, but to the opponents. If this is so, then Matthew had two traditions of the same or closely similar saying, in the one case (Mark) to the D, and in the other (Q) to the O. We have already noted Matthew's desire not to omit anything from his sources. If this principle operates here, then we can say with a fair degree of probability that Matthew, not wishing to exclude anything, inserted the AO version (Q) at 19:19 and the AD version (Mark) at 5:32. His placing 19:9 one verse late, and so causing the audience contradiction with Mark 10:11, would then be due to his conflating Mark and Q at this point. By delaying the audience change from O to D this one verse he is able to agree with the O audience in his Q source, even though following Mark. He then compensates by giving the 5:32 version Mark's D context. Determined to include everything, he then adds the section about *porneia* from his M source to both 5:32 and 19:19, accomplishing a rather neat conflation of three sources for the same saying. The audience disagreement between the AO and the AD versions remains unexplained; but we can perhaps thus understand the skillful manner in which Matthew handled an awkward situation.

At times it would seem that one or another editor has changed the audience of a logion in his source because of his desire to include material in a collation on the basis of theme. For example, Luke 16:16-18 contains three logia directed to the O (log. 109, 26, 34). These are paralleled in Matt. 11:12-13 (ADG); 5:13 (A1), and 5:32 (A1). These three sayings in Luke are bound together by the theme of the law, and their connection with the L material that precedes and follows is tenuous at best, reflecting a Lucan collation at this point (Q plus L). If, as we have suggested above, the Q version contained an O audience, then it would seem that Matthew has placed these three sayings in two different collations on the basis of theme, the one (11:12-13) dealing with John the Baptist, and the other (5:18, 32) with the law. The fact that Matthew's audience in 11:7-30 is ambiguous may suggest a studied ambiguity to gloss over the audience change.

Or it may be that the above reflects the lack of clarity of the original source itself. It is a curious thing that in the three sections where there is decided audience obscurity (Matt. 11:20-30; Luke 9:23-27; 13:22-30) in each case there is some kind of disagreement between the sources in connection with or immediately preceding the ambiguous section. Luke 13:18-21 is AGO while the parallels in Mark 4:30-32 and Matt. 13:31-32 are both A1; and then Luke 13:22 f. begins an obscure section with a very weak editorial comment, *Eipen de tis auto,* directing the following logia to the vague *autous.* Luke 9:23-27 begins with the obscure *Elegen de pros pantas,* and is paralleled in Mark 8:34 with a clear A1 audience and in Matthew with *mathetais autou* (D). Matthew 11:20-30 begins with the direction of the logia to the ambiguous *poleis,* and then as we have noted there is an audience contradiction in the Q material preceding this ambiguous section. This all could reflect a pattern of audience obscurity in the earlier sources, which then resulted in the logia being differently identified by the editors.

In the above three categories of agreement-disagreement, the dominant impression is one of agreement among the sources and editors: agreement on audience within a corresponding disagreement on all other elements; agreement where the audience factor seems to be the main principle holding together a conflation of logia; agreement in a complex audience situation where the running change in audience in an earlier source is followed slavishly by the Evangelists. We have found the editors at times disagreeing with one another due to the contradiction of their sources, or the ambiguity of the sources, or some confusion on the audience categories. We have seen them willing to change the audience in order to fit into a context where the similarity of one logion to another in wording or theme seems to have been a stronger principle of conflation than that of audience. The scarcity of these examples of disagreement would seem to make them the exception rather than the rule.

MARGINAL READINGS

The question arises concerning the marginal readings. There is, for example, an audience addition from Cyril (Lect. 11:3) to

Mark 16:15 to the effect that " they who know not are excusable, but ye, the apostles, who have in my name cleansed lepers and cast out devils and raised the dead, ought not to be ignorant of him for whom ye do these wondrous works." [9] This is a dramatic illustration of a consistent pattern in the Synoptics. Out of the thirty-four cases where the marginal reading makes some change or addition to the audience reference in the text, more often than not superfluous details are added to sharpen the audience reference; *but never once does the marginal reading ascribe to the logion an audience different from that in the text.* At times there is disagreement over detailed designations, for example, " disciple " for " twelve " (Mark 6:7), or " lawyer " for " scribe " (Luke 11:53); but these are always within the list of those terms regularly used to identify the same audience group. It is unmistakably clear that those responsible for the marginal changes conceived of the audience in terms of the same four groups we have been describing and were careful to preserve this group identity. As long as the audience remained in the same general classification there seemed little compunction against refining or even modifying the details.

In this chapter we have noted certain patterns pointing to a characteristic use of the audience by the various redactors and in the several sources and forms. Certain audience situations are the special concern of particular sources; and some forms tend to be most often used in logia directed to specific audiences. The Evangelists show characteristic patterns in their use of the audience. They all tend to collate their sources, and audience is one common principle of collation. There are illustrations of significant independence, but mostly we have discovered a rather slavish following of the sources on audience as on other matters. Usually when one editor disagrees on audience there is some visible reason, and Audience Criticism has proven to be a useful tool in identifying the activity of the editors as well as other critical characteristics of source and form. The one conclusion that transcends all others in this section is that all Evangelists and all sources show a percentage of agreement on audience that stands out above every other type of agreement in the Synoptics. There is a stability to the audience tradition that makes it unique among all Synoptic phenomena.

Chapter IV

SYNOPTIC DISCONTINUITY

At this point it is necessary to take note of one clear phenomenon emerging from our study. There are several lines of evidence pointing to the intensely interesting probability that a distinct line must be drawn between the E material of editor and narration and the A material of the logia of Jesus, tied as they are very closely to particular audience situations. This distinction we shall call discontinuity, and the purpose of the present chapter will be to discuss the evidence for this as an important tool for probing to the heart of our problem: the understanding of the origin, validity, use, and meaning of the audience phenomenon.

VERBAL DISCONTINUITY

To begin with, there is a clear discontinuity between the verbiage of the E and A material. One of the first studies that alerted me to this phenomenon was that wherein the entire Synoptic text was examined exhaustively for word patterns. This was only possible with the aid of the 7070 computer. A word pattern is defined as an occasion when a particular word in the text exhibits some distinctive usage or some high degree of correlation that makes it stand out. It was the introduction of this new category of audience as a correlation factor that opened up this insight. Now the wording of the logia could be correlated with the audience, and out of this comparison so many word patterns emerged that the logia were seen to stand off by themselves from the more obviously editorial material with a unique identity and integrity. To give this some measure of objectivity, three categories (a), (b), (c) will be used to distinguish the " quality " of a pattern.[1]

CHART XV. *Word Occurrence, E vs. A*

In this chart the number of different Greek words showing patterns of exclusive usage within the E or A stratum is compared according to the quality of pattern.

Stratum	Quality Category			Ratio of Exclusively A or E to Total Pattern Words
	(a)	(b)	(c)	
A	29	24	42	95/309
E	37	22	14	73/121

The chart above shows a clear verbal discontinuity between the E and the A material. There are 309 words within the logia showing distinct patterns of correlation between audience and wording. These words then can be called " characteristic " of the teachings of Jesus to particular audience situations (cf. Ch. V and Appendix B). Compared with this, there are 121 words characteristic of some aspect of the E stratum, whether editor, source, or someone speaking out of a particular audience (cf. Appendix C). These then are characteristic of the E material. Each of these bodies of words stands in distinction from the other, and this is what we are calling " discontinuity." Within these two collections of pattern words, 95 occur exclusively or almost so in the logia and 73 in the editorial material. They are particularly characteristic of A or E. The fact that the logia contain a total of almost three times as many pattern words as the editorial tradition sets it off sharply with a unique verbal integrity that is surprising to say the least. We shall develop this material at length in the next two chapters. What we want to underscore here is the difference, the discontinuity, between these two bodies of words.

This verbal discontinuity becomes more sharply defined when we compare the internal analysis of each collection of words. The A group contains an abundance of patterns that cut " horizontally " across all sources and through all Gospels. Almost every one of the 309 words, whether exclusively A or not, shows a horizontal pattern with respect to some audience. In contrast to this, within the list of 121 E pattern words only 55 show " vertical " patterns running " down " through a source, a Gospel, or some particular audience. The remaining 66 show no pattern except that of being characteristic of the E stratum generally. We find five words characteristic of Mark, nine of Matthew, and eighteen of Luke.[2] Besides these there are ten words characteristic of those speaking within an opponent audience (EO), and three peculiar to those within the

CHART XVI. *Exclusively A and E Pattern Words*

All are quality category (a).

E Words		A Words	
agele	hieron	halas	luchnos
aitia	kategoreo	amen	merimnao
akolutheo	krazo	ampelon	misthos
alabastron, pheugo	laos	adikias, talanton	numphios
apeggeilan, ochlos	lian	anaginosko, ouai	oikodespotes
Barabban	horion	ho huios tou anthropou	oligopistos
didache	poreuomai	geenna	opheilo
dunamai	parachrema	dechomai	peteinon
enantios	plethos	ergates	porneo
eperotao	ploion	eukopoteros	sapron
epitimao	presbuteros	exothen	Satan
zeteo	Petros	therismos	speiro
thaumazo	siopao	katakrino	skandalon
therapeuo	teleo	krouo	toioutos

disciple audience (ED). Beyond these, there are no clear and specific patterns among the E words. The plain fact is that the overwhelming number of verbal patterns cut horizontally across the sources, rather than vertically down through the sources. I find no verbal patterns whatsoever peculiar to any one of the Forms. There is clearly some basic verbal distinction that must be made between the editorial material and the logia.

This verbal discontinuity is sharpened even more when we compare the actual words peculiar to each Synoptic layer. The Appendixes will give the complete list. It will help to vivify this point if the exclusively A and E pattern words of category (a) are compared.

In the chart above, the most striking observation is the almost complete absence of words with Christian theological overtones in the E list. This holds true throughout all 121 E pattern words. The few words that might be called theological, such as *doxazo, arneomai, zeteo, aiteo, phobeomai, apothnesko, apodokimazo, daimonion,* are used mostly in a nonreligious way. There are very few words in this list that become theological terms in Paul or the rest of the New Testament. This is contrasted enormously with the A list, where most words are replete with theological content. The E list deals with externals, with superficial details, with nouns of person, place, or object and verbs of motion, description, or narration. One might say, this is all one could expect, since narrative description is the job of the editorial material. We could expect more, however, if there were a strong " dogmatic " interest on the part of editor or source. The significance lies in the clear demonstration of the lack of theological discussion, orientation, or even active vocabulary within the characteristic editorial material. Generally, with regard to both total lists, certain patterns emerge. Most names of persons, places, and Old Testament figures are E. This material stands out in its special interest in words with the kind of rational, liturgical, legalistic, political orientation peculiar to first-century Judaism: " festival, unclean, unleavened, truth, it is permitted, bill of divorce, Caesar, soldier," etc. In other words, the E tradition has such a surprisingly non-Christian flavor, especially when placed in contrast to the logia, that we see that verbal discontinuity is also *ideational* discontinuity. We will see more of this later.

Before leaving this study, we must deal with two more matters. The first is the verbal evidence for the intrusion of the Evangelist into the logia wording. There are twenty-five words that show a clear pattern of E usage, but with a few examples of A usage. If we say that the E pattern establishes these as characteristic of the editorial tradition, then their occurrence in a logion would cast doubt on their originality as a word of Jesus. The following is the listing.

CHART XVII.   *E Words with Some A Occurrence*

akatharton (AO)	*dierchomai* (AO)
aletheia	*didasko* (AO–EO)
apeggeilan (AO)	*doxazo*
apethanen (AO)	*eperotao* (AO)
exestin (AO–EO)	*epitimao*
apostolos (AO)	*arneomai*
aule (AGO–AO)	*euphraino* (AO)
Bethsaida	*hupostrepho*
Biblion (AO)	*ochlos*
David (AO)	*presbuteron* (AO)
deomai	*sphodra*
diaperao (AO)	*Kaisar* (AO–EO)
didaskale (EO)	

Within the list above there are four words showing a source pattern, all in the special Lucan source (S4): *apostolos, dierchomai, euphraino* (all A), and *hupostrepho*. These four would seem to be the most likely candidates for words inserted into logia by a particular source or editor. Among the twenty-five words above, sixteen reveal a striking pattern of orientation toward the opponent audience, either Jesus speaking to that audience, or an opponent speaking to Jesus. This could suggest that these words are editorial insertions since they are mostly used by the E. The fact of this audience pattern makes us pause in dismissing them too easily as unauthentic, since this word-audience correlation could reflect Jesus' use of current and particularly appropriate terminology to the opponents.[3] The clearest fact about this evidence is its scarcity, which tends to minimize the activity of the Evangelist in the creation of logia, while showing the abundant evidence for an editorial stratum with a certain cohesive integrity.

One more phenomenon needs to be examined, that of words used only once. A total examination of the Synoptic *hapax legomena* might force us to change some of the above estimates. Hawkins lists 373 such words in the three Gospels. Actually, a sampling of the 71 Synoptic words beginning with the letter *a* reveals a curious confirmation of the thesis of these pages: There are 37 E and 34 A *hapax legomena,* with no apparent patterns of any kind. If this is any indication of the rest of the picture, then it would suggest that the A and the E traditions are about equally filled with *hapax legomena,* further illustrating the integrity of each as a unique body of words, and suggesting the shakiness of any argument based on *hapax legomena.*

ARAMAIC DISCONTINUITY

One of the most interesting lines of evidence for discontinuity is that of the Aramic lying behind the Gospels. Since the days of Dalman, the most extensive and cautious treatment of this evidence has been the study of Matthew Black, wherein he outlines the many ways in which the Greek text of the Synoptics could be examined for the underlying Aramaic.[4] Out of an exhaustive analysis of grammar, syntax, vocabulary, Semitic poetic forms, translation and interpretation of Aramaic, Black comes to one conclusion which he feels can be established. " Where any one Semitic or Aramaic construction could be observed recurring, its distribution showed that it tended to be found most frequently, and sometimes exclusively, *in the words of Jesus.* The same conclusion emerged from a study of the translation and mistranslation of Aramaic in the Gospels. . . . We have to do with a translation-tradition, sometimes literal, mostly, however, literary and interpretive, but generally bearing the stamp upon it, in one feature or another, of its

Aramaic origin. Whether that source was written or oral, it is not possible from the evidence to decide. The only other place where evidence could be adduced of Aramaic influence of any extent outside the sayings of Jesus in the Synoptics was in the Marcan narrative or in non-dominical sayings and dialogue." [5] Black suggests that this last could be construed as evidence of the kind of Greek that an Aramaic-speaking Jew would write. Even more specifically, Black points out that asyndeton, the omission of conjunctions that normally join coordinate words or clauses, is, on the whole, contrary to the Greek language. In view of this, the fact " that asyndeton should so preponderate in the words of Jesus and be virtually absent in the longer narrative portions of the Synoptics . . . points to the conclusion that a sayings-tradition, cast in translation Greek and reflecting faithfully the Aramaic construction, has been utilized by the Evangelists." [6] Clearly, Black's analysis draws a sharp distinction between the editorial and the logia material.

The computer has turned up a new phenomenon that seems to add weight to Black's conclusion. An exhaustive study of every word in the Synoptics in every one of its usages, cross-correlated for the E and A traditions, reveals a very curious fact. Certain verbs show a regular absence of the imperfect and aorist tenses in the logia, but an abundance of these as well as other tenses in the editorial material. There are twenty-three such verbs that have appeared so far, and the patterns are clear enough to reveal some kind of linguistic reality producing this phenomenon. When one remembers that the Hebrew tense system has only completed and incompleted action, and that consequently the Greek aorist and especially the imperfect would find limited usage in translating the

CHART XVIII. *Words Showing Aramaic Discontinuity*

ago	*dunamai*	*krazo*	*teleo*
aiteo	*eggizo*	*lego*	*pheugo*
arneomai	*echo*	*laleo*	*phobeomai*
akolutheo	*zeteo*	*horao*	
ginosko	*thaumazo*	*poreuomai*	
ginomai	*kathemai*	*siopao*	

CHART XIX.   *Computer Audience Analysis of* Laleo

Verb Form	A	E	Verb Form	A	E
lalei	AD		*lalountos*		EK
lalei	AD		*lalountos*		EK
lalei	A1		*lalountos*		ER
lalei		EO	*lalountos*		ER
lalei		EO	*lalountos*		ET
lalein	AD		*lalountos*		ET
lalein		EG	*lalountos*		ET
lalein		EK	*lalountos*		ET
lalein		ER	*elalesa*	AD	
lalein		ET	*elalei* (imp.)		ED
laleite	AD		*elalei*		EK
laleisai (aor. inf.)		EG	*elalei*		EK
laleisai		EK	*elalei*		EK
laleisai		EK	*elalei*		EK
laleisai		ET	*elalei*		ER
lalesete (aor.)	AD		*elalei*		ER
lalesete	AD		*elalei*		ER
lalesete	AD		*elalei*		ER
lalesousin	AD		*elalei*		ET
lalethenton (aor.)		EK	*elalesan*	AD	
lalethentos		EK	*elalesate*	AD	
lalethesetai	AD		*elalesen* (aor.)		EK
lalethesetai	A1		*elalesen*		EK
lalo	AD		*elalesen*		EK
lalon	AD		*elalesen*		ER
laloumenois		EK	*elalesen*		ET
laloumenon		ER	*elalesen*		ET
laloun	AD		*elalesen*		ET
lalountos		EK	*elalesen*		ET
lalountas		ET	*elalesen*		ET
lalountes	AD		*elalethe*		EK
lalountes	AD		*elaloun*		EK
lalounton		EK	*lelalemenois*		EK

Aramaic verb, one is introduced to the unique possibility that this Synoptic tense pattern reveals the Hebrew orientation of the A material and the Greek orientation of the E.

One of the clearest examples of this distinction between E and A usage of verbs can be seen in a detailed study of the verb *laleo* in all its Synoptic usages.

In the listing above two patterns stand out: the imperfect never occurs in the A material and the aorist seldom does. The infrequent departure of the aorist from this pattern could be explained by the observation of both Black and Wellhausen that at times a Greek aorist has the force of a Semitic perfect.[7] Black takes this to be an illustration of translation Greek, however. That this " new " evidence by itself is decisive is doubtful. Taken together with the studies of Black, Wellhausen, Dalman, and others, it is more impressive. Certainly one can say with a high degree of probability that the A material generally must be distinguished from the E by its Aramaic orientation. The fact of the Aramaic flavor of some of Mark's narration would mitigate this judgment, but not negate it. The pattern is clear.

AUDIENCE DISCONTINUITY

Another illustration of this phenomenon lies in the difference between the E and the A strata in identifying the audience. For example, we have already seen the sociological, somewhat superficial terms used by the Evangelists in designating the audience (Ch. II). They are mostly described as *mathetai, allon hoi esan met auton, ochlos, Pharisaioi,* etc., with only rarely a designation that has any theological overtones (Luke 7:29; 10:29-37). On the other hand, Jesus in the logia is recorded describing or addressing the audience in a rich variety of terms almost every one of which has deep theological meaning.

We have already suggested that both the logia and the Evangelists identify the audience in terms of its " distance " from Jesus, its acceptance or rejection of him (Ch. II). In the list below it is strikingly evident that whereas the Evangelists refined this audience tradition into four clear categories (D, DG, GO, O), the Jesus of the logia seems to have viewed the audience context in basically a twofold sense. The phrase " He who is not with me is against

CHART XX. *Logia Words Identifying the Audience*

AD/ADG	AGO/AO
agathos	*hamartolos*
adelphos	*genea*
doulos	*gennemata echidnon*
elachistos	*kakos*
thugater	*poneros*
kalos	*sapros*
meizon	*hupokrites*
makarios	*huios geenes*
meter	*huios tou ponerou*
mikros	*huios tou aionos toutou*
mathetes	*Pharisaioi*, etc.
mikroteros	
huios tes basileias	
huios tou numphonos	
huios tou photos	
huios tes anastaseos	
huios theou	
hoi de kataksiothentes	
tou aionos ekeinou	

me " (Matt. 12:30) or " He that is not against us is for us " (Mark 9:40) is actually a kind of summary of Jesus' general attitude. He viewed the human situation as he viewed everything, in terms of the judgment of God (cf. *JGTJ,* Ch. X). For him there were only two kinds of persons. Men were either righteous or sinners, sons of the Kingdom or sons of the evil one, men of light or men of darkness, wheat or tares, alive or dead. Compromise was impossible, and indecision was tantamount to rejection. This crisis dualism is reflected in both the E and A traditions, but the E preserves it indirectly, while the A does so much more consciously and sharply, not only in the content of the logia, but in the very terms by which those in the audience are identified.

In the next chapter we shall see that the logia do indeed preserve the fourfold audience distinction, but this is done indirectly, in contrast to the E material where this somewhat stylized categorization appears quite deliberately. The Evangelists go out of their way to sharpen the fourfold distinction. Perhaps the clearest indication of this is the way in which the E distinguish much more clearly than the A between the AD and the ADG. In the next chapter we shall see that instead of separating the DG out as a special group, Jesus mostly addressed them in *company* with the D, forming a kind of " disciple block," which he addressed as one would a highly sympathetic audience and *as a whole*. At times he is concerned to separate the D out as a single group, but seldom if ever does he do so with the DG. They are the " rest," who follow him with the Twelve, and if he distinguishes them from the D at all it is more by default than design. This is perhaps the thrust of two obscure passages: the one is where Peter, like the Evangelists, wanting to make a clear distinction between the D and the DG, asks, " Lord, are you telling this parable for us or for all? " (Luke 12:41). The other is where Jesus assures the disciples, " What I say to you I say to all " (Mark 13:37), thus for him, at this point at least, minimizing this D–DG distinction. However this may be, it would seem that on several counts, there is clear discontinuity in the way in which the audience is viewed in the E and A material.

THEOLOGICAL DISCONTINUITY

The Jesus reflected in the logia is a creative mind who seems to have borrowed extensively from Rabbinic, popular, and Old Testament sources, but who rose above those sources with noticeable regularity (cf. *JGTJ*, 32 f.). The originality of the logia comes to unique focus when we see the A material differing significantly from the explicit or implicit theology of the E, whether it is the Evangelists or someone speaking out of Jesus' audiences. There is, for example, the manner in which the E and A material differ over the use of *pneuma* for *Satan* and his angels. By the first century it was common to view Satan as a member of the cosmos, a separate individual who stood in the most direct opposition to God (cf. *JGTJ*, 188). The word *pneuma* was, of course, a reference to God, and was also used to refer in both Old and New Testaments to man's psychic nature, to his highest endowment, that aspect of humanity most like God and most available to him (*JGTJ*, 157, 162). When, therefore, *pneuma* was used for Satan, one could see him presented in the highest proportions as a distinctly personal being, or even a rival God. It seems clear that Jesus' contemporaries conceived of Satan in this fashion. The question is whether or not Jesus did the same. Audience Criticism reveals a very interesting pattern.

CHART XXI.   Pneuma-Satan *Compared*

Pneuma refers to man's highest nature

E	Mark 2:8; 8:12; Luke 1:47, 80; 8:55; 10:21
A	Mark 14:38; Matt. 5:3; 9:55 (margin)

Pneuma refers to the Holy Spirit

E	Mark 1:8, 10, 12; Matt. 1:18, 20; 12:18; Luke 1:15, 17, 35, 41, 67; 2:25, 26, 27; 4:14
A	Mark 1:10, 12; 3:29; 12:36; 13:11; Matt. 12:28; 28:19; Luke 4:14, 18; 11:13

Pneuma refers to *Satan* or his angels

E	Mark 1:23, 26, 27; 3:11, 30; 5:2, 8, 13; 6:7; Matt. 8:16; Luke 6:18; 7:21; 8:2; 13:11
A	(Mark 9:25); (Luke 10:20); Luke 11:24, 26

The chart above shows Jesus using *pneuma* (*ruach*) about as his contemporaries did, with one startling exception. He seems reluctant to use *pneuma* as a description for *Satan*. This charted discontinuity becomes even sharper by two refinements in the above: in Mark 9:25, Jesus, in using *pneuma* for Satan, is not giving an independent judgment, but is quoting the child's father; in Luke 10:20 he does use *pneuma* for the demons, but he is merely reiterating what his *disciples* have told him (v. 17), and correcting them: " Do not rejoice in this, that the spirits are subject to you " (v. 20). This leaves only one case, in a parable, where the logia record Jesus voluntarily using *pneuma* for an unclean spirit. As I have attempted to show elsewhere, the reluctance to use *pneuma* in this common fashion is joined by other evidence to suggest that Jesus did not share the popular belief in Satan as a rival God or a separate psychic being (*JGTJ*, 191). Instead, the logia show Jesus speaking of Satan as a symbol for *men* in a problem-ridden and sinful condition, a view decidedly discontinuous with his generation, and, it would seem, with the Evangelists.

The use of the phrase *basileia tou theou* (*ton ouranon*) gives an illustration of discontinuity between the A and that part of the E stratum which describes the attitudes of various ones in the audiences. In the logia, Jesus presents a Kingdom of God that is intensely spiritual, predominantly personal, and embraces both the present and the future *eschaton*. Some logia emphasize the present sovereignty of God, some the future *eschaton,* and some give a balanced reference to both the present and the future (*JGTJ,* Ch. VII). When the Evangelists are clearly giving their own summaries of this doctrine, they speak of the Kingdom in general terms, remarkably lacking in interpretation: " He welcomed them and spoke to them of the kingdom of God " (Luke 9:11; cf. also Luke 8:1; Matt. 4:23; Mark 1:14-15). Every other occurrence in the E stratum reflects the use of the Kingdom idea by someone other than an Evangelist: John the Baptist (Matt. 3:2), Isaiah (Luke 1:33), the disciples (Luke 19:11; Mark 11:10), Joseph of Arimathea (Mark 15:43), the thief on the cross (Luke 23:43). There we find the Kingdom pictured in highly Jewish terms (Matt. 3:2; Luke 1:33; Mark 11:10) as an imminent, political (Mark 11:10; Luke 1:33; Matt. 3:2) or eschatological reality (Mark 15:43; Luke 23:42; 19:11; 1:33; Mark 11:10). Both of these expectations Jesus soundly rejected.[8] What this reflects is exactly what Luke indicates in one of his brief editorial summaries: " They *supposed* that the kingdom of God was to appear immediately " (Luke 19:11; italics mine). What is missing here is Jesus' characteristic emphasis on the present, inner, dynamic activity of the Kingdom as God's sovereign presence (*JGTJ,* Ch. X). The Evangelists seem to understand this Kingdom concept found in the logia, but appear reluctant in the obviously editorial material to do anything but describe it in the most general terms. Those in Jesus' audiences appear not to understand, and so this discontinuity is evident.

One general pattern emerging in this theological comparison is that the cosmology of the E is characterized by a superficial, externalized unsophisticated use of certain theologically loaded terms, while the logia show a depth of spiritual maturity and sophistication that stands in stark contrast. For example, the Evangelists and their contemporaries are reflected using *ouranos* in various ways: as a modifier of angels (Luke 2:13), as a circumlocution for God (Luke 19:38), as the locus of apocalyptic signs (Mark 8:11; Luke 11:16), but mostly as the domain of God or angels or the Spirit in a crudely physical manner. Heaven is up, and identified with the sky, and so spiritual phenomena come " down " to men, in rather primitive, cosmological fashion (Matt. 3:16; 28:2; Mark 1:10; 6:41; 7:34; 16:19; Luke 22:43; 9:54; etc.). The logia, on the other hand, give a vastly more sophisticated picture. Jesus does use *ouranos* in the more crudely contemporary and Jewish sense, but the curious thing is that this is almost always to an opponent audience. Most characteristically, and mostly to the disciples, he speaks of *ouranos* in close connection with the person of God, a presently existing spiritual dimension wherein men are related to God in a very special and intensely personal way (*JGTJ*, 86). The chief exception to this lies in Mark, ch. 13, in some highly questionable apocalyptic intrusions.

The word *aggelos* shows this same discontinuity. In its fourteen occurrences in the E material, the angel appears as a three-dimensional creature who can be seen and heard and who ministers to men.[9] The thirteen appearances of *aggelos* in the logia show Jesus making cryptic references to the possibility of angels taking part in the physical affairs of men (Matt. 26:53), and four times he identifies them as heavenly creatures distinct from the person of God (Luke 16:22; Mark 13:32; Matt. 13:39 f.; 13:49); but two of these are parables of the *eschaton,* and the parable of the rich man and Lazarus is completely untypical of his teaching (*JGTJ*, Ch. XII). Most typically, the logia present angels as references to the presence, the glory, the judgment of God active among men in decidedly personal, highly sophisticated fashion.[10] It would seem justified to generalize that Jesus' cosmology is, in its highest expression, discontinuous with that of his contemporaries, including the Evangelists. One can doubt very seriously if they understood the cosmology of the logia.

This general theological sophistication of the logia stands out when we see discontinuity in the use of certain rather common terms. The word *genea* is a perfectly normal word used by the Evangelists in a strictly temporal sense (Matt. 1:17; Luke 1:48). The logia, however, picture Jesus using this term eleven times, in three senses: a collective gathering of people bound together by biological affinity, by temporal affinity, or by moral affinity. The overwhelming stress is on *genea* as a moral-spiritual designation: an " evil generation," a " faithless generation " upon whom will come the blood of all the prophets (Mark 8:38; 9:19; Luke 11:50; etc.). Another example is *adelphos,* which describes a purely biological relationship in its editorial use; but in the logia it takes on a distinctly technical, theological meaning. These are the ones who do the will of God (Mark 3:31-35); and *adelphos* becomes a technical term for the disciples of Jesus. The word *dechomai,* as used by the Evangelists, describes the generally superficial act of receiving a person into one's city (Luke 9:53), or taking up a person or object into one's hands (Luke 2:28; 22:17). In its logia use, the term becomes intensely theological, a reference to receiving Jesus, his disciples, the Kingdom, and God in existential and saving depth.[11] The verb *aiteo* shows the same discontinuity. It has two main meanings in the Synoptics: five times Jesus uses it to describe prayer (e.g., Mark 11:24), and four times a simple request (e.g., Mark 10:38). Not once, however, in its six occurrences do the E use *aiteo* to refer to prayer.[12] In these and other ways (cf. Ch. V), the superficial level at which the E material operates must be sharply contrasted with the theological sophistication of the logia.

In summary, this chapter has taken note of several patterns of discontinuity that serve to draw a line of distinction rather clearly between the E and the A material. The editorial stratum simply does not look the same as the logia. The A material is emerging as an integral body of sayings within several source-redactor traditions: a kind of hard core of data treated with sufficient respect by the editors as to reveal these characteristic patterns. Audience Criticism up to this point is tending to support the view that only in the smallest degree are the writers of the Gospels authors, creating the logia themselves.[18] More evidence is necessary, however, before this hypothesis approaches anything like probability. For this we now turn to the full examination of these " horizontal " patterns of continuity within the A material. It is in this next study that the uniqueness and integrity of the logia will become most apparent, their discontinuity from the editorial stratum most believable, and their historicity most possible.

Chapter V

AUDIENCE CONTINUITY: WORD AND PRAXIS

We shift our discussion then to the logia, and more exactly to that intimate correlation between logion and audience which we have seen emerging at various points in this study. When one compares an individual term, technique, or idea of Jesus as it relates to audience at one point against its usage throughout the entire Synoptic tradition, a high degree of continuity is revealed. This consists of three types of patterns: word patterns, praxis patterns, and theological patterns. In this and the next chapter, these will be presented as fully as possible.

VERBAL CONTINUITY

Computer Word Study. In Appendix B there are listed 309 words and phrases that have patterns of one kind or another.[1] These can be called " characteristic " of the teachings of Jesus in the Synoptics. As has been pointed out, this concept of the word pattern is not new. T. W. Manson lists 191 such terms in an appendix to his book *The Teaching of Jesus.* What is novel is the surprising number of examples revealed by the computer. This is especially interesting when one sees that these 309 do not include many on Manson's list not solidly enough established as patterns. The following chart shows the distribution of these words in terms of the three quality categories we have been using.

CHART XXII. *Pattern Word Correlation*

Figures indicate the number of different words showing patterns, arranged according to quality of pattern and audience "blocks."

Pattern Quality Category

	(a)	(b)	(c)
D and DG	58	97	53
GO and O	27	43	22

It will be noted in the chart above that the ratio between categories (a), (b), and (c) is the same throughout these two audience blocks. The words to the disciples have about the same quality of continuity as those to the opponents.

A brief look at some of these terms will underscore the striking nature of the patterns. The word *amen,* for example, occurs fifty times in the Synoptics, each time on the lips of Jesus. The phrase *ho huios tou anthropou* is found on forty-three separate occasions, exclusively in the logia. The noun *ampelon* has twenty-nine uses in the Synoptics, each one in the teachings of Jesus. When one considers that *amen* and *ho huios tou anthropou* have almost no place in the Old Testament, and that *ho huios tou anthropou* and *ampelon* are not used again in the New Testament,[2] these Synoptic patterns stand out with special force. The fact that *amen* occurs forty-five of the fifty times in a disciple situation, and *ampelon* twenty-four of the twenty-nine times in an opponent context raises further interesting possibilities.

There are also groups of words that tend to cluster about a particular audience. For example, there are nineteen peculiarly Jewish terms that are almost exclusively directed to the opponents (O and DO): *apodekateuo, David, epigraphe, exestin, entole, thuso (thu-*

sian, thusiasterion), Ioannes, Iona, hieron, krateo, Mouses, naos, nesteuo, nomos, paradosis, sabbaton, Abraam, omnuo phragmos.[3] Many words stand out not just in their limitation to a particular audience, but because of their peculiar appropriateness for that audience. For example, *kakos* is almost exclusively AO, while *kalos* is mostly AD (14 AD, 4 AO). The word *Kaisar* is thoroughly opponent oriented (6 AO, 7 EO), suggesting the nervous political concern of this opponent stratum. The two verbs *pascho* and *sozo* show Jesus' special attention to suffering and salvation in talking with the disciples. The verb *speiro* reveals a peculiar affinity for mixed audiences, especially those of the disciples (10 A1, 3 A4, 8 AD); and we see here a metaphor especially well adapted for just such occasions: the sower sowing the seed of the word in those soils most prepared and likely to bear fruit (Mark 4:1 ff.). There is not one use of this verb to an opponent audience, or in editorial narration. The rest of this chapter will be spent in going deeply into such patterns of correlation.

CHART XXIII. *Pattern Word Saturation: Audience and History Correlation*

These figures represent the ratio of the number of occurrences of pattern words to the total number of *important* words (nouns, verbs, or others characterizing a person's speech), correlated according to audience and historical section.

	Pattern Words	Total Words	Percentage Saturation
AD	504	2,795	18%
ADG	114	585	19.5%
A1	288	1,110	26%
AGO	58	292	(20%)
AO	504	1,540	11.5%
H6	73	517	14%
H7	65	294	(22%)
Totals	1,211	6,894	17.5%

The chart above is representative of the saturation of the logia with pattern words.[4] The average for the entire logia tradition is

17.5 percent. This would suggest a hard core of verbal data characteristic of Jesus in his Synoptic teachings. We note also that the highest word pattern ratio occurs generally with logia given to the sympathetic audiences (D, DG, A1), and the lowest in those to the unsympathetic groups. Either Jesus is recorded speaking more characteristically to the disciple groups or his typical verbiage is preserved more accurately in logia to such audiences.

We are especially interested in the high saturation of pattern words in the A1 situation and the Passion Narrative (H7), and in the low percentage within the Marcan Apocalypse (H6). The Passion Narrative is noted for its earliness and general stability, and this could be reflected in this high verbal stability. Mark, ch. 13, on the other hand, is often considered an editorial compilation prior to Mark; and when one compares the 14 percent word saturation in the apocalypse with a 20 percent saturation in Mark generally, this chapter separates itself from the rest of Mark in this, another way. Furthermore, when the 26 percent saturation in the A1 tradition is compared with the 17.5 percent overall ratio, the suggestion arises that there is something about the presence of the DG that is especially conducive to the preservation of characteristic verbiage. One is reminded that there were scribes in the DG group. The possibility that there is a correlation here is very suggestive, but will have to await more evidence.[5] The intensely interesting fact to be noted is that these patterns cut across all sources and appear in the work of all editors. This suggests a verbal stability not dependent upon editor or source, and raises the distinct possibility that we have here some statistical indication of actual verbal history in the Synoptics. It is possible that in this limited collection of words we are dealing with the *ipsissima verba* of Jesus. This hypothesis will be tested at length in Chapters VII and VIII.

As we pursue this method one step farther, it becomes possible to extract those Greek words with the highest likelihood of being translations of the actual words of Jesus. According to this logic, these would be the category (a) words occurring only in the logia, and addressed only or mostly to an individual audience such as AD or AO. Such words would have a sufficient number of narrowing limitations to reduce the possibilities of interpretation to a minimum. The following list is what emerges according to this system of limitations.

amen	*oligopistos*	*ho huios tou*
adikias	*opheilo*	*anthropou*
geenna	*peteinon*	*katakrino*
ergates	*skandalon*	*numphios*
therismos	*toioutos*	*oikodespotes*
krouo	*talanton*	*ouai*
merimnao	*dechomai*	*anegnote*
misthos	*exothen*	*eukopoteros*

A word needs to be said here about the problem of translation. Can one really call a Greek term the *ipsissimum verbum* of Jesus? When one reflects that there are over twenty dialects of Aramaic, and we cannot yet be certain which one Jesus spoke, this problem becomes very difficult indeed. The cautious Delitzsch went no farther than producing a *Hebrew* New Testament, and one can appreciate his caution. Others, like Dalman, Torrey, Burney, and Black have attempted to recapture the actual Aramaic of Jesus, and one sees that at points this is perhaps not impossible. Actually, for our purposes, it is unnecessary. The fact of the Greek word pattern, cutting as it does widely across various sources and forms, says that whatever may be the actual Aramaic word, the patterns in the Greek reveal a general stability behind the Greek at these points that must also apply to the Aramaic. It is true that at times there are several Aramaic words that could be translated by a particular Greek term, and that on occasion there is evidence of the mistranslation of an Aramaic original. This gives us pause in demanding too exact an interpretation of *ipsissima verba*. What we are arguing here is that even granted exceptions and mistranslations, in a massive study such as this, these patterns are so broadly based that they have a stability that overcomes the exceptions. When several sources and editors agree independently and often that a particular Greek word accurately translates the kind of thing Jesus was accustomed to say about certain topics to certain audiences, it would seem that we have here the kind of inadvertent testimony that approaches very closely to *ipsissima verba* despite the translation problem.

CHART XXIV. *Pattern Word Correlation: Form and Source*

This chart shows the percentage ratio of pattern words to total words within each correlation.

	FA	FS	FP	FL	FM	S1	S2	S3	S4
AD	23	19	13	13	—	20	17	15	12
AO	16	13	11	—	—	15	18	15	7
A1	—	22	24	—	—	20	19	26	—

In further refining this verbal analysis, we have concentrated on the three most abundant audience situations (Chart III) under the assumption that they will be sufficiently representative of the total picture. The most obvious fact here is the movement in the chart above from left to right in the form categories and with some exceptions in the source categories. The apothegm contains the highest pattern word saturation, then the saying, then the parable, then the legend, and least of all the miracle story. If the apothegm circulated as a kind of illustrative unit, one could see where the exact wording would be especially important, like a sermon illustration where the punch line must be preserved exactly for telling effect. The fact that there are too few pattern words in the miracle stories to show up on such a chart may be instructive in assessing their exact, verbal historicity. With regard to the source correlation, we see the general superiority of Mark and Q, Matthew's high saturation in the A1 material (the Sermon on the Mount is 22 percent) and Luke's unique verbal independence.

In summary, two major observations might be made. In the first place, such verbal audience analysis opens up many new possibilities for analyzing old questions. Secondly, it is clearly possible on the basis of scientific criteria to talk seriously about the *ipsissima verba* of Jesus. Furthermore, when we see the abundance of logia pattern words, and compare this with those in the E tradition (Appendix C), the arresting possibility arises that we can be more certain that the words of the logia represent the words of Jesus than we can that the E words represent those of a particular Evangelist. There are more and sharper patterns, and more clearly demonstrable continuity in the wording of the logia than in that of the editorial tradition. The fact that we are talking about an average of 17.5 percent of the logia words does not deny the historicity of the rest. It only says that with this audience-critical method it is this much which can be demonstrated. When one remembers that we have omitted from the charts above all category (c) word patterns, about one third of the total (cf. Appendix B), and that other terms will emerge from the theological study revealing different kinds of patterns, then the number of words laying claim to this unique stability should be increased. The fact that we are talking only about a percentage of the logia words should give special comfort neither to the critical conservative nor to the liberal. It should serve, however, to challenge a deep-rooted assumption within modern scholarship that it is not even possible to talk about the actual words of Jesus.

Metaphor Study. As we continue our verbal study, it is reasonable to take another sampling of logia material wherein patterns are revealed; that is, the metaphors ascribed to Jesus. Since it is clear that Jesus was a preacher who consistently taught in metaphor, it would seem that here we come to a stratum laying particular claim to closeness to his authentic mind. Patterns at this level should have peculiar significance. There are sixty-two parables yielding this kind of data, within which are twenty-two basic metaphors employed as the following chart indicates.

In the chart below, three general observations might be made. The first is that the basic agriculture metaphor with its many variations is the most solidly demonstrated, although it shows no distinct audience pattern. The second is that the pattern metaphors in the AD material show a curious *personal* fixation, with those pertaining to money, servant-master, and the body predominating. A third important fact is that the AO pattern metaphors cluster around the more social experiences of dinners, weddings, and houses.

CHART XXV. *Parable Metaphor Study*

This shows the various metaphors correlated according to audience patterns, with pattern quality indicated.

AD PATTERN

> Salt (b) (log. 21, 194, 195)
> Light (b) (log. 22, 23, 24, 144, 324)
> Treasure-money-business (b) (log. 47, 49, 57)
> Servant-master (a) (log. 49, 204, 219, 221, 222, 237, 242, 263, 269, 280)
> Parts of the body (c) (log. 48, 160, 162, 163, 170)

AO PATTERN

> House (b) (log. 67, 125, 127, 138, 220)
> Dinner (b) (log. 233, 241, 242, 281, 282)
> Father-son (c) (log. 236, 279)
> Wedding (c) (log. 77, 281, 282, 324)

NO AUDIENCE PATTERN

> Agriculture (b) (log. 63, 64, 79, 131, 140, 143, 147, 148, 149, 151, 161, 217, 225, 263, 279, 280, 325)
> Door (c) (log. 60, 61, 227, 324)

This parable study is strengthened by a more general analysis of metaphorical terms where the different orientation between AD and AO becomes even more sharply evident. These words are more often used with one audience or another, but do not necessarily show patterns.

In the listing below, the words more characteristic of Jesus' teaching to the disciples (D and DG) cluster about four themes: (1) the harvest; (2) servant-master; (3) the parts of the body; (4) money, treasure, reward. The terms more typical of the AO and AGO teaching continue their orientation toward eating and banquets, and one notes the absence of the more personal and plebeian themes characteristic of the words to the disciples. This is the same general pattern found in the parable study. Clearly there is a difference in the type of metaphor Jesus is recorded using when speak-

AD, ADG Metaphorical Words

therismos	pur	protos
therizo	ous	hrabdos
thalassa	pule	hriza
krouo	sitos	broche
misthos	phulake	talanton
akanthas	elachistos	chalkos
agros	sperma	ergates
argurion	agrupneo	therismos
ekkopto	diaskorpizo	katheudo
zume	etairos	ballantion
thesauros	thrix	brugmos
thronos	kleronomeo	klauthmos
kopos	mesonuktian	pous
speiro	oikiakos	chiton
katharizo	orao	chreiopheiletes
oikonomeo	peruzonnumai	sapron
paidion	poterion	oikodespotes
poimaino	dendron	karpos

AO, AGO Metaphorical Words

neos	askos	cheilos
daktulo	geiton	oinos
epiblema	georgos	Iona
lestai	phragmos	gemizo
deipnon	numphios	

ing to the disciples and the opponents. Especially appropriate is the orientation of the servant-master metaphors to the disciples, and the dinner metaphors to the opponents.

In-Depth Word Studies. In some ways the most striking patterns appear in detailed studies of particular words. It is here that the consistent integrity of word usage suggests most plausibly a single mind behind these various occurrences. One of the most interesting examples of this is the word *doulos,* especially as it occurs in the parables of Jesus. There we find him using this term in consistent ways to identify the disciples of his audience. The correlation between audience and logion is striking. In ten different parables he identifies one of the key figures as a *doulos*. In every one the way in which the figure of the *doulos* is used is dependent upon whether Jesus is addressing an audience of disciples (D or DG) or one of opponents. Of this number there are seven parables addressed to a D or DG audience.

Matt. 10:24 ff. The Parable of the Disciples and Their Teacher (D)
Matt. 18:23 ff. The Parable of the Unforgiving Servant (D)
Luke 12:41 ff. The Parable of the Faithful and Unfaithful Servant (D)
Mark 13:34 The Parable of a Man Going on a Journey (D)
Luke 12:35 ff. The Parable of the Waiting Servants (D)
Luke 17:7 The Parable of the Unworthy Servant (D)
Matt. 13:24 ff. The Parable of the Wheat and Tares (D/DG)

In every one of these parables the exegesis demands that the *douloi* of the parable be equated with some group in what might be called the " disciple tradition ": the prophets, Jesus' contemporaries or those who would be in the same close relation to Jesus and the Kingdom in the future (cf. *JGTJ, ad loc.*). In three cases the identification of the servants of the parables with Jesus' immediate disciple audience is especially clear: Matt. 10:24-25, " A *disciple* is not above his teacher, nor a *servant* above his master "; Matt. 18:35 where Jesus applies the parable to his D audience with the words, "So also my heavenly Father will do to *every one of you* . . ."; Luke 17:9-10, " Does he thank the *servant* because he did what was commanded? So *you also* . . . say, ' We are unworthy *servants* ' " (italics mine).

It is significant that in every parable of this group the center of attention is on the figure of the servant. This would be natural if Jesus were identifying his audience with the *douloi* of the parable. It is also noteworthy that in all of these parables the servant stands in a special relationship to the Lord. He is given a charge of responsibility to watch, to be faithful, to open the door, to do what is commanded, all of which are characteristics of discipleship, and in every case to a D audience. The parable of the wheat and tares is especially interesting in that this rather aggressive, judging tendency on the part of the *douloi* of the parable is exactly what Jesus often warns the Twelve against.

On the other hand, there are three parables containing *doulos* addressed to an O audience:

> Mark 12:1-12 The Parable of the Vineyard
> Matt. 22:3 ff. The Parable of the Marriage Feast
> Luke 14:17 ff. The Parable of the Great Feast

In all of these the following is true: (1) The central figure is someone other than a *doulos;* he is a wicked husbandman or a reluctant guest. (2) The *douloi* have a secondary place as liaison between the lord and the main characters. Their function is that of transmitting the lord's invitation, or reminding men of his demands. (3) The exegesis demands the identification of the main characters with those in Jesus' audience who are antagonistic to his message, and the identification of the *douloi* with some aspect of the disciple tradition. The audience is clearly and consistently reflected in the parable.

It would seem that in *doulos* we have a term describing with peculiar exactness the fellowship with Jesus and the Kingdom to which he called men. It is not difficult to understand such usage when we remember the meaning of *ebedh* in the Old Testament. There the people of God are described in terms of this rich concept. Abraham, Isaac, Moses, Joshua, Caleb, Job, David, Hezekiah, Zerubbabel, Eliakim are all called servants of God. Israel as the Lord's servant is to have a mission to the nations (Isa. 42:19). Israel as the servant is the chosen witness of God (Isa. 43:10), and is the messianic servant himself (Isa. 42:1). Here is *ebedh* saturated with the long-established concept of some person or group especially dear, especially close, especially obedient to the Lord, and so especially commissioned by him. Where could Jesus have found a better word into which to pour his concept of the " New

Israel," the "New Servant"? The obvious implication is that in this *doulos* phenomenon we have a particularly clear reflection of the single mind and practice of the historic Jesus shining through the Synoptic tradition from depths beyond the manipulation of editors, or the creative activity of communities. This possibility will be explored more fully in later chapters.

A second example of such continuity of word and audience comes in the use of the phrase *basileia tou theou*. It is becoming increasingly common to interpret the Kingdom of God in a three-fold sense. (1) It is the presence of God's sovereignty in men's lives: "Son, go and work in the vineyard today" (Matt. 21:28). (2) It is the final consummation of God's purposes (Matt. 25:1-13). (3) It is God's sovereign purpose and presence through-out time and eternity like a field of grain growing now and eventually to be harvested (Matt. 13:24-30; *JGTJ*, 126, 129, 134). Joining the exegesis of all *basileia* passages to an audience analysis reveals some very interesting patterns as the following chart indicates.

CHART XXVI. *The Time of the Kingdom*

The figures refer to the number of logia units where one or the other of these three time aspects of *basileia* is stressed, counting each occurrence in each source.

	AD	ADG	A1	AO	AGO
Present Kingdom	16	3	12	9	2
Future Kingdom	8	1	1	1	0
Eternal Kingdom	13	0	2	0	0

In the chart above we see that when using *basileia* to a D or DG audience Jesus gives a fairly balanced emphasis on a Kingdom embracing both present and eschatological future. If anything, the stress is on the present. In dramatic contrast is his use of this term with the O and GO. Only once is he recorded stressing the future, eschatological Kingdom with the opponents (Luke 14:15), and never both present and future. The stress is almost entirely on the present nature of the Kingdom. In Chapter VI we shall see this phenomenon occurring in the clearest light. The Jesus of the logia seems reluctant to speak of the future *eschaton* to the opponents. This suggests that it is only to the disciples (D and DG) that Jesus gave his full teaching about the Kingdom, and one is tempted to see Mark 4:10-12 as a fairly accurate summary of this practice: " To you [disciples] has been given the secret of the kingdom."

There are many other illustrations of such continuity developing out of the study in depth of particular words and phrases. For example, we have already pointed out that the phrase *ho huios tou anthropou* occurs in forty-three separate logia, and never again in the New Testament. The *ipsissima verba* impression is strengthened by the patterns emerging from a deeper study of the phrase. We note that it occurs mostly to a disciple audience.[6] Its use to describe a suffering Son of Man is found only in the AD and ADG material.[7] The eschatological Son of Man is discussed fifteen times with the disciples, and only twice with the opponents (Mark 14:62; Luke 22:69). It would seem that here again the full picture of a present and future, suffering and kingly Son of Man is given only to the disciples. From the opponents, the Jesus of the logia withholds certain aspects of this concept almost without exception. He taught in a highly selective manner.

We have shown the discontinuity between the use of *ouranos* in the E and A material (Ch. IV). At this point we can add another pattern emerging from a study of this aspect of Jesus' cosmology. The word occurs as a circumlocution for God six times, and in each case to an O audience.[8] It is used on nineteen occasions to modify God, always in a personal sense (" My heavenly father "), always in a judgment context, and always either to a D or a DG audience. The Jesus of the logia is surprisingly consistent in using *ouranos* in a personal, judgment sense only to the disciples, and as a circumlocution for God only with the opponents.[9]

PRAXIS CONTINUITY

Arising at many points in this study has been the suggestion that Jesus was a selective teacher, speaking consistently in particular ways to certain audiences. One of the most brilliant illustrations of this comes from the " incredible theory " that he explained his parables only to his disciples.

> " And he said to them, ' To you has been given the secret of the kingdom of God, but for those outside everything is in parables.' . . . With many such parables he spoke the word to them, as they were able to hear it; he did not speak to them without a parable, but privately to his own disciples he explained everything." (Mark 4:11, 33-34.)

Not only the logion but Mark's editorial comment affirms the basic hypothesis of Audience Criticism: Jesus consciously adapted his teaching to his audience, explaining the parables principally to those who had eyes to see and ears to hear.[10] The standard approach to this matter has been to assume that this theory has been superimposed upon the tradition, because " such was utterly inapplicable to the teaching of Jesus." [11] He pitied the multitude and " would not wish to darken, but to enlighten them." [12] Two whole generations have followed Jülicher in insisting that Jesus did not use such allegory as that occurring in the explanations of the parables to the disciples.[13] What I am suggesting here is that this entire approach has been so indebted to a priori, deductive, nonscientific logic that certain clear and rather simple facts have been buried in the storm of protest to this " incredible theory." If one is willing to allow the text to speak for itself, and to examine all the evidence, what emerges is a pattern of such striking clarity that it stands as one of the leading illustrations of Synoptic continuity. There is abundant, inadvertent testimony that this was a common and widespread practice of Jesus.

Actually there are two issues here: (1) Do Mark 4:11, 33-34, and the many parallels to this idea found elsewhere describe a historic practice of Jesus? (2) Did Jesus use such allegory as is found in Mark 4:13 ff.? In order to get at these questions, we will have to refine the concept of parable " explanation," that is, the means of making the parables clear to the audience. Instead of one type of explanation, there seem to be at least four that can be identified in the material. We shall be using the term " parable " in its wide Semitic sense where *mashal* is used with no distinction between a comparison, a parable, or an allegory, and where even the term *hayedah* has the same loosely defined usage. As Manson suggests, the place to begin a discussion of Jesus' parables is not with the narrow usage of the rhetoricians of the West, but with the Old Testament where *mashal* is used in a variety of ways, including allegory (*The Teaching of Jesus,* p. 67). Since the discoveries at Qumran, such a necessarily Hebrew orientation for interpreting the Synoptics has become quite clear.

Semiallegorical Explanations. This category designates the explanation that may most correctly be called allegory, although not according to the rigid definition of Jülicher in which every point of the parable has a parallel in the explanation. Even in the three most allegorical, the parable of the wheat and tares (Matt. 13:24-30), the parable of the sower (Mark 4:13-20), and the parable of what defiles a man (Mark 7:15-23), many of the main elements are not interpreted. The most that can be said is that they are modified " semiallegory." These explanations usually occur as a separate unit at the end of the parable, sometimes on the same occasion as the parable, and at other times on a separate occasion.

Thematic Explanations. This category describes the type of explanation setting forth the main theme of the parable and giving its application usually as a compact unit at the end of the parable. If this explanation is taken away, the parable is still intact, although unexplained: for example, " Watch therefore, for you know neither the day nor the hour " (Matt. 25:13).

Contextual Explanations. This category describes the situation where the explanation comes in the literary or historical context of the parable. It often comes in the form of a question or phrase introducing the parable, or in the dialogue that follows it. In any event, as a result of the context there is no doubt as to the meaning and application of the parable.

Internal Explanations. This refers to the explanations given as an intimate part of the parables themselves, as running commentaries upon them. In some cases it is difficult to classify these as parables because they are so explicit. The parable of the sheep and goats is a case in point (Matt. 25:31-46). Under this category will be included those parables where the meaning is so obvious that one receives the impression that it has been explained, or that it needs no explanation.

When these four categories of explanation are correlated with the various audience types, the following are the results.

CHART XXVII. *Parables Explained and Unexplained Correlated According to Audience*

AD	AD (A1)	AGO (AA)	AO
Semiallegorical			
Matt. 13:49-50	Mark 4:13-20		Matt. 21:28-31b
Matt. 13:37-43	Luke 6:43-45		Mark 3:26
Mark 13:29-30			Luke 15:8-10
Mark 7:17-23			Luke 15:1-7
Luke 11:11-13			
Thematic			
Matt. 25:13	Mark 4:22	Luke 4:23	Matt. 22:11-14
Matt. 20:16	Luke 12:16-21	Luke 18:9-14	
Luke 18:1-8	Luke 19:11-28		
Luke 16:1-13			
Luke 17:7-10			
Luke 12:39-40			
Contextual			
Mark 9:49	Matt. 5:13-16		Luke 10:36-37
Mark 9:50	Luke 7:31-35		
Mark 13:34			
Luke 11:5-8			
Luke 12:35-38			
Internal			
Matt. 13:52	Luke 6:41-42	Luke 13:28-29	Luke 14:7-11
Matt. 25:31-46	Luke 6:47-49		Luke 11:39-41
	Luke 7:41-50		Luke 16:19-31

Parables Unexplained

Matt. 13:45-46	Matt. 13:33	Luke 12:58-59	Matt. 12:43-45
Matt. 13:44	Mark 4:26-29	Luke 13:6	Matt. 22:1-10
Luke 12:42-46	Mark 4:30-32	Luke 13:24	Mark 2:21
Luke 21:42-46		Luke 13:25-27	Mark 2:22
			Mark 3:27
			Mark 2:19-20
			Mark 12:1-12
			Luke 14:16-24
			Luke 15:11-32
			Luke 5:39

Totals: Explained (D, DG = 30)   Unexplained (D, DG = 7)
                    (GO, O = 12)   (GO, O = 14)

In the chart above there are twice as many parables explained as unexplained. This suggests there need be no battle between those who insist that Jesus veiled his message and those who maintain that he intended to be understood. They are probably both right. The distinguishing criterion is the audience. More importantly we note the inverse ratio of explained to unexplained parables. There are thirty explained to the disciples and twelve to the opponents, while seven remain unexplained to the disciples and fourteen to the opponents. When we see that this phenomenon is duplicated in all sources except L, we would seem to have a clear pattern supporting Mark 4:11, 33-34, as a general principle describing an actual homiletic practice of Jesus. At least the Jesus of the logia generally explained his parables to the disciples and left them unexplained to "those outside," who, having ears, did not hear. Jesus' use of parables in the logia seems to have been a selective one determined by the spiritual preparation of his audience. The dividing line was whether they accepted or rejected him, whether they were disciples or opponents.

The fact that there are exceptions to the rule calls the pattern into question. Some parables are explained to GO and O audiences, and left unexplained to the D and DG. The problem is lessened when we consider that the Marcan passage describes what is probably only a general principle, and the categories we have set up are only rough standards. A perfectly consistent picture is what should arouse our suspicions. If this were a description of an actual practice of Jesus, then it would have to be viewed not as an undeviating, artificial literary creation, but as a general, practical rule of thumb, used in the heat of life situations, where there would inevitably be exceptions to the rule. Actually, a further pattern emerges with regard to the exceptions. In every case except two the parables explained to a GO or O audience are either direct warnings against some sin such as pride, or are illustrations for the purpose of winning an argument. They do not deal with the Kingdom of God. One exception, the wedding robe (Matt. 22:11-14) is a parable where the thematic explanation is in doubt.[14] The other, the rich man and Lazarus (Luke 16:19-31), is a Jewish parable commonly known and self-explanatory (cf. *JGTJ,* 218). This would argue further that Mark was right in refining this principle by quoting Jesus to the effect that when he deliberately explained a parable *dealing with the Kingdom of God, the heart of his gospel,* he did so only to the D or DG.

The modern critical attitude toward these parable explanations is typified by Jeremias, who dismisses them as the additions of the early church, or as, in the case of Matt. 13:37-43, " the work of Matthew himself." [15] He points to the " impressive number " of examples of words, phrases, or grammatical constructions in this passage exhibiting the linguistic characteristics of the Evangelist. I have already pointed out that only thirteen of Jeremias' thirty-four examples are actually words, phrases, and grammatical constructions peculiar to Matthew; and every one of these has either a verbal or ideational parallel or direct counterpart in some other source in the Synoptic logia (*JGTJ,* 136). There is some slight evidence of Matthean style and vocabulary, but when one subjects this question to an exhaustive analysis, Jeremias' objections simply disappear. The total facts are these. In the eleven parables where semiallegorical explanations occur, there are a total of 265 important words in the basic parable and 263 such in the explanations. In the parables there are fifty-four pattern words, or 20 percent, that are characteristic of Jesus' language. In the eleven semiallegorical explanations there are seventy-one pattern words, or a total of 28 percent, that lay strong claim to being characteristic of Jesus. If anything, these explanations, given mostly to the D and often privately, are more typical of the mind of Jesus than are the basic parables. When one examines these explanations, they reveal more of the most characteristic theology of Jesus than do the parables. This is clearly one reason they appear to the modern exegete as being different from the parable. The factor that lends a new understanding is that of the audience. Many of these parables are given to nondisciple audiences and partake of all the reserve and restriction of material given to the opponents. But the explanations are given to the disciples, and the often dramatic shift in mood, language, and theology is merely typical of logia given to those who had eyes to see. This will be demonstrated at length in Chapter VII. It is only when Mark 4:10-12 is not taken seriously on its own terms that exegetes have the kind of trouble Jeremias has with these explanations.

There is much more evidence supporting this practice of explaining parables to the disciples. Luke 10:23-24, although in an entirely different context from Matt. 13:16-17, still retains one contextual element with regard to the logion, " Blessed are the eyes which see what you see! " They both agree that this was given privately to the disciples. The teaching about marriage given to the opponents in Matt. 19:4-9 is explained to the disciples, with the added comment, " He who is able to receive this, let him receive it " (v. 12). The incident of the withered fig tree, whether actual history or the actualization of a parable, is explained privately to the disciples (Mark 11:20-25). It is certainly possible that the principle enunciated in Mark 4:11, 33-34, is a theory imposed upon the Gospel by the early church. The widespread, subtle, intimate manner in which this emerges as a general pattern throughout the Gospels, however, would seem to cast grave doubt upon such an explanation. For this to be true, one would have to posit some kind of wholesale collaboration or intricate rewriting of the entire parable tradition on the most obtuse and technical level, and this seems most improbable. As Vincent Taylor says about the

"Messianic Secret" of Mark, "The agreement is too astonishing to be the work of art." More probably it is the reflection of historical reality.[16]

There are many other illustrations of such characteristic praxis in the logia. One of the most typical is the regularity with which one can identify the audience within the very symbolism of the parable, for example, in the use of the *doulos* symbol. An especially clear example is Luke 12:35-36: "Let *your* loins be girded and *your* lamps burning, and *be like* men who are waiting for their master to come home from the marriage feast" (italics mine). The oracular quality of the formula "Truly I say to you" is unduplicated in any similar literature of the period. The note of warning and imperative is typical and links the logia closely to the prophetic literature: "Watch therefore. . . . If . . . better that, . . . beware." There are many characteristic phrases that permeate the sources, such as "The kingdom of God is like," or "for my name's sake," or various combinations of the son metaphor: "sons of the kingdom," "sons of Satan," "sons of light," etc. (*JGTJ,* 187). Perhaps most typical of all is the way in which Jesus is portrayed seizing on a historic incident and immediately turning it to theological account, for example, Luke 13:1-9, "Unless you repent you will all likewise perish" (v. 5).

This then is the hypothesis emerging from these pages: the many patterns of continuity in the use of words and homiletic practice are so widespread, so brilliant, that we are driven to the possibility that here we have a demonstrable reflection of an authentic mind shining at certain points through the process of Gospel formation. One of the most certain ingredients in this picture of Jesus is his activity as a selective teacher, deliberately adapting his teaching to his audience.

Chapter VI

AUDIENCE CONTINUITY: THEOLOGY

The correlation between logion and audience can be investigated in one final way, in the theological continuity that gives coherence to the material. This lies not in isolated proof texts, nor in the use of single words or phrases, but rather in outstanding ideas that emerge from exhaustive study and represent a kind of internal consensus within the logia tradition, whatever be the words used to express them.

Now theology is not a mathematical exercise, nor is it something that can be divided up into units like logia or words. If Jesus had an idea of God, for example, it could be expected to interfuse and color everything he said or did, subtly or overtly. Nevertheless, with anyone who thinks and speaks consistently about theology, whether Jesus or a modern theologian, there are inevitably certain characteristic " high points " that become the trademark of that mind, to the extent that one can recognize his thought immediately, or see it reflected in his students generations later, and these can be tabulated and correlated. Certainly the phrases " Ground of Being," " Theology of the Word of God," or " Revelation and

Reason " call to mind Tillich, Barth, and Brunner with a surety that will identify their thought for years to come. One of the surest results of my study of the Synoptics has been the awareness of the depth and sophistication of the theological ideas found in Synoptic logia (cf. *JGTJ*). The richness of Old Testament reference, the creative newness in the use of current ideas, the inner integrity of thought, all point to the logia as a highly " theological," deeply mature body of thought. As such, they reveal many characteristic theological " high points."

In this chapter we shall attempt to identify those ideas typical enough to reflect the kinds of patterns for which we have been looking. These pattern ideas will then be cross-correlated for source, form, and audience, just as we have the words that form them. The question is, Did Jesus speak in special ways to certain audiences? Did certain forms consistently contain certain ideas? Do particular sources specialize in particular concepts? If the patterns are strong enough, then we are led to another hypothesis that attends upon those of previous chapters. If it is possible at certain points to re-capture the *ipsissima verba* of Jesus, it ought also to be possible to recover his " *ipsissima mens*." We ought to be able to talk about the " theology of Jesus."

There are two focuses for this chapter. The first is the general picture of the theology of the Synoptics, correlated for source, form, and audience. The second is the more specific study of Jesus' view of the audience to summarize the extent and manner in which this factor can be for us a hermeneutic tool. There is, of course, an in-creased danger of subjectivity in this kind of theological analysis. Every idea identified will be the result of prior exegesis. Such is inevitable, and about all one can do is recognize the danger, and strive to minimize it. The exhaustive, inductive method of this study should help to reduce the angle of subjectivity but will never eliminate it.

BASIC THEOLOGICAL PATTERNS

Since this is not a book detailing the theology of Jesus, the following list will be incomplete. It will contain those concepts exhibiting some of the most outstanding patterns, as further illustration of the intimate correlation between the logia tradition and the audience.

1. *The Justice of God.* Of all the theological ideas controlling the Synoptics, this is by far the most significant. As I have attempted to demonstrate at length, this concept of God literally consumes the mind of the Jesus of the logia (cf. *JGTJ*). Fundamentally the Synoptic concern for justice derives directly from that of the prophets in the Old Testament. It centers upon no specific term so much as a galaxy of terms revealing a characteristic twofold tension between four basic aspects of God's nature: between the love of God and his wrath, between his imperative and his condition. These four ideas hold together in the Old Testament and Synoptic logia as a kind of " theological complex," each always implying the other, whether the word *mishpat* or *krisis* is used or not. It is this theological " syndrome," this inextricable correlation of ideas, which identifies God and his relations to men as justice and judgment. It is in the interaction between such love and wrath, between such imperative and freedom, that the whole drama of man's salvation is enacted. This, I take it, is *the* characteristic pattern of Synoptic thought. So widespread is it that no particular patterns of source or form are evident. There are, however, certain patterns of audience that will be seen in this purely representative list.

2. *The Present Crisis.* The crisis of God's judgment has two temporal points of focus, the historical present and the *eschaton.* In the logia, the overwhelming stress is on the present crisis with 144, or 42 percent, of all logia in all sources and all forms except FM and FL being specially concerned with the judging, separating, challenging, imperative confrontation with God within history. Jesus lays the sword of a terrible alternative across the souls of men.

They are either wheat or weeds, good or bad fish, faithful or unfaithful servants, wise or foolish virgins, fruitful or unfruitful trees,
saved or lost, light or dark, forgiven or unforgiven. This crisis separation focuses mostly upon the actions of men in history, as they
choose for or against the Kingdom of God (*JGTJ,* 179 ff.). More
exactly, an audience analysis of this material reveals that Jesus
was more concerned to stress the historic than he was the eschatological judgment of God with those *other than the Twelve,* as the
following chart will make clear.

CHART XXVIII. *Comparison of Audience Emphasis
on Present and Future Crisis*

Figures represent the percentage of all logia to that audience.

	AD	ADG	A1	AGO	AO
Present Crisis	23	33	65	42	60
Eschaton Only	20	6	1	0	11

The striking feature in the chart above is that the differential between the present and eschatological crisis rises sharply as one
moves away from the AD toward the AO. Jesus gave a balanced
emphasis on God's judgment in present and *eschaton* to the D (log.
151, 154, 193, 221, etc.), but his concern with the other audiences
was almost exclusively for the present. This is the same pattern observed in our study of *basileia* and represents one of the most defensible of all patterns deriving from this study.

Another distinction that can be made within this concept of crisis
is that between Jesus' emphasis on God's love and on his wrath.
Here again certain clear patterns develop. The stress on love and
wrath varies directly in relation to the distance of the audience
from Jesus in its sympathy and acceptance. The emphasis to the
disciples (AD, ADG, A1) is in roughly inverse ratio with that to
the opponents (AGO, AO). When talking about the present crisis,
Jesus is clearly pictured adapting his emphasis to his audience,

CHART XXIX. *Comparison of Audiences in Jesus'
Emphasis on Love and Wrath*

Figures represent the percentage of logia making a particular emphasis
in relation to all present crisis logia to that audience. For example, 51
percent of all AD passages dealing with the present crisis stress the rewards
of God's love.

	AD	ADG	A1	AGO	AO
Love	51	60	45	12	12
Wrath	30	20	13	50	52
Both	21	25	42	40	36

stressing love with those who accepted him (log. 94, 105, 196,
etc.) and wrath with those who did not (log. 134, 137, 215, 160,
224, etc.). Another striking fact is the increase in emphasis on
both love and wrath as the situation shifts from AD to AO. This
type of saying is especially strong in the crisis tension between
God's love and wrath that formed the heart of Jesus' evangelistic
appeal. It is in such passages that men would be most sharply
driven to make a choice for or against Jesus and the Kingdom
(log. 129, 131, 233, 279, 218, 70, etc.). As we might expect, this
appeal occurs most often to DG, GO, and O audiences.

This present crisis then becomes an intense concern for inner
piety as distinct from the externalism of the opponents. As one
might expect, the emphasis on cleansing the inside of the cup as
well as the outside occurs chiefly with the O (log. 215, 76, 131,
296, etc.). It does, however, infuse all that Jesus said about the
present crisis. He was concerned for the light of God's glory, the
treasure of his sovereignty, the purity of his presence *within*, ex-
pelling the demons and giving new value and life to the soul (e.g.,
Mark 8:38; cf. *JGTJ,* 179–208). This concern for the inner
man is one of the clear characteristics of the logia, involving all
sources, forms, and audiences.

3. *Jewish Concerns.* Jesus was a Jew, and inevitably his teaching
reflected that fact. There are 115 logia showing some concern for

the kinds of theological and practical matters dear to the heart of first-century Judaism. A curious pattern immediately presents itself. The logia emphasis on Jewish matters varies inversely as the distance of the audience from Jesus.

CHART XXX. · *Relative Emphasis on Jewish Matters*

Figures represent percentages of all logia to that particular audience.

AD	ADG	A1	AGO	AO
15	14	28	40	67

Here is clear evidence for adaptation to the audience. To the disciples (D, DG) Jesus says relatively little about these matters. He seems unconcerned to raise such issues as fasting or Sabbath observance or matters dealing with the Temple. The high percentage of stress on such concerns to the opponents would seem to reflect *their* interest rather than his. The constant theme that runs through this material in varying fashion is a kind of tension between Jesus' approval and his disapproval of Judaism. To the Twelve, he sees his person and mission fulfilling the Old Testament (log. 337, 352, 261, etc.); but he is sharp in his rejection of such things as legalistic Sabbath observance, fasting, tithing, and especially ritual cleanliness (log. 163, 184, 302, 215, etc.). In his preaching to the larger group of disciples (ADG, A1) he seems to go out of his way to identify with the Old Testament, its law, its righteousness; but then he turns this all against the audience by insisting that they go beyond the narrow righteousness of scribes and Pharisees to the true, inner, Kingdom piety of the Old Testament (log. 1, 69, 259, 28, 35, 46, 287, 288, 289, etc.). It is not difficult to see here the seeds of Paul's concept of the true Jew (Rom. 2:28-29).

With the opponents on the other hand, we see the mood shifting, and Jesus becoming much more concerned to show his sympathy for Judaism, but also to condemn the sterile legalism of his day. He shows his approval for those things which are " old," for the prophets, Moses and the Law, for David and the sanctity of the

Temple, for the *Shema* and the Old Testament in general (log. 80, 210, 284, 286, etc.). But he is constant in his criticism at one supreme point: they have put the tradition of the elders before God and his Kingdom, before men and their needs, and before their own inner righteousness (log. 159, 114, 115, 117, 233, etc.). There is an abundance of material here which is fairly well summarized in the parables of the new and old wine and the new and old garment. There is at once a continuity between his gospel and Judaism, but there is also a drastic difference. This message comes into sharpest focus with the opponents.

There is also in these Jewish-oriented logia a certain narrow, parochial, even legalistic strain that runs quite counter to the broader, more prophetic, antilegalism that is the dominant motif. This runs through logia to all audiences. Jesus is concerned that not one iota of the law be relaxed (Matt. 5:19), and his advice to the rich young ruler is to keep the commandments (Matt. 19:16-22). He seems to indicate that being a " son of Abraham " has something to do with Zacchaeus' salvation (Luke 19:9), and at several points indicates that for him the evangelistic mission should be restricted to the " lost sheep of the house of Israel " (log. 57, 85, 95, 164, 165). One fact gives us pause: there is a clear source pattern in this material as the following chart illustrates.

CHART XXXI.   *Source Study of Logia Jewish Concerns*

Figures represent numbers of logia. In line three, numerators indicate the percentage of the 115 Jewish logia in each category. The denominators give the percentage of total logia found in each source category.

	S1	S2	S3	S4
Narrow Legalism	2	2	7	2
Beyond Legalism	8	8	18	6
Percentage Ratio	30/43	25/25	25/15	10/10

In the chart above it is clear that the logia stress is predominantly on going beyond the current Jewish legalism. It is also evident that Matthew's special source (S3) has not only the greatest interest in legalism but also the greatest interest in Jewish matters in general. The percentage ratio of Jewish material in S3 in line three is 10 percent above the ratio of S3 to the total 352 Synoptic logia, while the other sources are average or below average. For this reason, and the fact that the more narrowly legalistic logia stand in clear contradiction to the total stress of this body of material, we must hold such narrowness and legalism suspect. It represents what one might call an antipattern. Somehow this parochialism must be reconciled with the rest. Either it represents some special interest within the early community, and the preponderance of S3 argues in this direction, or it must be accommodated to the great majority of logia, perhaps as Jeremias has done in seeing Jesus instructing his disciples to *begin* their mission in Israel as a " precondition " to the arrival of the universal Kingdom of God.[1]

4. *Jesus' Teaching About Himself.* There are approximately fifty-eight logia where Jesus is pictured saying something about his person and mission. This shines through all sources, forms, and audiences with a regularity that reveals a distinct pattern of self-consciousness. The chief stress to all audiences lies in the prophetic role wherein he confronts men with the crisis of God's judgment: " I came to cast fire upon the earth " (log. 223, 101, 76, 197, etc.; cf. *JGTJ,* 237 ff.). One even more characteristic stance within this emphasis is in the fifty-five logia where he sees himself as the very crux of the crisis. There is a strange crisis " egotism " in this material that shows Jesus insisting that acceptance or rejection of him is the same as acceptance or rejection of the Kingdom: they are to go out *in his name;* to lose their lives *for his sake.* It is *his presence* that makes the present time so significant. It is *he* who is greater than Moses or the Temple, or the Sabbath, or Jonah (log. 103, 187, 116, 168, etc.). The testimony to this strange egotism is unanimous and abundant.

But within this material, there are even sharper patterns. For example, to the disciples (mostly D) this crisis egotism is more personal: " for my sake . . . in my name . . . he who loves father or mother more than me . . . he who receives you receives me " (log. 93, 187, 102, 104). Furthermore, there is a dominant suffering motif that occurs almost exclusively in logia to the Twelve, involving such pattern words as *pascho, paradidomi, pino, poterion, mastigoo* (log. 173, 314, 264, 351, etc.). As we have already noted, Jesus gives his full picture of the Son of Man, present, eschatological, suffering, and kingly, only to the disciples. The eschatological role assigned to the messianic figure, presumably, for the editors, that of Jesus, occurs almost exclusively in the AD material (log. 252, 324, 325, etc.).

With the opponents, on the other hand, we find curiously enough the strongest emphasis on Jesus' person and mission. Twenty-one percent of all AO logia make this personal stress as compared with 13 percent of the AD logia. Comparatively speaking, there seems to be a greater concern on Jesus' part to identify his own role in speaking to the opponents than to the D. The prophetic mission of warning and call to judgment predominates in the AO logia, and comes perhaps to clearest focus in the parable of the wicked husbandmen (Mark 12:1-12; cf. *JGTJ,* 67 ff.). In the opponent material there is this one further pattern: Jesus presents himself as superior to the Jewish religion, its institutions and its historic figures (log. 116, 119, 135, 136, 137). There is a certain logic to this emphasis. A man who spoke as he did would inevitably arouse most sharply in such an audience this crucial question: Who is he and by what authority?

5. *Teaching About God.* This general theme of God's justice comes to its most pointed expression in thirty-nine logia where there is direct and explicit teaching about God (cf. *JGTJ,* 51 ff.). One cannot study these without seeing here a description of God that is clear, vivid, and arresting. Fifteen are parables where two general metaphors stand out: God is a man of authority, a judge, the owner of a vineyard, a king, the lord of servants (log. 281, 252, 204, 148, etc.); God is a father with various kinds of sons (log. 58, 197, 279). These images occur in all audiences, but the father image is strongest with the AD (log. 58, 93, 161, 277, 197). In the AO, the stress is on the seeking, demanding, imperative nature of God. There is a slightly greater stress on God in the disciple

material; but generally the most consistent pattern is the picture of the God of justice, whose love, wrath, imperative, and condition stand in creative and redeeming tension.

6. *The Total Demands of the Kingdom.* Another characteristic theme is that of the absolute claims of the Kingdom to total obedience, total priority, total self-abnegation. There are twenty-five logia with this emphasis in all sources, and the interesting thing is that these are all directed to disciple audiences (AD, A1, ADG; cf. log. 28, 40, 152, 153, 261, 262, etc.). There is an apparent logic to this, for it would only be with those who had made the initial response to Jesus that these total demands would have any meaning.

7. *Ecclesiastical Emphasis.* There are eighteen logia devoted to a discussion of what from our later point of view we could label as " church " matters, whether the word *ekklesia* is used or not. As might be expected, twelve of these are directed to the D audience. These logia contain a certain ingroup feeling, where trouble between the *adelphoi* is dealt with (log. 29, 30, 38, 56, 199, 203, etc.). They reflect an early disciple fellowship within which were inevitably certain tensions. By far the most dominant theme is the question of authority. Ten logia deal with it and two curious patterns emerge. The first is a tension between the giving of authority to the disciples (log. 174, 200, 201, 199, 261, 269, 335, 350) and the denying of it (log. 266, 290, 291, 292): " You know that . . . their great men exercise authority over them. But it shall not be so among you " (Mark 10:42, 43); " You are not to be called rabbi . . . father . . . masters " (Matt. 23:8-10). The second is a source pattern where all but two (log. 269, 335) of the passages giving authority to the Twelve occur in the M source. This could reflect some kind of conflict between the Jerusalem church and the Marcan wing, but the warnings against authority in M suggest it is not so much a contradiction in fact as in emphasis. That is, Jesus gave the disciples authority, but warned them against authoritarianism. The M source then for its own reasons stressed the mat-

ter of disciple authority, while Mark, Q, and M all warned against abusing these prerogatives, as in the parable of the faithful and unfaithful servant (Luke 12:42-46), or the warning against lording it over the Gentiles (Mark 10:42-43). The M passages stressing authority might well constitute what we are calling an antipattern, reflecting more the emphasis of the Jerusalem church than that of Jesus.

8. *Antiapocalyptic Logia.* There are seventeen logia where Jesus is pictured warning against expecting an early arrival of the eschatological Kingdom or *parousia*. In these sayings he rejects the concern for days, hours, and signs, for looking here or there, all symptoms of that apocalypticism so widespread in first-century Judaism (log. 306, 314, 319, 320). This day will come when no one knows: sudden, unexpected, delayed (log. 220, 221, 246, 307, 319, etc.). The striking thing about this material is that it occurs in all sources, but exclusively to the D audience. It seems that the Jesus of the logia felt that only with the Twelve was it worthwhile or even possible to counter the prevalent apocalypticism.

9. *Emphasis on Faith.* Beyond the above are certain lesser theological patterns in quality categories (b) or (c). One of these is the message on faith, given only to the disciples. Six AD logia stress faith in prayer and in following Jesus (log. 181, 275, 276, 336, etc.). Six to the DG stress faith as an ingredient in Jesus' healing ministry (log. 69, 81, 83, etc.).

10. *Emphasis on Forgiveness.* A similar theme, also reserved for the disciples (AD, A1, ADG), is that concerning forgiveness. Faith, forgiveness, healing, and discipleship go together, and forgiveness is the mark of the true servant of the Kingdom (log. 45, 203, 204, 277, etc.). The nine logia occur in all sources.

11. *Selective Theme.* In nine logia Jesus stresses the selective nature of his teaching. It is only those who have eyes to see or ears to hear who will understand. It is only the good soil that will

receive the seed and bear fruit, only the houses of " sons of peace " who will receive the disciples and be blessed (log. 142, 143, 256, etc.). Each of these is given to the disciples (AD, A1, ADG).

It would seem fairly clear by now that certain theological " high points " stand out in the Synoptic logia. Some of these cut across all sources, forms, and audiences in such abundance that we have universal testimony to a theology in the logia that reveals a unique integrity and continuity. Other themes show more subtle and exact patterns of correlation where certain ideas occur only or mostly to certain audiences or in certain sources. From this it would seem quite clear that the kind of continuity we have found in the words and praxis of Jesus occurs to a unique degree in the ideas that bind many logia together into theological complexes showing regular audience patterns. So far as we can see, there are no distinct theological patterns involving form. It would seem that form pertains more to verbal and literary style than to theology.

JESUS VIEWS THE AUDIENCE

Throughout the book we have noted that to describe the audience of a particular logion is to say something about its meaning, and, indeed, about the answers to certain critical questions. At this point it becomes possible to pull together all we have learned about Jesus' concept of the audience, and sharpen it as a hermeneutic tool.[2]

1. *Disciple Block.* As we have already pointed out, one of the chief characteristics of Jesus' audience conception was his thoroughly theological view. For him there were only two kinds of persons: those who were for him and those who were against him; those who had accepted the Kingdom of God and those who were rejecting it. These we have called the Disciple Block (AD, A1, ADG) and the Opponent Block (AO, AGO). It is the Evangelists who are the most concerned to distinguish between the four audience groupings. Nevertheless, Jesus is recorded making some use

of these more careful group distinctions in his teaching. He taught in special ways to each group.

The twelve disciples — The Jesus of the logia had a clear and well-developed conception of the Twelve as a distinct group. This is seen in at least nineteen words or phrases which he reserves exclusively for them. Among these are four terms that predominate and show audience patterns: *mathetes, adelphos, doulos,* and *mikros.* The word *mathetes* occurs five times on the lips of Jesus, each time to a disciple audience (AD, A1, ADG). In Matthew and Mark it always identifies the Twelve as those who are not above their teacher (Matt. 10:24), who are compared to prophets and righteous men (Matt. 10:42). Luke records a wider usage where the disciple is one who comes to Jesus renouncing himself and his loved ones (Luke 14:26); and these are the salt of the earth. In this latter usage *mathetes* must probably refer to the DG as well as the D.

Adelphos occurs six times in the logia, and always to the disciples (AD, AL, ADG). The identification of the *adelphoi* with the *mathetai* can be made in every case, and is especially clear in Matt. 12:49-50: " And stretching out his hand toward his disciples, he said, ' Here are my mother and my brothers! For whoever does the will of my Father in heaven is my brother, and sister, and mother.' " Here is a technical term used regularly by Jesus in Mark, M, and L, to describe those whose acceptance of God's will is their acceptance of Jesus. In Matthew the term is closely linked with *ekklesia* (Matt. 18:17).

We have already discussed Jesus' use of *doulos* to designate the disciples in his parables. This term seems closely restricted to the Twelve, and is especially prominent in Jesus' vocabulary. There is an interesting parallelism in Matthew between this term and the other three: " A *disciple* is not above his teacher, nor a *servant* above his master. . . . Whoever gives to one of these *little ones* even a cup of cold water because he is a *disciple*. . . . You are all *brethren*. . . . He who is greatest among you shall be your *servant* " (Matt. 10:24, 42; 23:8, 11; italics mine). The stress in this servant image is on the obedience of the disciples to God's commands, especially the demand to be faithful.

One of the most interesting of these is *mikros,* which is a term of endearment occurring in five logia, all AD. The *mikroi* are those who believe on Jesus (Mark 9:42), whose angels God always beholds (Matt. 18:10). They are those whom God does not will to perish (Matt. 18:14), those members of Jesus' " little flock," to whom God wills to give the Kingdom (Luke 12:32). One is tempted to see here the possible root of those sayings where the disciples are described as the " least " (*mikroteros*) in the Kingdom of Heaven (Matt. 11:11; Mark 4:31; Luke 9:48). *Mikroteros* then becomes a play on *mikros,* that is, a description of a disciple.[3] In all these terms we see Jesus drawing a careful circle about this special group: sometimes the larger body of disciples, but more often that small fellowship most intimately related to him, the D.

The terms Jesus used to identify the twelve disciples generally reflect his affection for them, his hopes for them, his approval of them. They are a " little flock," " brethren," " good men," " blessed ones," " sons of the kingdom," " sons of light," and " sons of God." One is therefore not prepared for the discovery of the extent to which an exhaustive survey of the logia reveals his criticism of them. They are men of little faith, foolish, and slow of heart to believe (log. 222, 252, 351, 336). They consistently fail to understand his message, his person, and his purpose until he cries out to Peter that he is not on the side of God but of men (log. 175, 163, 257, 143, etc.). They are vain, exclusive, legalistic, unforgiving, complaining, inclined to be pompous, striving for preferment, anxious to lord it over others (log. 185, 188, 203, 204, 265, 266). His constant disappointment over them takes the form of a running series of parables where some of them are described as unfaithful servants, as men not waiting for their master to return; weak, timorous sheep who will betray him and be scattered by the rigorous demands of discipleship (log. 221, 222, 237, 143, 204, 329, 330, 336, 338, 340). The logia are noteworthy for their almost complete absence of praise for the Twelve; and this pattern generally agrees with the negative estimate given in the E material. If anything, the logia would seem to be slightly more positive.

There are sixty-seven logia wherein Jesus describes the mission of the disciples, thirty-four of which are AD, and the rest ADG or A1. In that mission teaching given to the D there are forty-seven pattern words, with the following eleven used more than once: *ethnos, axios, dechomai, heneka, amen, phobeomai, hora, hetoimazo, aionios, pino, kleronomeo.* In this material there are several leading ideas occurring often enough to constitute patterns. The Twelve are warned that they will be persecuted, rejected, divided, killed, like sheep among wolves, like those who must carry their own cross (log. 98, 102, 94, 95, 96, 90, 91, 262, 265). But even as they are beset by these troubles, they are to " fear not," for God will instruct them, guide them, and protect them (log. 86, 93, 96, 98, 305). An important theme revolves around the demand that they be true and obedient servants, and they are especially exhorted to be awake, wise, and prepared for the coming of their master (log. 219, 220, 221, 222, 320, 325). The verb *gregoreo* seems characteristic of this theme (cf. also log. 237, 242, 325, 204, etc.). It is a kerygmatic mission primarily, and the center of their proclamation is Jesus and the Kingdom (log. 97, 100, 106, 188, 307, etc.). He gives them authority to bind and loose, to baptize, to heal the sick, to raise the dead, to cast out demons (log. 320, 350, 174, 200, 85, etc.); but this authority pattern must remain in category (c) because most of these references are S3. This emphasis is modified by Jesus' warnings against the abuse of authority (log. 265, 323).

In preceding chapters, certain critical patterns have emerged involving the D. We have seen that there are almost three times as many logia directed to the disciple block as to the opponents. More exactly, 43 percent of all logia are given to the D audience. The teaching to the Twelve then constitutes the focus of the logia tradition. We have found the Marcan source containing the highest percentage of material to the D, followed by M, then Q, and finally L. Mark might then be called the strongest disciple source. We found all forms of logia directed to the D, but the most typical for the AD material was the didactic form (FS). Most legends are in the AD orbit, and miracle stories occur mostly to AD and ADG. We have seen also that verbal patterns occur most often in the disciple block, with 18 percent of all important AD words showing such patterns (Chart XXIV). Certain metaphors are also used consistently with the Twelve, especially those of the harvest, the servant-master relationship, those involving parts of the body, and those dealing with money and business. Not only does the Jesus of the logia use many forms, words, and metaphors consistently with the Twelve, but he is regularly pictured explaining his parables to the disciples (D, DG), while leaving them unexplained to the opponents "outside." Curiously enough these explanations to the disciples contain a slightly higher percentage of pattern words than do the parables themselves.

One of the deepest insights of this study has been to the effect that it was to the Twelve that Jesus gave his most characteristic, most balanced, most " total " teaching; and as one moves away from the D to the DG, the GO, and finally the O, so do certain principles of selectivity go into increasingly sharp operation. It was to the D that Jesus gave a fully balanced picture of the justice of God as both present and eschatological, both love and wrath. It was to the D that he presented the Kingdom of God as God's sovereign presence at work within history, at the *eschaton* and transcending all time. It was to the D that he spoke of himself as the Son of Man both in the present and at the *eschaton,* both as a kingly and a suffering figure. It was to the D that he taught cosmology in his most characteristic, personal, and " vertical " sense (cf. *JGTJ,* 91 ff.). It was to the D that he seems to have given a concept of Satan far beyond the first century in its sophistication. It would seem abundantly clear that it was to the D that the Jesus of the logia most characteristically and completely spoke his mind.

There are other examples of theological continuity typifying Jesus' approach to the D. For example, he most often spoke to them about God, and here the father image and the stress on love is the strongest. If we say that Jesus gave his most characteristic teaching to the D, then we must see him as one for whom a concern for Jewish institutions was not typical. One might say that where he is the most non-Judaistic he is most himself. This accords well with the pattern of antiapocalypticism which is a message he reserves entirely for the D. It is only with them that he warns of the impending destruction of Jerusalem and the Temple (log. 303, 308, 309, 310, 311, 312, 317, 318). In fine, it is with the Twelve that Jesus is pictured being the most balanced, the most personal, the most didactic, the most creatively original, and therefore the most radically contrary to current and established ideas. This would seem to reflect a keen sensitivity to his audience, and to the practical exigencies of popular teaching and preaching. Again, this makes a certain common sense: if one must be radical, new, and creative, let him be so in the inner circle where he is most likely to be understood or at least given a sympathetic hearing. It is for these that the " mystery " of the Kingdom must inevitably be reserved.

The disciple crowd — Moving slightly away from this " ground zero " of the logia, we come to Jesus' teaching to the sympathetic multitudes, containing as it so often did the Twelve and others so close to being members of the inner circle that there seemed to be no problem later in filling Judas' place. As we have suggested, Jesus is not as careful in distinguishing the DG from the D as were the Evangelists. There is, however, enough evidence to suggest that for him they constituted an identifiable group; primarily as those who were disciples in their own right, but without being part of the Twelve. There are two designations common to Jesus' teaching to the ADG or A1 situations. These are men and women of faith (log. 69, 81, 83, 165, 267); they are " blessed " ones who hear and keep the word (log. 214, 12-20). Beyond these two, most other terms used by Jesus for the Twelve also at times can refer to the DG. Perhaps the most noticeable distinction is the dominant theme of praise that contrasts sharply with his almost universal criticism of the D.

The DG are also included in Jesus' mission instructions at various points in the Synoptics. Generally speaking his directions to them follow the same lines as those to the D: they are to proclaim the Kingdom by teaching and preaching, and by letting their light shine through deeds of mercy and service (log. 16, 23, 327, 144,

24, 72, etc.). They will be persecuted, but they must trust God for strength and deliverance (log. 53, 54, 86, 90, 91, 208, etc.). If anything, with the DG there is a greater stress on total commitment as a requisite for participation in this mission (log. 71, 205, 234, 259).

The ADG material (including A1) also reveals certain critical patterns that help to identify this as a distinct group in Jesus' mind. Twenty-nine percent of all logia are given to the DG or A1 audience. The Q source is especially strong in this tradition (Chart II). Since this regularly represents a preaching situation, it is to be expected that a high percentage of parables should be here (Chart XI). This larger disciple audience seems to be the typical preaching situation, characterized by Matthew in the Sermon on the Mount. The high percentage of miracle story merely underscores one of our definitions of the DG as those whose faith was sufficient for Jesus' healing ministry.

There is a shift with the ADG–A1 logia to a stronger Jewish emphasis than with the AD material. Jesus seems to identify almost deferentially with the Jews and the Old Testament (log. 1, 69, 259, 26, 27, 28, 30), but then turns this against his audience by demanding that they go with him beyond Jewish legalism to the fulfilling of the law (log. 24, 28, 30, 33, 36, 37, 38, 41, 42, 46). In the A1 teaching particularly there is a strong S3 predominance, with fourteen of the nineteen logia which reflect this theme being from the M source. There is some evidence for the kind of narrow Judaism we have noted in the AD teaching, but again this is all located in the M source (log. 26, 27, 28, 43, 59, 57), and must be taken in the light of the dominant theme of a basic sympathy for Judaism coupled with the demand that men go beyond legalism to the deeper fulfillment of the law. In this Jewish emphasis, there seems to be a special attempt on the part of Jesus to accommodate to the orientation of the audience.

Throughout this stratum there is a strong element of the judgment of God as we have been defining it. There is some teaching revealing the continuity between God's historic and eschatological judgment: the house on the rock, the one who enters " life " maimed, the fruitful seed, are already judged when the storm and harvest of eschatological testing come (log. 67, 33, 147, 31, 66, etc.). But the stress here is overwhelmingly on the crisis in the historic present: upon the blind receiving their sight now, the nearness of the Kingdom now, being true salt, fruitful seeds, good treasure now; and this is placed in the sharpest contrast to hypocrisy and unfruitful, bankrupt, worthless spiritual death, *now* (log. 44, 21, 42, 48, 63, 176, etc.). There are at least twenty-seven logia to this audience emphasizing reward to those who hear and do the will of God, whose names are written in heaven, that is, those who are " blessed " ones (log. 214, 209, 18, etc.; cf. *JGTJ,* 199 ff.). This is the sharp point of this whole body of material, reflecting it would seem the committed nature of at least part of this audience. But then there are also twenty-eight logia with a strong emphasis either on the tension between God's love and his wrath, or upon wrath alone, again it would seem reflecting the uncommitted nature of other segments of this larger disciple audience. It is a *corpus permixtum,* and the imperative to make peace with their accuser lest he turn them over to the judge seems to indicate this kind of highly charged preaching situation (log. 31, 21, 45, 29, etc.).

Along with this focus on the historic crisis, the ADG material makes a strong plea for the kind of inner purity, inner light, inner treasure, inner fruit that is the characteristic mark of the presence of the Kingdom of God within a life (log. 32, 22, 48, 65, 63). There is a tension between the inner and outer man that is particularly evident in Jesus' teaching to the disciple crowd, and further underscores the note of crisis imperative.

The only real emphasis on what can be called a " social ethic " occurs in this audience stratum, mostly in the Sermon on the Mount (log. 24, 36, 37, 39, 122). Jesus is far more interested in the Kingdom as an inner presence than he is in good works themselves, and it is this lack of stress which constitutes the pattern at this point.

One of the most apparent characteristics of these ADG–A1 logia is their omission of certain elements found in the AD teaching. The most notable lack is that of the balanced and total emphasis to the Twelve. There is little eschatology, and what there is deals only with the wrath of God. There is none of the AD teaching about Jesus as the crux of God's judgment, what we have called his "crisis egotism," and little concern to describe his person or mission. There are no parables describing God, relatively little ecclesiastical concern and almost none of the sharp criticism of the audience so typical of the AD logia. Clearly, the logia give us a picture of a Jesus who spoke in different fashion to the larger crowd of disciples than he did to the Twelve. We have moved away from the total message to a more selective version; not far, but far enough to be apparent.

2. *The Opponent Block.* There is a much sharper distinction that must be drawn between the disciples in general (D, DG, A1) and the opponents (GO, O) than that between the two groups of disciples. It is here that we see most clearly the simple, twofold theological distinction in Jesus' mind between those who were for him and those who were against him.

The opponent crowd — Moving even farther away from the intimately sympathetic AD situation, we come to the teaching directed to the unsympathetic crowd. There are only twenty-four logia in this stratum, and so any patterns found here must be in category (b) or (c). Again, the chief impression is the lack of balance and totality. For example, there is no eschatology, and little reference to the love of God. The single teaching about God pictures him as one who will destroy those who are rich in this world's goods, but not rich toward him (Luke 12:16-21). The emphasis is all on the present crisis, and there the stress is on God's wrath toward the unfruitful trees, toward those who are greedy, defiled within, who will perish because they refuse to repent (log. 225, 217, 160, 224). He is highly critical of this audience, and we see an escalation of his criticism over that to the AD: they are like children in the marketplace who will not be pleased. John wailed and they did not weep. Jesus piped and they did not dance (Luke 7:31-35). There is some evidence of accommodation to his Jewish audience in his deference to John the Baptist (log. 108, 110), in his reference to the fulfillment of the Old Testament (log. 4, 108), and in his insistence that they go beyond Jewish legalism to the inner righteousness of the publican, the true fruitfulness of those " least " in the Kingdom of God (log. 160, 253, 225, 108).

There are also a few technical patterns in this layer of tradition. The AGO has a high percentage of S4 and FA, reflecting the commonly observed polemical interest of Luke. There are no miracle stories, and this seems to justify Mark's summary comment on the opponent character of the synagogue in Nazareth: " He could do no mighty work there . . . because of their unbelief " (Mark 6:5-6). One final thing must be said at this point. There is a shifting, provisional sense to the opponent crowd reflected in the use of the words *laos* and *ochlos* to refer to both the DG and the GO. This describes a " mood " rather than a fixed commitment or a description of position or party. The GO can and do become DG; and the disillusionment of the Passion Week suggests that in the minds of the Evangelists there are DG who became GO, along with Judas. It is the very uncertainty of the crowd that makes Jesus' theological distinction between DG and GO ultimately the more correct: some are for him, the others are against him.

The opponents — Even as the focus of Jesus' teaching to the sympathetic audience was upon the Twelve, so the AO material is the focal point of the opposition. In a sense these Jewish officials are the " antidisciples." There are certain terms that Jesus reserves for them, such as *poneros, hupokrites, gennemata echidnon,* and in a burst of graphic metaphor he says of the O, " Let them alone; they are blind guides," plants " which my heavenly Father has not planted " (Matt. 15:14, 13). The distinctive character of this group in the mind of Jesus is revealed not only in these typical designations but also in the abundance of critical, verbal, and theological patterns converging on this audience. Twenty percent of all the logia are given to the O. All sources are well represented, with S1 having the highest percentage (Chart II). All forms occur in this audience situation, but the most abundant is FA, showing the polemical nature of these logia. One curious critical pattern shows the AO material having the greatest concentration of logia where questions can be raised regarding the accuracy of the audience identification. We have noted (Chart XVIII) that most of the A words that may be E intrusions are in fact AO. Furthermore, there are a number of AO logia with no O pattern words whatever, but with many AD pattern words, suggesting sayings that are not characteristically opponent oriented (log. 134, 138, 168, 233, 229). Other AO logia could with some justification be identified as A1 (log. 132), AGO (log. 135, 168), AA (log. 281, 282), or AY (log. 215, 229). There is some evidence therefore that the AO tradition has less audience clarity and certainty than the AD, although we are reminded that the comparative percentage agreement between AD and AO logia is fairly close (Chart VIII).

The importance of this audience stratum is underscored by the many pattern words oriented toward the opponents, and the fact that 11.5 percent of all important AO words are pattern words (Chart XXIV). The metaphor pattern centering on the banquet motif reveals one of those " natural " patterns with a certain commonsense logic. As the rather typical, idealized locus of the teaching to the Twelve was in some " private place," so that for the AO was the social occasion, the dinner, suggesting that the meal with Simon the Pharisee was chosen by the Evangelists as a typical opponent-oriented incident (Luke 7:36-50).

The largest recurring result of our audience survey has been the insight that Jesus gave his total, balanced, most characteristic message only to the D. This pattern continues as we see the imbalance, the highly selective nature of the material to the O. We are now at the opposite end of the spectrum, the farthest away from the intimate, inner circle wherein Jesus could most completely be himself. Now he is on the defensive, under constant attack, and the logia reflect this in many ways. For example, we have seen that he does not characteristically explain his parables to the O, seemingly despairing of their ability to understand the " mystery " in depth. His typical crisis message, especially in his use of *basileia,* focuses on both present and future, but with the O, overwhelmingly on the present.[4] His crisis teaching deals with both the love and the wrath of God, but the greatest stress on wrath occurs to the opponents. These are the ones whose blasphemy against the Holy Spirit will "never" have forgiveness, whose hearts are evil and empty and far from God (log. 129, 138, 159). They are the lost, the forsaken, the dead, the evil generation (log. 236, 229, 168) who at the *eschaton* will render account for every careless word (Matt. 12:36-37). This concentration on woe for the opponents was apparently observed by the early editors, and typified in the collections of woes brought together on the basis not only of content *but of audience*. In the unanimous opinion of the editors it was typical of Jesus to warn the opponents of the wrath of God.[5]

Jesus' selectivity is further seen in the growing accommodation to the Jewish point of view as we move from AD to AO. We have shown his relative lack of concern for Jewish matters, and his rather shockingly non-Jewish teaching to the D. With the O, one finds an almost awkward deference to Judaism, an almost solicitous accommodation to the Jewishness of the opponents. We have noted the surprising scarcity of reference to the *basileia tou theou* with the AO (Chart XXVII). At this point we can add another observation that brings this into bold relief: the emphasis on repentance, forgiveness, inner purity, righteousness, obedience to the Old Testament commandments and works showing true religion, the reference to the prophets, to Moses, to David, to the sanctity of the Temple, to the *Shema* and the Old Testament in general, that is, the references to specifically Jewish concerns, are all stronger in the AO material than his characteristic message of the Kingdom. This emphasis on more traditional religious matters clearly shows a pattern of adaptation to this most sensitively Jewish audience. Again, there is a certain practical logic to this that makes it what one might well expect from a clever practitioner of the arts of teaching and preaching. The striking thing for us is that this has been so well preserved in the Synoptic tradition.

The opponent material reveals Jesus setting himself in clear and aggressive opposition to his audience. Sixty-five percent of all AO teaching shows that Jesus was the aggressor. It is true that there are many apothegms here containing questions showing aggressiveness on the part of the religious officials. There are, however, many more sayings and parables where the origin of the denunciation is Jesus himself. The pattern seems to be that this was a two-sided battle, where Jesus himself provoked most of the opposition. There are eighty-seven logia where his criticism is sharply evident. Whereas he criticized the Twelve for putting *themselves* before the Kingdom, Jesus criticized the opponents for putting *their religion* before the Kingdom of God. They put the traditions of the elders before justice and the mercy of God (Mark 7:3); they put ritual legalism before their concern for men (log. 114, 118, 211); they put external purity before their own inner righteousness (log. 293, 114, 279, 298). In this stance, they were unable to understand the working of God in and through him (log. 126, 273, 78); they did not enter the Kingdom themselves, and they hindered those who were entering (Luke 11:52). "You blind guides," he cries out in a characteristic summary, "straining out a gnat and swallowing a camel!" (Matt. 23:24). If the logia are any indication, Jesus was an intensely critical person, and one can perhaps see why not only the opponents, but at times his own disciples, were set against him.

This Jewish accommodation carries over to his description of his own person and mission. The twenty-one AO logia containing this theme reflect the same crisis message running throughout his teaching about himself; but the prophetic image of warning and call to repentance is stronger here (log. 76, 135, 228, 229), and he describes himself in more typically Jewish ways, as greater than the Temple, Jonah, Solomon, or the Sabbath (log. 116, 136, 137, 119). This prophetic theme continues in the nine AO logia describing God. There he is most consistently pictured as a seeking, demanding God of justice whose judgments on men because of their resistance to his invitation must issue mostly in wrath (log. 233, 235, 236, 240, 280, 281, 282, 295, 174). Beyond these themes, the major pattern in the AO logia, as in ADG and AGO, is the absence of those other ideas given only or mostly to the D. This clear contrast between the teaching to the Twelve and that to the opponents, as that between the disciple block and the opponent block, stands as one of the solid results of the present study.

AUDIENCE CRITICISM AS A HERMENEUTIC TOOL

At this point it should be possible to apply the concept of continuity to certain questions raised in Chapters II and III. There we saw the care with which the audience was recorded, and the agreement between the sources. Our analysis of the various types of continuity showed an intimate correlation between logion and audience at every level. This should help us to interpret the audience phenomenon. It would seem highly probable that the audience was of great importance to those who recorded the tradition *because they believed the message of the logia itself was audience-centered.* They believed the Jesus of the logia taught selectively, accommodating his message to his audience to such a degree that the nature of the audience became an important part of the message of the logion itself. This was then preserved with unique fidelity, for anyone knowing about Jesus would have realized that the audience was needed for the correct and meaningful reproduction of his teaching. This means to us that the audience has become a hermeneutic factor of first importance. It means that we cannot really understand what the logia are saying until we understand the audience to which they are attributed. It means that to know the audience is to know in advance something about the kind of characteristic teaching we can or cannot expect to this audience. When these major patterns of verbiage, praxis, and theology are contradicted, such antipatterns alert us to material that is either out of context or out of keeping with the Synoptic picture of Jesus.

Before leaving this subject, we must recall something said earlier to the effect that this exhaustive, horizontal analysis does not replace the more traditional critical disciplines of Source, Redaction, and Form; it rather precedes and informs them. In this " club sandwich " of induction and deduction called the scientific method, these more " vertical " disciplines must refine and correct the massive, horizontal approach. It would seem, however, that when a selective study in depth of some individual question leads to conclusions that run significantly counter to one of these broad patterns of theology, verbiage, or praxis, such conclusions must be secondary to the testimony of the total Synoptic material to itself. Everything we have said about scientific induction, about the pattern, about horizontal and exhaustive analysis would suggest that the evidence derived from this method is of the strongest kind.

Chapter VII

EXPLAINING THE PHENOMENA: REDACTION, SOURCE, FORM CRITICISM

Moving from the hermeneutic exploitation of our study, we come finally and inevitably to the question that has been insinuating itself between the lines at almost every point. What is the meaning of these various audience phenomena for the history of Synoptic formation? Our investigation has revealed four major facts: (1) The Evangelists are more careful to accurately preserve the audience than they are any other element of the logia context. (2) They agree with one another consistently to a higher degree on the nature of the audience than on any other point of comparison, including the wording of the logia. (3) A clear line of discontinuity must be drawn between the ideas and linguistic orientation of the Evangelists and that of the logia, setting the latter apart as a separate and distinct body of material. (4) A series of verbal, praxis, and theological patterns cut horizontally through the logia to such an extent that it is apparent there is a greater continuity and inner integrity to the logia than there is to the obvious words, ideas, or practice of any single Evangelist, or of all the Evangelists put together. Out of these four large results has emerged one all-embrac-

ing conclusion: the lively, intimate, and consistent correlation between audience and logia has revealed a universal consensus that
logion and audience were inseparable. Jesus was a selective teacher
whose crisis message was a net sifting one audience from another.

Our question now is to what historical conclusions these large
results and other more detailed observations lead us. We move then
to science as " policy " as we attempt to gather together these
data and construct some theories that relate the isolated phenomena to this historical question in some coherent way. We need to
explain the origin and meaning of these phenomena. What, if anything, do they say about the historical authenticity of the material?
Can we really talk seriously about the *ipsissima verba* and the
ipsissima mens of Jesus? Answers to these questions will involve
every critical discipline of Synoptic scholarship and should tell us
something more about the practical uses of Audience Criticism.

REDACTION CRITICISM

Evidence for the Redactor as Author. There are a number of
possibilities for explaining the origin and meaning of the audience
phenomena. They tend to cluster around four of the major critical
disciplines. For example, in the wake of Bultmann's early work on
the Synoptics, it has been common to attribute the audience data
to the Evangelist or redactor.[1] This has been part of a general en-
thusiasm for explaining most Synoptic questions in terms of the
special interests of the editors.[2] Certain it is that our study has
found much evidence of the redactor at work. We have shown, for
example, how all the Evangelists went out of their way to indicate
the audience, and how they were much more concerned than the
logia tradition to distinguish clearly in an almost stylized way between the four basic audiences. The redactors are clearly conscious
of Jesus' selective teaching, and reflect this in such remarks as
Mark 4:33-34, or in the eschatological collection in Mark, ch. 13.
Actually, wherever we find a collation on the basis of audience, we
have testimony to the redactor's belief in the importance of this
selective principle.

The disagreement between the Evangelists is an especially good tool for getting at the characteristics of a particular one. The similarity of one logion to another seems to have caused Luke to locate a saying improperly. Both Matthew and Luke change the audience of logia from their sources in order to include material in a collation on the basis of theme. There are also indications of vocabulary or style characteristic of one or another Evangelist, as the following list details.

Mark	Matthew	Luke	
euaggelion	aigupton	anapempo	epilambano
euthus	Babulonos	aner	pimplemi
thambeo	enthumeomai	apographe	ethos
periblepo	onar	apostolos	euphraino
akathartos	sphodra	brephe	hupostrepho
thalassa		diaphulaxai	hrema
dekapolis		diasozo	egagon
ploion		dierchomai	egeneto
opsias		de	eie
kat idian			
Petros			
peran			

In Chart XVII we noted twenty-five Greek terms characteristic of the E material generally, but containing some use in the logia, suggesting the vocabulary of the editor. It is also noteworthy that all three Evangelists tend to give periodic summarizing generalizations which clearly reflect their opinions. As Luke says of the disciples, " they supposed that the kingdom of God was to ·appear immediately " (19:11). In general, Matthew seems to follow his sources most slavishly, and Luke gives the most evidence of independence both in the choice of words and in the handling of the sources.

There are also some indications of theological commentary. In Mark 12:12, for example, the editor interprets a parable and affirms Jesus' audience orientation when he comments: " They . . . feared the multitude, for they perceived that he had told the parable against them." In a parenthesis, Mark explains the meaning of an Aramaic word: " Corban (that is, given to God)." Luke's interpretation of the parable on humility (14:7-11) is quite clear: " Now he told a parable to those who were invited, when he marked how they chose the places of honor. . . ." We note also Luke's insertion of *dokei* (8:18b), Matthew's explanation of the logion in 16:12, his interpretation of an obscure figure of speech in 12:28, and his explanation of a parable with the addition of the one word *scholazonta* (12:44).

Beyond these detailed evidences, one sees the influence of the editor in the general flavor and orientation of a Gospel. For example, the editor of Mark appears to be a Jew, familiar in intimate ways with the language, customs, geography, religion, institutions, climate, and other such details of Palestinian life. He is much oriented toward the sea of Galilee, toward boats and Jesus' crossing back and forth over the lake. He has an eye for outdoor detail, for mornings and evenings, for sunrises and sunsets, and his focusing of Jesus' ministry in the house in Capernaum strengthens the Petrine orientation found in his most abundant use of the word *Petros*.[3] The author seems to know much detail about Jesus, his private conversations with the D, and his reactions to various people. He knows the names of persons and obscure districts and villages that figure in Jesus' ministry. He is a man especially impressed by action, and his Gospel shows Jesus and the D constantly on the move, very busy, overwhelmed by crowds. We have noted his activity in making theological comments; but such is usually quite clear, and often rather awkwardly introduced. The largest and most skillful editing job is that of ch. 13, and there the editorializing consists in the alternate arrangement of the sayings about the *eschaton* and the destruction of Jerusalem, presumably by someone prior to the final editor of Mark (*JGTJ*, 146).

Evidence for the Redactor as Transmitter. The primary impression gained in this study is that of the redactor as a transmitter, recording and providing settings for the logia that came to him from many sources, with an almost slavish attention to detail. There are three principal types of evidence pointing in this direction.

1. The first has to do with the high percentage of agreement between the redactors on the details of the logia that can be compared. We have shown a general agreement on wording and audience of approximately 90 percent in the reproduction of both the Marcan and Q sources. There is an almost 90 percent agreement on all items of context in Matthew and Luke's reproduction of their Marcan source, and in the FM and FL material the agreement is almost 100 percent. The Evangelists all agree that Jesus adapted his teaching to the four basic types of audience, and they agree unanimously and almost without exception that wording and audience are inextricably related.

The highest agreement comes in their attributing logia to a particular audience. Some of the most striking illustrations of this carefulness come in those places where the Evangelists direct the same logion to the same audience but in entirely different blocks of material such as the Sermon on the Mount, Luke, ch. 17; Mark, ch. 13; or Matt., ch. 23. In these cases, the logia had to be evaluated individually for audience, which suggests that the audience-logion correlation was attached to or inherent in each logion prior to its editing by the redactor. This raises a very important possibility for explaining this phenomenon of agreement. The inner logic of the logion itself may have been the source of this audience agreement. The editors may have merely been giving the audience that any editor would naturally have given to that kind of saying. Thus the audience would be the choice of the editor and the agreement preconditioned by the plain logic of the saying.

Such is apparently true with certain logia. The sayings " Woe to you, . . . for you build the tombs of the prophets " clearly demands an O audience. " Here are my mother and my brothers! " is surely to be directed to the disciples. The problem is that other sayings do not contain such evident logic: " Get behind me, Satan " is given to the D, and " The kingdom of God is in the midst of [within] you " is given to the O. In order to get some objective leverage on this question, an experiment was conducted with several groups of laymen, ministers, seminary students and professors. A representative sampling of twenty logia was lifted out of its audience context. Each person was then instructed to assign to these logia one of the four audiences which he believed to be the accurate one. He could do this from his knowledge of the Synoptics, and for some this was considerable, or he could base his choice on the intrinsic logic of the saying itself. The results show a 45 percent agreement between these persons and the Gospel writers in the exact audience identification. This is to be compared with an average 70 percent exact agreement between the Evangelists in reproducing Mark and Q. If this logion sample was truly representative, and if these subjects in any way paralleled the disciple tradition, then it would seem that the audience of approximately 45 percent of the logia could be identified by the redactor himself, either from his general knowledge of Jesus or from the logic of the saying. This, however, leaves 25 percent that must be accounted for in other ways. Most of this remainder seems to have been due to the careful copying by Matthew and Luke of their Marcan and Q sources. All of which leads us to a high regard for the treatment of the logia material on the part of these Evangelists. There is a sense of sanctity inhering in their transmission of the teachings of Jesus that warns us strongly against attributing too much changing or authoring of logia to these redactors. Primarily they were cautious and slavishly attentive transmitters.

2. A second type of evidence pointing in the same direction is found in the clear line of discontinuity that must be drawn between the E and the A material. The editorial stratum reveals vertical patterns of words and ideas contrasting sharply with those of the logia. The almost complete absence of Christian theological content in the words peculiar to the editors argues strongly against attributing any significant " dogmatic " interests to them other than those of reporting faithfully the words of Jesus. The Aramaic flavor of the logia compared with the Greek orientation of the E material further supports this discontinuity. Any thesis favoring abundant redactional activity in the logia must be thoroughly chastened by this phenomenon of discontinuity (cf. Chapter IV).

3. The manifold illustrations of continuity within the logia show

clearly that most patterns of words, ideas, or praxis cut *horizontally* across all Gospels rather than vertically down through any particular one. This fact, perhaps more than any other, simply forbids us to stop with the redactor in examining the origins of this material. These editors are manifestly transmitting to us material that achieved its continuity prior to them. Furthermore, the fact that we can detect such continuity so often, and in such detail, demands a carefulness in the preservation of detail that is outstanding to say the least.

This all leads us to propose a simple axiom regarding the use of the redactor as a critical tool for examining the logia. *Where the redactor is the most surely at work, he is the most clearly at work.* His original comments, creations, and editorializing can generally be detected. His work consists mostly in parenthetical insertions, in explanatory comments in the narration, or in the selection and arrangement of the logia. Otherwise, the evidence points to a unique stability in the details of the logia that demands their origin prior to the redactor, and a peculiar carefulness on his part in reproducing them.

SOURCE CRITICISM

Going more deeply into the process of Gospel formation, we come to a second possibility for explaining these various audience phenomena. It is quite possible that this agreement and continuity was given to the logia by the sources that the redactors used. The correlation of audience and source has been fruitful in producing new data, and in explaining some of the audience phenomena. The four major sources show patterns indicating characteristic activity on the part of their authors and editors. Beyond those commonly observed, our study has turned up several new observations, supporting the identity of these as distinct sources. For example, there is a decided movement from Mark's high interest in the single, more intimate audience situations to a preference for larger audiences in Luke's special source. That is, the sources show audience orientation as the following refinement of Chart VII shows.

CHART XXXII. *Source Audience Interest*

	High Interest	Low Interest
S1	AD, AO	AGO, ADG, A5
S2	ADG, A1	ADG, AO
S3	A1	ADG, AO
S4	AGO, ADG	AD, AO, A1

These orientations for the various sources could of course be those of the redactor; but the other evidence for the independent identity of these as sources antecedent to the redactor argues for their inclusion as source phenomena. There are also indications of verbal continuity within these four major sources. The verb *euphraino* occurs six times, each in a logion, and each in Luke's special source. The noun *euaggelion* occurs in six logia, all but one (Matt. 24:14) in the Marcan source.[4] Perhaps more significant is a further refinement of Chart XXIV which shows S3 with the highest average saturation of logion pattern words (18.6 percent), then S1 with 18.3 percent, S2 with 17.6 percent, and S4 with 6.3 percent. The one clear pattern is the relative verbal independence of the L source.

There are also certain patterns of theological continuity appearing in these sources. We have seen that S3 has the greatest interest in Jewish matters, and the most evidence for the narrow legalism that stands as an antipattern in contrast to Jesus' consistent teaching in the logia. There is also a curious fixation on the love of God in S3 with logia describing the present crisis. It would seem that one can find subtle evidences of the editors of these sources at work, particularly in their special interest in one or another of the general logia teachings.

But we must go farther, for there is a distinct possibility that these audience phenomena may derive from an even earlier stratum, from the author-editors of certain " protosources." This, of course, is an old thesis, that behind Mark, Q, M, and L lie such early written materials as a passion narrative, lists of testimonies to Jesus' Old Testament fulfillment, genealogies, John the Baptist stories,

mighty work tracts, conflict stories, parable tract groupings, apocalyptic tracts, hymns and liturgical worship material, etc.[5] Audience
Criticism supports the separate identity of some of these. For example, the logia contained in miracle stories are directed mostly to
the DG audience, suggesting an audience-oriented miracle tract
grouping (Chart XI). The apocalyptic sayings are given almost
exclusively to the disciples, pointing to the D-oriented collection
in Mark, ch. 13, as such a separate body of material. There is also
a suggestion coming out of this study that the stability of the
Marcan logia, their inner consistency, and the carefulness in their
reproduction argues for a very early basic collection that could
point to an " Ur Markus " or a " K " source (Parker), or to Papias'
" Oracles." A detailed study of such protosource hypotheses is beyond the bounds of the present study.

It does seem that Source Criticism aids us considerably in explaining the phenomenon of audience agreement. In Chart IX we
note that exact agreement on all contextual factors, including audience, is almost exactly the same in the Marcan tradition (85%).
This suggests that the agreement on audience is largely the result of
Matthew and Luke copying the Marcan source. If we say that approximately 45 percent of these logia could have been given an
audience by the redactor or source editor merely as a result of their
intrinsic logic, then this would leave about 40 percent of the Marcan
audience identification as a direct result of the redactors copying
Mark. When one talks not of " exact agreement," but " general
agreement," we see in Chart X that in using the Marcan source
the audience agreement is 98 percent or 10 percent higher than all
other elements of the Marcan context. It would seem that this 10
percent audience overplus represents a margin of agreement not
explained by reference either to intrinsic logic or to source. One obvious possibility will be discussed in Chapter VIII. It could well
represent the historic factor of simple, accurate recall.

The Q comparison in Chart IX shows a 47 percent exact agreement on audience. If we say again that 45 percent of the audience
agreement in Q is the result of intrinsic logic, this only leaves an
unexplained 2 percent, showing a basic difference in the exact re-

production of the Marcan and Q audience tradition. The comparison between Mark and Q on audience agreement becomes more similar if we take the " general agreement " in Q (#1 and #2) which then is 83 percent. This again suggests that approximately 40 percent of this general agreement in Q is due to Matthew and Luke copying the same source. So in both Mark and Q we have three factors emerging for explaining the audience agreement: (1) the intrinsic logic of the logia (45%); (2) the result of copying Mark or Q (40%); (3) an unexplained overplus in Mark of 10 percent which could be due to accurate recall. Why Q should have such a lower percentage of exact audience agreement than Mark remains a question.

Beyond this, Source Criticism falters in its ability to explain the audience phenomena. It is evident that all redactors and all sources agree on every major conclusion of our study: the carefulness in preserving the audience, the discontinuity between the E and A material, the many patterns of continuity that lie subtly and inextricably embedded in the logia-audience combination. For any editor or protoeditor to have been that consistently perceptive at a level only discoverable through an exhaustive analysis of all three Gospels is very hard to believe. Such an explanation would require a massive degree of editing that would place impossible requirements on the process of Gospel formation. It would seem, rather, that these patterns drive us below the level of source for their explanation. There must be some deeper cause for this consistency that antedates and supersedes the work of those who collected and edited the sources.

FORM CRITICISM

One of the most important possibilities for explaining the audience phenomena lies within the discipline of Form Criticism. Bultmann has insisted as a basic principle that consistency of theme reflects a consistent *Gemeinde* or the " laws " of tradition rather than a consistent person behind them.[6] The thrust of Bultmann's analysis is to drive us behind the redactors or the sources back to the early community as a creative sociological entity. The form of the logia is the result of the use to which they were put by the community in preaching, teaching, and debate. Following this logic one would have to say that the patterns we have noted in this study represent the *kerygma,* the faith of the early church. They permit us to penetrate to this early sociological level, but no farther.

In applying the discipline of Form Criticism to the historical question, it would be well to begin by reviewing the results of the correlation of audience and form. The insights from this study may be summarized under three headings. (1) There is a direct correlation between audience and form (Chart XI). (2) The nature of the form is directly related to agreement between the redactors. The high agreement for example in FM, FL, and FA logia suggests there is something about the narrative-related form that stabilizes the logia tradition. (3) Form enables us to discover certain things about the history of logion origin and transmission. This high agreement in the Mark and Q tradition on FM and FL suggests stories well rehearsed and brought into standardized form long before being included in Mark and Q. The high literary agreement between the Evangelists with FS and FP suggests that certain blocks of sayings and parables were joined together prior to the work of the Evangelist. It is apparent that the concept of form can help to explain some of the data of this study.

But now we come to the harder question. Do the phenomenon of form and the results of form-critical analysis preclude our discussion of the historical Jesus? Granted the ability of Form Criticism to reveal the early community at work, especially in the standardizing of legends and miracle stories, does this sociological approach sufficiently explain the phenomena of continuity and discontinuity? Before we can attempt an answer, it is necessary to examine the very concept of form itself, and the interpretation given it by Bultmann, to see if this is a correct assessment of the obvious evidence of Synoptic forms. As I see it, there are not one but at least two possibilities for explaining the data of form.

1. The fact that the FM and FL show the highest agreement, for example, could be the result of their being more intimately con-

nected with the life of the early church than were the FS and FP, which could then support Bultmann's dictum that they were *created* by that church community.

2. On the other hand, the high agreement between FL/FM and AD/ADG (Chart XI) could mean, not that the D and DG created the legends and miracle stories out of whole cloth, but that *by their very nature* these logia demanded a particular form, which in turn demanded a particular context for that form to have meaning. That is, Jesus did his miracles chiefly before the D and DG simply because the requirement of faith was built in to the miracle. That which is called legend, *by its intrinsic nature* involved Jesus in interaction with the D and DG. A correct reporting would then inevitably have produced this correlation. One might say that the FM and FL by their essential nature demanded a particular literary, historical, geographical, and audience context, and so these tended to be stable in the tradition. The stability of wording would suggest an early standardization of the story, either through oral repetition, or early fixing in written form, or both.

This leads to an interpretation of form data that stands at variance with that of classical Form Criticism. A legend, for example, demands a certain written form involving much historical narrative simply by virtue of the material. One couldn't report such a saying in any other way. The apothegm demands a rounding off at the end and the imbedding of the logion in a brief narrative framework because that is the natural way to reproduce such a saying. It occurred in a dialogue situation, flashing with the brilliance of the true bon mot, and so it must be reproduced. The saying and the parable stand alone by their very natures, and so need no narrative setting: the one is a didactic device, the other a more hortatory, homiletic mode (certainly by Jesus as much as by the early church). The higher percentage of wording agreement with the FP and FA would then be a function of the nature of the form. The apothegms were short, and correct wording was important to make the point. Parables required more careful wording than the sayings because of their more poetic, literary form. Such an interpretation takes the focus away from the creative activity of the early church and puts it on the logion itself, as used by Jesus and reproduced by the redactor in either oral or written form.

When, therefore, we see a close relationship between form and agreement, and between form and audience, we seem to have indicators pointing in the direction of this alternative interpretation. FM and FL by their very nature demand accuracy of La, Ha, and Ga, and so they have it. FP and FS do not demand this accuracy, and so they do not receive it. The FA is a form where there is such an intimate relationship between the saying and the surrounding event that the one cannot be told without the other; but the attention to La, Ha, and Ga is not as demanding as that of the FM and FL. This is exactly what is revealed in Chart XII.

The fact that some forms occur most often to certain audiences argues in the same direction. The nature of the audience as O demands a particular type of argumentative saying, which in turn demands the apothegm to reproduce the saying event. The nature of the audience as A1 prompts a certain crisis message, which is most effectively presented to the crowds in the form of parables. Mark enunciates this general approach to the crowds (A1): " And he taught them many things in parables " (Mark 4:2). The nature of the audience as D prompts a certain more intimate, more didactic message. He had already won them over. Now they must be instructed. The form most suited to this type of material is the saying. This is epitomized in the didactic scene at Caesarea Philippi (Mark 8:27-33). In summary, when we find the FA occurring most often with the AO and AGO, the FP with the AGO and A1, and the FS with the AD, it would seem that the Synoptics give us an inadvertent and unusually exact picture of the kind of form-audience correlation that simple logic would dictate. Some of this could be editorial and some could very well reflect the deeper historical situation. There is absolutely no need for the tortuous interpretation of the phenomenon of form that has too long dominated Synoptic scholarship. The evidence seems to argue that the form of a logion is the result, not of the use to which it was put in the early church, but rather of the intrinsic nature of the logion, asserting itself in history and commending itself to those who recorded the tradition. If this is true, then form does not necessarily preclude us from going beyond the form to the historical situation. In fact, form may be an aid to the recovery of this most primitive history.

The Inadequacy of Classical Form-Critical Explanations. The logic of Form Criticism actually denies some of the conclusions of its chief exponents. If the logia circulated independently, and were the product of the early church, they could hardly have at the same time been the product of any particular redactor, especially one writing in the late first century. A line must be drawn between what Bultmann called a " community product " and what for the redaction critic is more a *literary* product. In the heart of his discussion of form in *The History of the Synoptic Tradition,* Bultmann seems to have sensed this contradiction and avoided making form a literary device. He presents the Evangelists as those who were conservative in handling the tradition, giving us an essentially " unaltered " life of Jesus (pp. 343, 354, 356, 363, 366). The form would then be an *oral* product. But in the concluding section of this book he emerges as a full-blown redaction critic, making the redactors or their predecessors *literary* creators, expanding cult legends, creating apothegms and audience situations, and all conditioned by dogmatic motives (pp. 343–345, 371). If we are going to say that the logia circulated " independently," then it would seem we must allow them to be more independent of redactor or editor than Bultmann or the entire post-Bultmannian emphasis would allow.

Behind this confusion and apparent contradiction lies a basic weakness in Form Criticism. Throughout this critical movement there has been a continuous refusal to make any distinction between the clearly editorial material and the logia.[7] It is this problem almost more than any other that haunts Bultmann and his disciples, as it haunted Wrede before him. If there is one clear probability emerging from our study, it is that one must see a discontinuity between the E and the A material that simply denies the dogmatic activity of the redactor in either creating or altering the logia tradition to any great extent. We have seen ample evidence of the redactor at work. But the fact is that most of the patterns cut *horizontally* across all Gospels, all sources, and all forms rather than vertically down through any particular ones. The minute one admits the existence of such a distinction, a doctrinaire Form Criticism demanding to explain the entire history of the Synoptic tradition as the activity of the redactors or early source editors becomes impossible.

But if Form Criticism will not permit us to say that form is a redactor's product, then by this same logic we are driven with Bultmann to say that form must have arisen along with the *kerygma* within the oral period and in essentially oral form. Bultmann's conclusions here are much more plausible in terms of form-critical axioms than are those of the so-called post-Bultmannians. If this is so, then the logic of historical skepticism still stands, supported by a highly creative oral period. The early church as a creative community authored some and altered most of the sayings of Jesus to such an extent that it is impossible to get through to the level of primitive history.

But this does not seem to us to be the case. The two results of our study that stand immovably in the way of this form-critical thesis are the phenomena of continuity and discontinuity. For the many horizontal logia patterns to have been the product of a creative early church, certain highly improbable things would have to be true about that early community and the process of Gospel formation.

1. There would have to be a widespread knowledge of these "created" patterns sufficient to account for their appearance in all the sources. This would mean that those in the church would have to have created the complicated usage of the word *doulos,* for example, or the specialized use of *ho huios tou anthropou* in a suffering and eschatological sense only with the D, and then spread the knowledge of these complicated patterns throughout the early church in a very short time. It would mean that the pattern of explaining parables only to the D would have to have originated within the minds of some in the early community, and somehow been communicated to all who were transmitting this material. It

would mean that the broad spectrum of audience-logion correlation regarding, for example, the present and future crisis, or the love and wrath of God, would have to be the result of the creative activity of the church, universally known and widely understood. It would mean that the restriction of Jesus' teaching about his suffering, his crisis egotism, his antiapocalypticism, his emphasis on faith, forgiveness, and selective teaching only to the D audience would have to be the product of a commonly known thesis within the Palestinian church. It would mean that it was generally agreed that Jesus used the metaphors of body, salt, light, business, and harvest only in the AD logia, and those about weddings and dinners primarily with the nondisciples . . . or that all these patterns are the merest chance. All of this is so highly unlikely that one wonders at the history of this discussion which forces him to belabor such patent logic. On the contrary, the subtlety, complexity, sophistication, regularity, and widespread occurrence of these patterns drive them below and behind the social scene to a more unitive source. It is infinitely more likely that they represent an individual than a collective mind.

2. A theory of *Urkirche* creation would demand an editorial body capable of somehow controlling the editors of all sources and Gospels to such an extent that departures from the " pattern line " would be minimal. According to any presently defensible theory of Synoptic origins, this is highly improbable.

3. Such a theory would dictate a lack of concern for the facts of evangelical history that would allow a community to compose or drastically alter the original teachings of Jesus without complaint, opposition, or minority report. This is possible, but the evidence of agreement between the editors and of discontinuity between narration and logia suggests a conservatism on the part of the editors in handling the logia that cautions strongly against attributing such license to the early community of which they were a part.

4. For these patterns to have originated in the early church would require a widespread consensus regarding the teachings of Jesus at the deepest levels of refinement and usage. Certainly there

was general and conscious agreement on many things, for example, that Jesus adapted his teaching to the different audiences. But one looks in vain for the kind of *minutely detailed consensus* demanded by this alternative. Instead, we find the logia disagreeing with the editors in the usage of such terms as *ouranos, basileia, pneuma, genea, aggelos, adelphos, dechomai,* and *aiteo.* We find the logia within Mark, ch. 13, contradicting the apocalyptic tenor of the total chapter. Instead of agreement, we find the logia presenting one set of terms for the audience and the editors another, the logia having a more theological view of the audience and the Evangelists a more historical and ecclesiastical view. The entire body of evidence for discontinuity argues against any such broad and intimate consensus. The same is true of evidence for the special Jewish and ecclesiastical concerns of the M source, presumably the Jerusalem church, and of the many indications of misunderstanding of Jesus' mission and message on the part of all the early audiences, as well as the Evangelists, bitterly underscored by Jesus' constant criticism of his disciples.

In fact, there was no such unanimity between the Jesus of the logia and the editors or protoeditors; and the pattern of continuity running through the logia critique of the disciples reflects, not consensus, but constant misunderstanding between Jesus and these earliest members of the *Urgemeinde.* How could a community create that which it did not understand? How could it have created and passed on so as to preserve with such fidelity material that reflects so very many subtle patterns of unanimity and continuity?

This hard core of logia pattern material clearly antedates the work of the editors. It would seem also at this stage of the discussion to antedate the creative thought of the early community. Source and Form Criticism can indeed explain some of the data; but they fall short of explaining convincingly just those things which constitute the major new evidence of Audience Criticism. If there is any validity in this approach, we must look not only to the community but beyond the community for the ultimate explanation of these phenomena.

Chapter VIII

BREAKING THE *GESCHICHTE* BARRIER: HISTORICAL CRITICISM

There is one other obvious possibility. Within some apparent community consensus and creativity, the controlling element could be the single mind of the historical Jesus, wherein such continuity would be not only possible but perfectly natural and inevitable.

The general shifting of emphasis, the increasing audience selectivity, the accommodation of language, practice, and idea within the logia as Jesus moves from the D to the O audience in such subtle, complicated, and widespread fashion drive us to affirm the possibility that these patterns could reflect a unitary reality antedating, superseding, and overriding the early church. Within the climate of modern historical skepticism one hesitates even to make such a suggestion, but the logic is inescapable. The alternative that seems to explain the most simply and naturally those phenomena which cannot be explained by Redaction, Source, or Form Criticism is that these patterns constitute windows whereby we can break through the barrier of early church and editor back to the authentic life and teaching of the historical Jesus.

THE *GESCHICHTE* BARRIER

Such a suggestion immediately opens a Pandora's box of problems. Before we can seriously entertain such a possibility, we must face up to those obstacles which have barred this line of thought in recent years. These problems taken together form what we shall call the *Geschichte* barrier. For a quarter of a century it has been axiomatic that if one is to think critically about the Synoptics, it is neither possible nor legitimate to accept this historical alternative. Wrede assumed that there was no sure method of distinguishing the later interpretation from the "*Sache selbst.*" Bultmann went farther by insisting: " It is *not permitted* [italics mine] to go beyond the ' proclamation ' (*kerygma*), using it as a ' source ' in order to reconstruct the ' historic Jesus' with his messianic consciousness." He convinced an entire generation that " the Gospels lack any interest of a scientific, historical kind." [1] As a result, Bultmann fell back upon Kähler's convenient distinction between *Geschichte,* what the early church believed about Jesus, and *Historie,* what actually happened. Kerygmatic theology, stemming at least partly from Bultmann's skepticism, has since assumed that because one can't get through this *Geschichte* barrier, it doesn't really matter. [2]

This is a formidable obstacle, and has largely convinced the average critical mind of two generations. And we might be tempted to join the chorus, except for one large fact: this historical skepticism is based upon a methodology that is generally prescientific and that begs altogether too many questions. As I see it, there are seven major elements constituting the *Geschichte* barrier, each of which in one way or another exhibits this nonscientific methodology.

1. *The* Geschichte *Problem.* The first question has to do with what we are looking for when we talk of " authentic life and teaching." The old nineteenth-century quest of the historical Jesus attempted to draw a hard line between the Jesus of history and the Christ of the church's faith. Bultmann and his followers have rejected this dichotomy by redefining history along the lines pursued by Collingwood, Dilthey, and others where the distinction is made

between *Historie,* that which the historian can establish about the past, and *Geschichte,* that which has a vital relation to the present and future, that " inner history " of mind that stresses the manner in which the original reporters entered into the history they were reporting, and the ways in which the modern historian must also become existentially involved in the history he is interpreting. These facts are well known and need no extensive review here (cf. *JGTJ,* 17-22). What we would point out is that by defining the problem in these terms, Bultmann has made a genuine quest of the historical Jesus impossible. Like a self-fulfilling prophecy, the negative conclusions are intrinsic to the very manner in which the historical problem has been defined. This modern debate is a veritable jungle. What I shall attempt to do is draw an outline of the problem and sketch some new and hopefully more productive grounds for the future of the discussion.

Basically, the question of the historical Jesus has become polarized around two focuses: the *legitimacy* of the quest for *Historie* and the *possibility* of that quest. Within this forensic ellipse there are many corollary problems that will be outlined below; but all that is said will revolve around these two points of focus.

The semantic problem — The first aspect of the *Geschichte* problem has to do with the very way in which Bultmann has set up the debate. The distinction between *Historie* and *Geschichte* is an artificial one that tends to beg the question. If *Historie* represents the hard facts of " outer history," and *Geschichte* is to be distinguished meaningfully from it, then *Geschichte* should represent something clearly distinct from *Historie*. It should refer to *nothing but* the inner or interpretive element of faith or point of view. This distinction would then be useful for theoretical discussion. But, as Bultmann recognizes, one cannot separate *Geschichte* absolutely from *Historie*. Fact and interpretation interweave inextricably in the writing of history. This very truism shows the artificiality of the distinction. An absolute category (*Historie*) is contrasted with a relative one (*Geschichte*), a simple with a complex, and we see that they are not coordinate categories. They are like a sloppy lecture outline where one point overlaps onto the other, and where confusion is inevitable. If we are to permit a substantial and genuine element of outer history in *Geschichte*, then the distinction from *Historie* is meaningless, or at best, confusing. If we are not, then we have begged the question.

The problem of faith — A second corollary to the *Geschichte* problem is the matter of faith. Lying behind most Bultmannian or post-Bultmannian discussions of the problem is a kind of " Historiophobia " which has tended to react against a serious consideration of *Historie*. This is an old problem for German theology. It has its more immediate roots in the work of Martin Kähler as expressed in Bultmann and those in his tradition; but its deeper roots would seem to lie in the thought of Martin Luther, with his stress on justification by faith alone, and in the confrontation of the German Reformation with the Renaissance and its insistence on the supremacy of reason. Emil Brunner's *Revelation and Reason* is still perhaps the classic work on this problem. " The unbelieving search for security " is the canard often hurled at those said to be too concerned over *Historie,* and one is instructed by the Lutheran orientation of so many of those who, like Carl Braaten, draw back in horror from " the monstrous claim . . . that now because of scientific historiography we have ' a second avenue of access ' to the person of Jesus." [8] This fear of nineteenth-century liberalism, a kind of high tide of Renaissance penetration into German theology, is understandable; but for those who have not yet canonized Luther, this fear can be expected to be less than traumatic.

Within this supreme emphasis on faith being grounded in the existential encounter with Christ, there is one large problem, that of the psychology of faith. There is a lack of psychological sophistication to this Historiophobia. It is rare when anyone who talks about the supremacy of faith over intellectual conviction takes the trouble to describe what he means by faith, and yet that is the heart of a very great confusion. What is needed is the recognition that anything involving the human psyche, like faith, must necessarily be a compound of the conscious and subconscious aspects of the human mind. Faith is an amalgam of rational belief, and what we might call " subrational encounter," somewhat in the terms made popular by another Lutheran, Emil Brunner. This means that when one talks about faith not being dependent on rational activity, one is demanding that somehow faith not be inevitably involved (and in that sense dependent) with the conscious mind, which is psychological nonsense.[4] Personal maturity is based on the unity of the subconscious and the conscious elements of personality. It would seem legitimate to posit that maturity of faith also involves the union of the conscious and subconscious elements of that faith. Such a divided mind is exactly one of the causes of this Historiophobia, which is just as much a sickness as any phobia: the inability of the conscious mind to accept rationally what the subconscious affirms existentially.

Years ago Donald Baillie noted a strange phenomenon in German theology: an essentially conservative Lutheranism linked with a radical critical liberalism.[5] What was then a phenomenon has today become a problem; and it is this writer's suggestion that many of the apparent contradictions within the *Geschichte* barrier are the result of this basic theological-critical schizophrenia. Faith without belief is pathological faith. The problem for Christian belief at this point is the Jesus problem, the possibility of finding genuine *Historie* in the Synoptics to sustain the rational validity of the *kerygma*. Certainly the continued insistence on the legitimacy of the quest for the historical Jesus bears testimony to the rational demands of faith.[6]

When one faces a serious frustration, there are usually two ways to go for relief: either withdraw or attack. Faced with the frustration of existential encounter without the rational support of historical belief, Bultmann seems to have compensated by withdrawing to existentialism. In an interview in 1962, I said that I saw a logical connection between his critical skepticism and his shift to existential theology in his later work, having found no evidence of such an interest in any of his writings prior to the publication of *Die Geschichte der synoptischen Tradition* in 1921. His answer was quite clear. He said: " Naturally, that is what happened. I was led to ask, how important is *Historie* anyway? " If the discovery of *Historie* is not possible, then the almost inevitable compensation is to insist that it is not important. One has fled from *Historie* to *Geschichte*. Regularly in studies stressing *Geschichte* there is a substratum of skepticism regarding the *possibility* of finding *Historie* in the Gospels.[7] There is not space to develop this further. One can only point to the psychopathology of the *Geschichte* problem and the need for faith in Jesus to encompass the total man in a healthy and unified interaction between subconscious and conscious, subrational and rational: in this instance between one's intellectual apprehension of Jesus as *Historie* and his existential encounter with him as *Geschichte*. It is only thus that Christian theology can retain its health, and herein lies the most practical legitimacy for the continued quest of the historical Jesus.

The epistemological problem — A third corollary to the *Geschichte* problem involves the entire field of epistemology. The whole fixation on the problem of faith in historical knowledge, whether it be the faith of the historian, or that of the early church, dramatizes the fact that faith represents the extension into theology of the whole problem of human knowledge. Faith, in all that it means, *is* religious knowledge. Whether we are saying that the early church had faith in Christ as Lord, or that we must have faith in order to understand Christian theology, and so a believing audience is better equipped to understand Jesus, we are in either instance affirming the action of the knowing subject in the process of knowing something about the noumenal world. In other words, this orientation of the historical discussion in terms of faith and *Geschichte* has plunged us into the maelstrom of the epistemological problem, from which there is as yet no certain escape. The implicit suggestion in Bultmann's separation of *Historie* from *Geschichte* is that if we cannot somehow recover *Historie* with *absolute objectivity,* it is not legitimate to talk seriously about it. This whole approach *implies* that unless the Biblical historian can solve the epistemological dilemma, it is not legitimate to seek the historical Jesus.

Certainly this is an impossible burden to place on Biblical historiography, and also an unnecessary one. In this post-Kantian, postexistential age, no one can deny the place of the human observer in any observation, or the difficulty if not impossibility of proving an *absolute* relationship between any datum of the noumenal world and the words or ideas in the phenomenal world used to identify them. Even physical scientists are coming to realize, as James Conant says, that "the structure of nature may be such that our processes of thought do not correspond to it sufficiently to permit us to think about it." [8] There is a certain relativity built into the three-dimensional nature of the human mind that limits our *absolute* knowledge at every point. In the realm of theology, this is the basis of the insight that what is loosely called faith or unfaith is an inevitable aspect of the total knowing process. But the point is this: granted the limitations of the human mind and the inevitable relativity of knowledge, this does not mean that we cannot know enough about the data of the objective world to talk seriously about them. As Bishop Berkeley reminded us years ago, there is something infinitely practical about knowledge of the objective world. We bump our shins against it, and for practical purposes, we know it is there. It doesn't matter that we can't prove its existence in some abstract, absolute sense; but it does matter if we don't take its existence seriously. The unspoken demand that somehow the historian must *prove* with a peculiar absoluteness the data of Synoptic history in order for the quest to be legitimate or possible is philosophically naïve. It is a kind of sub-rosa humanism that represents the Renaissance mind ill at ease within the Reformation, demanding to storm the gates of heaven, to know absolute good from evil, but frustrated at the knowledge that he is man and not God.

On the contrary, it is the practical acceptance of that which one can prove only in terms of relative probabilities, that has characterized the scientific mind in the twentieth century; and it is this that is essential to Biblical historiography if it is ever to achieve any scientific results. The Biblical historian does not need to solve the problem enunciated by Gorgias the pre-Socratic Sophist, and continuing in semantic garb to this day in modern philosophy, in order to get on with the job of historiography. Before we can really get through this *Geschichte* barrier, we must reconstitute Historical Criticism along new, scientific lines, and free it from the impossible baggage that has swamped it in the last generation. We need to begin asking the kinds of questions that permit genuine historical answers, and the epistemological question is not one of these.

Mention might be made of one further facet to this epistemological blind alley into which the discussion has been channeled by Bultmann's definition of the problem. This is the dilemma of what Wittgenstein called " language games." Each discipline of thought has its own axioms and postulates, words and ideas which compose the language game of that discipline. One can reason and prove certain things within that discipline, if one uses the tools peculiar to it, that is, the rules of that game. But when one goes to another discipline, the rules change, the language changes, and one must argue and reason within a different set of axioms. The point is that, according to Wittgenstein, one cannot argue across the boundaries of any one " game," using the words and axioms of that game to prove or disprove things within another.[9] It would seem that the *Historie-Geschichte* orientation of the quest for the historical Jesus runs grave risk of shipwreck on Wittgenstein's thesis. The data of *Historie* represent those of the three-dimensional world, and it would seem that the words and axioms used to demonstrate the probabilities within that historiographic language game should be those of the three-dimensional world. *Historie* should be validated historiographically. *Geschichte,* on the other hand, used in its pure sense, deals with a dimension of reality that is more psychological, philosophical, and theological; and it has its own very specialized vocabulary and its own peculiar axioms. When one attempts to validate *Historie* in terms of *Geschichte,* he is immediately involved in the problem Wittgenstein describes: he is using categories out of context, and is at least open to serious challenge. Much work needs to be done on this matter; but raising the question will hopefully serve as a warning against allowing the search for *Historie* to become hopelessly confused by the use of words, axioms, and categories completely out of context.

The historiographic problem — Out of the frustration of historical skepticism and the surprising excitement over the rediscovery of the existential aspect of knowledge as popularized by Bultmann in *History and Eschatology*,[10] one major casualty has been the rejection of *Historie*. Most existentialist historians insist that they are concerned for the objective facts of history, and some, critics of Bultmann, such as Van Harvey and Schubert Ogden, go to great lengths to show that Bultmann is willing to admit the importance of *Historie*.[11] One must admit the presence of quotations in Bultmann protesting his innocence; but the fact remains that *Historie,* though present, is lost and forgotten in the philosophical and theological discussions over *Geschichte*. In *History and Eschatology,* certainly one of the major statements of Bultmann's philosophy of history,[12] he affirms his concern for *Historie,* but actually mentions it only at the beginning and ending of the book. The rest is all *Geschichte*. What he *does* with *Historie* speaks so loudly one cannot really hear what he *says* about it. Any disclaimer by Bultmann against a rejection of *Historie* must be assessed against the *Grundschrift* of his entire system of thought, *Die Geschichte der synoptischen Tradition*.[13] He assesses the conclusions of that book in *Form Criticism: A New Method of New Testament Research:* " The investigation of the sayings of Jesus leads to a considerable uncertainty, but it does not end in complete skepticism. By no means are we at the mercy of those who doubt that Jesus ever lived . . . the character of Jesus, the vivid picture of his personality and his life, cannot now be clearly made out; but what is more important, the content of his message is or will be more clearly recognizable." [14] The objective facts of *Historie* have become so subservient to the faith of the early church that what remains as *Historie* is only *the fact that* Jesus lived. The content of his message is pure *Geschichte*. It is this historical skepticism which has been axiomatic for two generations of scholars.[15] The hard core of this historical problem is not its legitimacy, but its *possibility*. It is a problem of *Historie*.

This leads to another aspect of the historiographic problem, to what might be called the " Bultmannian captivity." There is a very real question as to whether or not the so-called post-Bultmannians have gone very far from their source. Harvey and Ogden have documented brilliantly what seems to be the fact, that there is little new in the " new quest " of the historical Jesus.[16] As I see it there are two elements that might be considered new in this movement. The one is a conservative reaction away from the " historical brink " to which Bultmann led it. There is a definite and quite vocal concern over *Historie:* " How is it possible for faith to be content with mere tradition? "[17]

The other new element is a basic illogic that attempts to talk seriously about *Historie* while still clinging to most of Bultmann's presuppositions, both critical and existential. For example, James Robinson attempts to establish *Historie* in the Synoptics by showing the similarity between the *kerygma* and the teachings of Jesus at the " deeper level of meaning." He begins his methodological reconstruction by arguing in a typically Bultmannian way that his method can affirm the historicity of only that part of Jesus in which he is *least Christian,* that is, when the *kerygma* shows traits the church could hardly have invented.[18] He operates from a kerygmatic stance thoroughly based on the historical skepticism of Wrede and Bultmann. But then Robinson performs a logical somersault by affirming that the Synoptics are most authentic where they are closest to the deeper meaning of Paul and the *kerygma,* in other words, where they are *most Christian.*[19] It would seem more logical to insist that we cannot have it both ways. You cannot use the early church both to discount and to establish the general historicity of the Synoptics.[20] The basic suggestion for methodology coming from this entire post-Bultmannian group seems to be that by establishing the *kerygma* in Paul, Acts, or the later Epistles, we can then work backward to the Synoptics, using the *kerygma* as a test for genuineness. In the beginning was the *kerygma*. But this is exactly the barrier we are describing, and the logical contradiction of using the church's faith as a test for the historicity of that which is assumed to be the product of the church's faith is a painful reminder that we are arguing in a circle. One cannot use the *Geschichte* barrier to break through the *Geschichte* barrier.

The historiographic problem becomes that of the search for *Historie* becoming sunk in a kind of philosophical swamp. The post-Bultmannian discussion has been an attempt to find a valid philosophical starting point for genuine historical research. Inevitably we are involved in the philosophy of history. But the problem is that historiography has been drowned out in the babel of tongues fighting a dozen philosophical battles on as many fronts. Tactically this has been disastrous. What has been going on is the quest for the *philosophy* of the historical Jesus.

What is needed, then, is what Stephen Neill calls "real historians." [21] It wasn't until the physical sciences broke out of the philosophical dilemmas of previous centuries that the scientific revolution began. Surely the time has come for the quest of the historical Jesus to break out of this nineteenth-century philosophical trap, and enter into the twentieth century by undertaking a practical, empirical, inductive study of the life and teachings of Jesus, where, even as we recognize our epistemological limitations, even as we accept the existential realities, even as we admit the inevitable activity of the early church, this recognition does not deter us from genuinely scientific historical research that searches for *Historie* on its own terms.

2. *The Argument from Form.* A second basic part of the *Geschichte* barrier has been the concept of form. This and other factors to be mentioned have militated against the *possibility* of the quest of the historical Jesus more than against its legitimacy. Bultmann interpreted this concept as revealing the use to which the Synoptic material was put in the early Christian community. The barrier to genuine *Historie,* then, is seen to envelop the logia of Jesus in the very form in which they come to us. But our study has suggested a different interpretation. Form is rather the function of the intrinsic nature of the logion, and by itself has nothing definitive to tell us about the historical validity of the material in general. It is only when form is surrounded by a whole host of other presuppositions that it gains the power to support Bultmann's thoroughgoing mood of skepticism.[22]

3. *The Argument from Motive.* One of the favorite means of attacking the validity of the Synoptic material has been that of attributing certain " motives " to those in the early church who gathered and recorded the logia. When evidence for these motives was discovered, then one could safely attribute this material to the early church, or a particular Evangelist. Wrede's book *Das Messiasgeheimnis* is, of course, one of the classic illustrations of this. Wrede's thesis has always had to beg one simple alternative. The " secret " motif in Mark could just as well have been the motive of the historical Jesus as of Mark. By itself, unaided by other presuppositions, the " Messianic Secret," which is surely found in Mark, argues neither for nor against historical validity.

One of the most influential examples of this approach has come out of the interpretation of Jesus as an apocalyptic figure who predicted the *eschaton* in the lifetime of his disciples. As E. F. Scott records, " It was believed . . . that the Lord would return at any moment to bring in the Kingdom, and there could be no purpose in writing down a record of him for a future age that would never come." [23] Since there was no motive for writing down the words and deeds of Jesus, we cannot look for early written reports, and thus any record of his life and teachings must be late, and strongly influenced by the early church. I have already attempted at length to show that Jesus' concept of the Kingdom was far more comprehensive than the consistent eschatologist would permit (*JGTJ,* 122–141). Our present study has shown that the pattern at this point shows Jesus warning against just such apocalypticism. Those passages, especially Mark, ch. 13, making him predict an early Parousia constitute an antipattern, and represent some kind of intrusion into the text. Furthermore, we have shown that even if Jesus and the entire disciple community were apocalyptists, this would not have robbed them of the motive for preserving his words and deeds, any more than it prevented Paul, or John, or the author of I Peter who wrote as late as A.D. 96, " The end of all things is at hand " (I Peter 4:7).

Perhaps the strongest argument against the abuse of this motive approach comes from the evidence for the clear discontinuity be-

tween the E and the A material, and for the patterns of continuity
cutting horizontally across the logia. A few vertical motive patterns have shown up, for example, the Jewish, ecclesiastical interests of Matthew's special source, but these are at a surprising
minimum. This argument from motive has provided an excuse for
some of the most extreme and bizarre exercises in " Thesis Exegesis," and reflects in this author's opinion more often the " motive "
of the modern exegete than that of the early church (cf. *JGTJ,*
25–26). The clearest motive we have observed in the Synoptics is
that of the Evangelists in preserving with a peculiar slavishness the
details of their sources, and of the earlier community in reproducing the words and ideas of Jesus with a surprising continuity.

4. *Strictly Oral Period.* One of the basic axioms constituting the
Geschichte barrier is the assumption that the original period of
Gospel formation consisted of a " strictly oral " development of
the Gospel material within the early church.[24] Aside from the
apocalyptic argument above, this is usually supported by insisting
that the early disciples were too poor or too uneducated even to
purchase the materials for writing, let alone transcribe the words
and deeds of Jesus.[25] Aside from the fact that the very name " oral
period " begs the question, the oversimplification of this position
shares the weaknesses of all such " nothing but " extremes. If the
" formation period " were a philosophical concept, then we might
concede that it could have been " strictly " one thing or another.
Instead it was a process and period of life, involving among many
other complexities, the completely unpredictable factor of the
human mind. We place ourselves in a very tenuous position if we
impose upon the chaotic imponderables of a living tradition too
neat and simple a pattern. Aside from this, our study has cast an
entirely new light on the question. The problem with this whole
discussion has been a loose and uncritical view of the disciple audience. If we see that beyond the Twelve, however literary or not,
extends a crowd of disciples, involving every kind of person from
the most tattered leper to men and women of position, wealth,
and education, among whom were most probably some scribes,

then the possibilities for literary activity among the disciples become enormous. This particular argument seems to this author to be one of the most fatuous examples of special pleading in this whole discussion and needs to be relegated to the limbo reserved for nonscientific methodology.

5. *Argument from Development*. Another common exegetical assumption contributing notably to this *Geschichte* barrier has been to the effect that wherever two of Jesus' logia resemble each other, this is necessarily the result of " development " within the primitive church, usually assumed to be from the simple to the complex. From the inception of Form Criticism, there has been much protest over the a priori nature of this particular method.[26] In this chorus of objection, there is one simple alternative that keeps asserting itself: if the Gospels show the development of a particular idea, parable, or figure of speech, what is to stop us from saying that this could equally represent the development within the mind of Jesus? To assume that development could only be within the early church simply begs the question.

There is a curious lack of humor and a sense of what is involved in the life of a traveling teacher and preacher in this argument that strongly suggests the academic isolation of those who beg this question. There seems to be an unspoken belief that Jesus could only have given one idea, parable, or metaphor on one occasion and in one form. This is patent nonsense as any itinerant lecturer knows. It is true that within the theological patterns presented in this study there are many forms and variations that the basic metaphor will take, and at times some " development " within the tradition would seem to be detected, for example, in the parables of the pounds and the talents. More often it would seem to us that these similar sections show so many important differences that it is much less tortuous to see them as similar but different sayings (cf. *JGTJ, ad loc.*). The suggestion that commends itself to us is that we are dealing with material bearing all the earmarks of abundant *repetition* by Jesus. The inherent continuity of the logia argues for the kind of repetition that would have enabled the disciples to fix these teachings firmly in mind. It would seem inescapable that the Twelve and even some of the DG would have heard Jesus' basic stock of material again and again, and in varying versions. This kind of repetition is exactly the type of thing common with Jewish rabbis and their pupils, who then recorded that " Ben Azzai used to say . . . ; R. Akiba used to say," that is, they said it many times.[27] With such repetition by Jesus, development within his own presentation would certainly have been possible, if not probable, and we must not beg this question.

Another objection to this argument from development is that one cannot assume that oral material always developed from the simple to the complex. Vincent Taylor showed years ago that in a controlled experiment forgetting of details operates more commonly than their enlargement.[28] Such an experiment, of course, cannot re-create the exact Palestinian situation. Stronger evidence comes from the comparison of the Gospel of Thomas with its parallels in the Synoptics. There are, for example, thirteen canonical parables reproduced in the Gospel of Thomas: two are longer than their Synoptic counterparts, *nine are shorter*. If this is any indication, it would seem that as the teachings of Jesus circulated in the community, both processes were at work, with the tendency to shorten predominant over that to expand.[29] In no case is there any significant change in the message of the parable.

6. *The Use of Parables.* One widespread assumption that has contributed greatly to the argument from development, and to much negative estimate of the parables, derives from Adolf Jülicher's insistence that Jesus never used allegory, and that his parables only had one point. When we find them with allegory, or with more than one point, we are justified in seeing here the work of the community. This is a very good illustration of the kind of doctrinaire and highly artificial axiom that becomes fixed in popular methodology, almost without one's knowledge, like something breathed in the air. How many have read Jülicher's *Die Gleichnisreden Jesu*? It has never been translated into English, and few seem to take the trouble to question this dictum. I have already chal-

lenged this on the grounds that Jülicher was imposing a Greek mode upon one who should be allowed to operate within the Hebraic use of the parabolic *mashal,* where allegory was common, and widely used by rabbis of Jesus' day (*JGTJ,* 28). Aside from this, our present study has offered two items of evidence that would hopefully lay to rest this particular example of deductive logic. If we take the trouble to begin with an examination of the text, rather than with a doctrinaire a priori, two things become clear. In the first place, the semiallegorical explanations to certain parables appear to be merely part of a widespread pattern wherein Jesus is consistently recorded explaining his parables to his disciples, and leaving them unexplained to those outside. The unconscious testimony of all sources is that this was Jesus' characteristic practice which Mark goes to some lengths to typify in ch. 4.

In the second place, we have noted the highly significant fact that the number of word and theology patterns in these suspected semiallegorical explanations equals and often exceeds those in the parables they are explaining. Jülicher's observation that anything so highly artificial as allegory could not be used in the heat of debate reflects an academic rather than a homiletic mind. Jesus was a preacher, and the parable is the form most common in preaching situations. Any preacher knows that the kind of semiallegory found in the parables is the stock-in-trade of the homilete, and such illustrations through constant repetition tend to take on a breadth of meaning impossible to circumscribe. In this author's opinion, there is almost no principle of exegesis more calculated to produce arbitrary and inaccurate parable interpretation than this one-point-only axiom. It is a relic of the pre-Qumran age where New Testament scholars turned to classical Greek models for interpreting the Synoptics and needs to be decently buried.

7. *Prefabricated Models.* One final source and characteristic of this *Geschichte* barrier needs mentioning. It has long been tempting to draw close parallels between the Synoptics and other types of literature, and then argue that the Synoptics must have been formed in the same manner. The Greek model motivated Jülicher as it did

Bultmann and two generations of scholars. Qumran has severely damaged the validity of the Greek parallel. Bultmann also drew close comparisons with German folklore, and from the " laws " of such lore constructed his model. The problem is that the literature on folk tradition reveals no agreement among the experts on any such " laws," [30] and one can't help noting Bultmann's complete dependence on Baumgartner for his understanding of the axioms of folk literature.[31] There is an obvious reflection of the Synoptics in the Mishnah, and Bultmann made massive use of Strack-Billerbeck in the later editions of *Die Geschichte der synoptischen Tradition.* The work of Birger Gerhardsson in *Memory and Manuscript* is the most recent extensive illustration of this approach. Although we would agree with many of Gerhardsson's insights, there is one basic danger in relying too heavily on this method. The Synoptics represent something absolutely unique in the history of literature. There is really no exact parallel. As I shall attempt to show in a forthcoming book, there are parallels with one type of ancient literature or another in the attempt to reproduce *ipsissima verba,* in the oracular quality of the logia, in the vividness of the narration, in the interaction between narration and logion, and even in the audience orientation, but there is no literature that puts these and other characteristics of the " Synoptic Mode " all together except the Synoptics. Unless we begin and end with the Synoptics themselves in constructing a model, we run a grave risk of superimposing an artificial and alien formation process upon the early church.

BREAKING THE BARRIER

But now let us depart from these traditional lines of debate. Some of them have taken us as far as they can; others represent an old-world methodology that needs to be replaced. Ours is a practical approach. We are assuming that in a commonsense way we can talk about historical persons even while admitting the relativity of such knowledge. We are suggesting that we can talk about the historical Jesus without necessarily jeopardizing the importance of faith. We are concerned to examine the Synoptics with a minimum of a prioris and let them testify to their own historicity. Most specifically, we have presented a method based upon the search for patterns constituting evidence for the existence of the data of the objective world. In applying these principles of search and restraint, of method and policy to the quest for the historical Jesus, and to the evidence derived from this study, a clear, historical logic emerges. To be a person, existing in the objective world, implies a certain uniqueness, regularity, and permanence, a certain " habit " of mind and action. If there be any evidence for the historical Jesus in the Synoptics, it should be reflected in these phenomena. It is exactly such patterns that are evident in the words, praxis, and theology of Jesus at a level so deeply imbedded in the logia, so widespread, so detailed, so distinct from the editorial patterns, that their most probable source is the unique mind of the historical Jesus coming through the process of Gospel formation reasonably intact.

The " Fix " Concept. In bringing this method to final focus, we need one more tool, this time taken from the lore of celestial navigation, a process not unlike that of historiography. Finding one's position at sea is a problem of bringing together coordinates that are the results of individual observations of the heavenly bodies. Each sun or star sight represents a mathematical " pattern." When its angle is calculated and related to the observer, the result is one line drawn across the chart, indicating that the ship is somewhere along that line. But before a " fix " can be obtained, several other such lines of position must be plotted from independent observations of different heavenly bodies. As these mathematical and geometric patterns converge on a point, so does one locate his position. Thus it is in Biblical historiography. Each of these patterns of word, idea, praxis, metaphor, or a complex of all, represents something objectively true about its source, as each star sight has independent validity. The historical Jesus is somewhere along that line. Then, when these various patterns are brought together, if there is a mutual convergence around a point, whether sharply or only generally defined, at that point we are justified in talking about a Synoptic " fix," about the historical Jesus. This convergence would be the compatibility, the overall continuity, the interdependence, of one individual pattern with another. Where one pattern clearly contradicts several others, that pattern stands like a bad star sight and needs to be discarded, modified, or somehow explained in the light of the converging complex of patterns. This is the antipattern to which we have already referred. Each pattern then says something historically valid about Jesus; and it is in the total complex of patterns *that are mutually compatible* that we should be able to find a genuine profile of the historical Jesus. At times this will involve word or theological patterns so sharply defined that we can talk about the *ipsissima verba* or *ipsissima mens* of Jesus. At other times, these patterns will be less distinct, and we will have to talk about the core of authenticity within a certain variety of verbiage or emphasis or even theological idea that is more the work of church or redactor. Historicity then will assume various guises, and be a matter of more or less at one point or another, rather than absolutely yes or no *in toto.*

Extent of Synoptic Historicity. One question remains. To what extent do the 352 logia show concentrations of patterns sufficient to constitute a historical fix? How much of the logia tradition is *Historie?* In examining this question, we go to Appendix A, where all the data of the various studies in this book are brought together into a comprehensive chart. First let us look at the possibility of talking about the *ipsissima verba* of Jesus. We have noted that 17.5 percent of all important words in the logia are pattern words (Chart XXIII). In Appendix A we see that 88 percent of all the logia have at least one pattern word. This would not be much in itself, unless such words were ones that in themselves contained theological patterns, such as *doulos* or *basileia,* and these words were being used in the peculiar ways that constituted those patterns. Of more importance would be the logia containing large pattern concentrations, and of these there are forty-six with 25 percent or more of all the words in the logion being pattern words. This is 13 percent of all the logia. There are twenty logia with 50 percent or more pattern words (log. 83, 116, 170, 48, 176, 339, etc.), three with as much as 80 percent (log. 104, 116, 170), and two with 100 percent pattern words (log. 81, 69). It would seem *probable* from this evidence that we can identify the *ipsissima verba* of Jesus with at least 17 percent of all the important words, and in at least 13 percent of all the logia. From this minimal figure, one could then open the *possibility* of the Greek translation of exact words of Jesus in approximately 88 percent of all the logia, and in an indefinite number of words that are used often, but do not show the clarity of category (a) or (b) patterns used in this estimate, for example, the seventy-six category (c) pattern words or phrases in Appendix B.

Beyond the *ipsissima verba,* it is even more probable that we can talk of the *ipsissima mens* of Jesus. Again looking at Appendix A, we see that 97 percent of all logia have at least one pattern of some kind. There are 91 percent with at least one theological pattern, 86 percent with patterns in each of two pattern categories, and 48 percent with significant concentrations of patterns in more than one category. This suggests the probability that the Synoptics contain a much higher concentration of the exact ideas of Jesus than of his exact words, in somewhere between 48 percent and 91 percent of all the logia.

There remains however a significant area of doubt that must be part of this historical summary. Twelve percent of the logia contain no pattern words, 9 percent reveal no theological patterns, and 3 percent have no patterns of any kind. There are antipatterns in over 7 percent of the logia. Added to this is the fact that Matthew and Luke disagree in their reproduction of the wording of Mark and Q an average of 14 percent, and in their audience designation an average of 9 percent. This gives us a rough average factor of doubt of approximately 9 percent in the several ways this can be calculated. It would seem that any statement about the historical teaching of Jesus must contain some such element of caution.

In conclusion, it would seem that the historical Jesus must ultimately be a composite discovery. There are in the Synoptics areas

of history where the " outer " element of *Historie* is predominant
and recoverable, but surrounded by areas where there is an increasing predominance of " inner " history, or, if we can use it in
this purer sense, *Geschichte*. In this complex and limited manner,
it would seem highly probable that we can indeed break through
the *Geschichte* barrier and talk of the authentic, historical Jesus.
Basic to all stands a body of logia possessing a rare stability and
integrity, reflecting a church deeply concerned from a very early
period to preserve the exact words and ideas of Jesus, and uniquely
successful in so doing.[32]

If this be true, then the obvious implication is a theological one.
The next task of Biblical scholarship is to reconstruct the authentic
theology of Jesus, where the element of *Historie* is at a maximum,
and use this as a basis for our understanding of Paul and John and
the rest of Christian theology in general. It is the more primitive
theology of Jesus that must stand in judgment on the *kerygma,* not
vice versa as in the post-Bultmannian program. Using this method,
I have attempted a beginning in *The Justice of God in the Teaching of Jesus*. The framework for such a theological reconstruction
has been laid out in Chapter VI of this book. Here we conclude
with the briefest miniature. The historical Jesus was a selective
teacher who spoke to people as they were able to understand, regularly adapting his teaching to his audience, and giving the totality,
balance, and entire range of his message only to the twelve disciples.
His mind was consumed by his sense of the judgment of God, and
the desperate need for men to yield themselves to His sovereignty.
The message itself and the methods he used were a sword, a net, a
seed, an invitation — selecting, sifting, and separating those who
received it from those who did not. He was a commanding, critical,
demanding person whose joy in life was deepened by a sense of his
terrible mission, to present in himself the very judging alternatives
of God's love and wrath. And he chose a cross, and predicted its
advent, and yet at every point rose above its dominion.

Appendix A

TOTAL LISTING OF LOGIA

Below is a total listing of every logion, with all correlated data derived from this study. The logion numbers are those used in the text of the book. Each symbol is explained in the Key to Abbreviations. The WP fraction refers to the " dominant " Gospel: Mark, and Luke for the Q source. The numerators in the WP fraction refer to the number of pattern words, the denominators to the total number of important words in those logia. The numbers with TP, PP, and MP give the number of such patterns per logion, all in categories (a) and (b). If there is a divergence in A, H, S, or F, the designations follow the order of passages as listed. The final list of numbers refers to the agreement categories for La, Ha, Ga, Aa, and Wa, reading from left to right, with the last number giving the type of comparison.

LOGION

1. Matt. 3:15, ADG, H2, S3, FL, WP 1/7, AP–1.
2. Luke 4:4, 8; Matt. 4:4, 7, AN, H2, S2, FL, WP 1/14, 111121.

3. Mark 1:15; Matt. 4:17, AA, H2, S1, FN, WP 2/3, TP–1, 111127.
4. Luke 4:21, AGO, H2, S4, FA, WP 0/3, TP–2.
5. Luke 4:23, AGO, H2, S7, FQ, WP 0/10.
6. Matt. 13:57; Mark 1:4; Luke 4:24, AGO, H2, S6/S1/S7, FA, WP 2/5, PP–1, 331117.
7. Luke 4:25-27, AGO, H2, S4, FA, WP 1/30, TP–1, PP–1.
8. Matt. 4:19; Mark 1:17, AD, H2, S1, FL, WP 0/7, TP–1, PP–1, 111118.
9. Luke 4:25; Mark 1:25, ADG, H2, S1, FM, WP 0/2, 111113.
10. Luke 4:43; Mark 1:38, AD/ADG, H2, S1, FN, WP 0/11, TP–1, 111233.
11. Luke 5:4, 10, AD, H2, S4, FM, WP 1/6, TP–1, PP–1.
12. Matt. 5:3; Luke 6:20, A1, H2, S2, FS, WP 1/6, TP–1, 322121.
13. Matt. 5:4, A1, H2, S3, FS, WP 1/5, TP–1.
14. Matt. 5:5, A1, H2, S3, FS, WP 2/6, TP–1.
15. Matt. 5:6; Luke 6:21, A1, H2, S2, FS, WP 1/5, TP–1, 322121.
16. Matt. 5:7; Luke 6:21, A1, H2, S2, FS, WP 1/5, TP–1, 322131.
17. Matt. 5:8, A1, H2, S3, FS, WP 1/5, TP–1.
18. Matt. 5:9, A1, H2, S3, FS, WP 2/6, TP–1, PP–1.
19. Matt. 5:10, A1, H2, S3, FS, WP 2/6, TP–2.
20. Luke 6:22-23; Matt. 5:11-12, A1, H2, S2, FS, WP 4/17, TP–2, 322121.
21. Matt. 5:13; Mark 9:50; Luke 14:34-35, A1/AD/ADG, H2, S1, FP, WP 3/11, TP–2, PP–1, MP–1, 333231.
22. Matt. 5:14, A1, H2, S3, FP, WP 2/9, TP–2, PP–1, MP–1.
23. Matt. 5:15; Luke 11:33, A1/AG, H2/H3, S2, FP, WP 2/8, TP–1, PP–1, MP–1, 333321.
24. Matt. 5:16, A1, H2, S3, FP, WP 6/10, TP–1, PP–1, MP–1.
25. Matt. 5:17, A1, H2, S3, FS, WP 1/8, TP–1.
26. Matt. 5:18; Luke 16:17, A1/AO, H2, S2, FS, WP 4/14, TP–1 (AP–1), PP–1, 333321.
27. Matt. 5:19, A1, H2, S3, FS, WP 3/16, TP–1 (AP–1), PP–1.
28. Matt. 5:20, A1, H2, S3, FS, WP 1/9, TP–2.
29. Matt. 5:21-22, A1, H2, S3, FS, WP 4/27, TP–4.
30. Matt. 5:23-24, A1, H2, S3, FS, WP 2/19, TP–3.
31. Matt. 5:25-26; Luke 12:57-59, A1/AGO, H2/H3, S2, FS, WP 4/14, TP–2, PP–1, 133331.
32. Matt. 5:27-28, A1, H2, S3, FS, WP 2/10, TP–2.
33. Matt. 5:29-30, A1, H2, S3, FS, WP 3/24, TP–2.

34. Matt. 5:31-32; Luke 16:18, A1/AO, H2/H3, S8/S2, FS, WP 2/12, TP–1, PP–1, 333327.
35. Matt. 5:33-37, A1, H2, S3, FS, WP 4/37, TP–2, PP–1.
36. Matt. 5:38-42; Luke 6:29-30, A1, H2, S2, FS, WP 2/30, TP–1, PP–1, 212121.
37. Matt. 5:43-45; Luke 6:22-28, A1, H2, S2, FS, WP 5/22, TP–2, PP–2, 212121.
38. Matt. 5:46-47; Luke 6:32-33, A1, H2, S2, FS, WP 3/13, TP–2, 212121.
39. Luke 6:34-35, A1, H2, S4, FS, WP 3/26, TP–2, PP–1.
40. Matt. 5:48; Luke 6:36, A1, H2, S2, FS, WP 0/6, TP–2, 212121.
41. Matt. 6:1-4, A1, H2, S3, FS, WP 12/39, TP–3, PP–1.
42. Matt. 6:5-6, A1, H2, S3, FS, WP 12/28, TP–3.
43. Matt. 6:7-8, A1, H2, S3, FS, WP 3/12, TP–2.
44. Matt. 6:9-13; Luke 11:2-4, A1/AD, H2/H3, S2, FS, WP 5/23, TP–5, 333221.
45. Matt. 6:14-15, A1, H2, S3, FS, WP 2/11, TP–2, PP–1.
46. Matt. 6:16-18, A1, H2, S3, FS, WP 12/28, TP–2.
47. Matt. 6:19-21; Luke 12:33-34, A1/AD, H2/H3, S2, FP, WP 9/23, TP–2, MP–1, 333221.
48. Matt. 6:22-23; Luke 11:34-36, A1/AGO, H2/H3, S2, FP, WP 10/20, TP–2, PP–1, MP–1, 333321.
49. Matt. 6:24; Luke 16:13, A1/AD, H2/H3, S2, FP, WP 2/17, TP–1, PP–1, MP–2, 333211.
50. Matt. 6:25; Luke 12:22-23, A1/AD, H2/H3, S2, FS, WP 7/13, TP–1, PP–1, 333211.
51. Matt. 6:26; Luke 12:24, A1/AD, H2/H3, S2, FS, WP 5/12, TP–2, PP–1, 333221.
52. Matt. 6:27; Luke 12:25, A1/AD, H2/H3, S2, FS, WP 1/6, TP–1, 333211.
53. Matt. 6:28-30; Luke 12:26-28, A1/AD, H2/H3, S2, FS, WP 6/26, TP–4, PP–1, 33221.
54. Matt. 6:31-33; Luke 12:29-30, A1/AD, H2/H3, S2, FS, WP 5/20, TP–3, 33221.
55. Matt. 6:34, A1, H2, S3, FS, WP 2/8, TP–1.
56. Matt. 7:1-5; Luke 6:37-38, 41-42, A1, H2, S2, FS, WP 9/34, TP–1, 112121.
57. Matt. 7:6, A1, H2, S3, FP, WP 0/11, AP–1, MP–1.

58. Matt. 7:7-11; Luke 11:9-13, A1/AD, H2/H3, S2, FS, WP 14/37, TP–2, PP–1, 333211.
59. Matt. 7:12; Luke 6:31, A1, H2, S2, FS, WP 1/9, TP–1, 111121.
60. Matt. 7:13-14, A1, H2, S3, FP, WP 4/19, TP–1, PP–1, MP–1.
61. Luke 13:23-24, AA, H3, S4, FP, WP 1/9, TP–2, PP–1, MP–1.
62. Matt. 7:15, A1, H2, S3, FP, WP 3/9, TP–1, PP–1.
63. Matt. 7:16-17, A1, H2, S3, FP, WP 8/18, TP–2, MP–1.
64. Matt. 7:18-20; Luke 6:43-44, A1, H2, S2, FP, WP 12/21, TP–4, PP–1, MP–1, 112121.
65. Luke 6:45; Matt. 12:35, AO/A1, H2, S2, FP, WP 7/16, TP–2, PP–1, MP–1, 333321.
66. Matt. 7:21-23; Luke 6:46, A1, H2, S2, FS, WP 5/32, TP–3, PP–1, 333231.
67. Matt. 7:24-27; Luke 6:47-49, A1, H2, S2, FP, WP 6/43, TP–3, PP–1, MP–1.
68. Mark 1:41, 44; Matt. 8:2, 4; Luke 5:13, 14, ADG, H2, S1, FM, WP 1/2, 111117.
69. Matt. 8:7, 10; Luke 5:9, ADG, H2, S2, FM, WP 4/4, TP–2, PP–1, 321111.
70. Matt. 8:11-12; Luke 13:28-30, ADG/AA, H2/H3, S2, FM, WP 5/31, TP–2, PP–3, MP–1, 333321.
71. Matt. 8:20; Luke 9:58, ADG, H2/H3, S2, FA, WP 2/11, TP–1, 333111.
72. Matt. 8:22; Luke 9:60, ADG, H2/H3, S2, FA, WP 1/6, TP–3, 133121.
73. Matt. 8:26, AD, H2, S3, FM, WP 2/4, TP–1.
74. Matt. 8:32, AD, H2, S3, FM, WP 0/1.
75. Matt. 9:2; Mark 2:5; Luke 5:20, ADG, H2, S1, FM, WP 0/4, TP–1, 111117.
76. Matt. 9:12; Mark 2:17; Luke 5:31, AO, H2, S1, FA, WP 0/10, TP–3, 111117.
77. Matt. 9:15; Mark 2:19-20; Luke 5:34-35, AO, H2, S1, FP, WP 7/14, TP–3, PP–1, MP–1, 111116.
78. Matt. 9:16; Mark 2:21; Luke 5:36, AO, H2, S1, FP, WP 3/13, TP–1, PP–1, 111127.
79. Matt. 9:17; Mark 2:22; Luke 5:37-38, AO, H2, S1, FP, WP 4/16, TP–1, PP–1, MP–1, 111127.
80. Luke 5:39, AO, H2, S4, FP, WP 3/7, AP–1.

81. Matt. 9:22, ADG, H2, S3, FM, **WP 4/4, TP–2.**
82. Matt. 9:24, AGO, H2, S3, FM, WP 1/4.
83. Matt. 9:29, 30, ADG, H2, S3, FM, WP 4/8, **TP–1.**
84. Matt. 9:32-38; Luke 10:2, AD/ADG, H2/H3, S2, FS, WP 4/10, TP–1, PP–1, 333211.
85. Matt. 10:5-8, AD, H2, S3, FS, WP 4/30, TP–2 (AP–1).
86. Matt. 10:9-10; Mark 6:8-9; Luke 10:4; 9:3, AD/ADG, H2, S1/S2, FS, WP 4/14, TP–1, 333227.
87. Matt. 10:11-13; Luke 10:5, AD/ADG, H2, S1/S2, FS, WP 5/22, TP–1, 133227.
88. Mark 6:10; Luke 9:4, AD, H2, S1, FS, WP 0/5, TP–1, 111113.
89. Matt. 10:14; Mark 6:11; Luke 9:5, AD, H2, S1, FS, WP 2/10, TP–1, 133327.
90. Matt. 10:15; Luke 10:12, AD/ADG, H2, S2, FS, WP 2/11, TP–2, PP–1, 133221.
91. Matt. 10:16a; Luke 10:3, AD/ADG, H2, S2, FS, WP 3/10, TP–1, PP–1, 133221.
92. Matt. 10:16b, AD, H2, S3, FS, WP 1/5.
93. Matt. 10:17-20, AD, H2, S3, FS, WP 6/23, TP–2, PP–1.
94. Matt. 10:21-22, AD, H2, S3, FS, WP 5/19, TP–3.
95. Matt. 10:23, AD, H2, S3, FS, WP 3/13, TP–2 (AP–1).
96. Matt. 10:24-25, AD, H2, S3, FS, WP 4/19, TP–2, PP–2.
97. Matt. 10:26-27; Luke 12:2-3, AD, H2/H3, S2, FS, WP 3/14, TP–1, 333121.
98. Matt. 10:28; Luke 12:4-5, AD, H2/H3, S2, FS, WP 6/13, TP–2, PP–1, 133121.
99. Matt. 10:29-31; Luke 12:6-7, AD, H2/H3, S2, FS, WP 1/18, TP–1, 133121.
100. Matt. 10:32-33; Luke 12:8-9, AD, H2/H3, S2, FS, WP 6/17, TP–4, PP–1, 133121.
101. Matt. 10:34-36; Luke 12:51-53, AD, H2/H3, S2, FS, WP 1/20, TP–2, 233121.
102. Matt. 10:37-38; Luke 14:26-27, **AD/ADG, H2/H3, S2, FS, WP** 3/12, TP–3, 333221.
103. Matt. 10:39; Luke 17:33, AD, H2/H3, S2, FS, WP 2/7, **TP–2,** PP–1, 133121.
104. Matt. 10:40, AD, H2, S3, FS, WP 4/5, TP–4.
105. Matt. 10:41, AD, H2, S3, FS, WP 4/14, TP–4.
106. Matt. 10:42, AD, H2, S3, FS, WP 2/11, TP–3.

107. Matt. 11:4-6; Luke 7:22-23, ADG, H2, S2, FA, WP 5/20, TP–3, 322111.
108. Matt. 11:7-11; Luke 7:24-28, ADG/A7, H2, S2, FA/FS, WP 7/40, TP–2, PP–3, 122211.
109. Matt. 11:12-14; Luke 16:16, ADG/AO, H2/H3, S2, FA/FS, WP 3/7, TP–2, 333331.
110. Matt. 11:16-19; Luke 7:31-35, ADG, H2, S2, FA/FS, WP 5/31, PP–1, 122121.
111. Matt. 11:21-24; Luke 10:13-15, AA/ADG, H2/H3, S2, FS, WP 6/40, TP–1, PP–1, 331311.
112. Matt. 11:25-27; Luke 10:21-22, AA/ADG, H2/H3, S2, FS, WP 8/28, TP–4, 233311.
113. Matt. 11:28-30, AA, H2, S3, FS, WP 1/18, TP–2 (AP–2).
114. Mark 2:25-26; Matt. 12:3-4; Luke 6:3-4, AO, H2, S1, FA, WP 1/18, TP–1, 111127.
115. Matt. 12:5, AO, H2, S3, FA, WP 4/8, TP–1.
116. Matt. 12:6, AO, H2, S3, FA, WP 2/3, TP–2.
117. Matt. 12:17, AO, H2, S3, FA, WP 1/6, TP–2.
118. Mark 2:27, AO, H2, S1, FA, WP 2/5, TP–2.
119. Mark 2:28; Matt. 12:8; Luke 6:5, AO, H2, S1, FA, WP 2/4, TP–2.
120. Mark 3:4; Luke 6:9, AO, H2, S1, FM, WP 3/8, TP–1, 111113.
121. Luke 6:24-26, A1, H2, S4, FS, WP 6/23, TP–1 (AP–1).
122. Luke 6:34-35, A1, H2, S4, FS, WP 5/20, TP–1.
123. Luke 7:13, 14, ADG, H2, S4, FM, WP 1/4, PP–1.
124. Luke 7:40-50, ADG, H2, S4, FA, WP 11/61, TP–4, PP–1, MP–1.
125. Mark 3:23-26; Matt. 12:25-26; Luke 11:17-18, AO, H2/H3, S1, FP, WP 3/20, MP–1, 133122.
126. Matt. 12:27-28; Luke 11:19-20, AO, H3, S2, FS, WP 1/13, TP–2, 133111.
127. Mark 3:27; Matt. 12:29; Luke 11:21-22, AO, H2/H3, S1, FP, WP 2/11, TP–2, MP–1, 133122.
128. Matt. 12:30; Luke 11:23, AO, H2/H3, S2, FS, WP 9/2, TP–2, 333111.
129. Mark 3:28; Matt. 12:31, AO, H2, S1, FS, WP 0/9, TP–1, PP–1, 111128.
130. Mark 3:29; Matt. 12:32; Luke 12:10, AO/AD, H2, S2, FS, WP 1/8, TP–2, 333321.

131. Matt. 12:33, AO, H2, S3, FP, WP 5/13, TP–2, PP–1, MP–1.
132. Matt. 12:34, AO, H2, S3, FS, WP 2/10, TP–3.
*
134. Matt. 12:36-37, AO, H2, S3, FS, WP 3/12, TP–2, PP–1.
135. Matt. 12:39-40; Luke 11:29-30, AO/AGO, H2/H3, S2, FS, WP 11/26, TP–3, 333221.
136. Matt. 12:41; Luke 11:32, AO/AGO, H2/H3, S2, FS, WP 4/12, TP–4, 233211.
137. Matt. 12:42; Luke 11:31, AO/AGO, H2/H3, S2, FS, WP 2/14, TP–4, 233211.
138. Matt. 12:43-45; Luke 11:24-26, AO, H2/H3, S2, FP, WP 1/30, TP–2, MP–1, 233111.
139. Mark 3:33-35; Matt. 12:48-50; Luke 8:21, ADG, H2, S1, FS, WP 4/12, TP–2, PP–1, 321117.
140. Mark 4:3-9; Matt. 13:3-9; Luke 8:4-8, A1, H2, S1, FP, WP 15/51, TP–3, MP–1, 111127.
141. Mark 4:10-12; Matt. 13:11-15; Luke 8:10, A1/AD/AD, H2, S1, FS, WP 5/18, TP–3, 111227.
142. Matt. 13:16-17; Luke 10:23-24, AD, H2/H3, S2, FS, WP 5/17, TP–2, 333121.
143. Matt. 13:18-23; Mark 4:13-20; Luke 8:11-15, AD/A1/AD, H2, S1, FP, WP 12/62, TP–5, MP–1, 111227.
144. Mark 4:21; Luke 8:16-17, A1/AD, H2, S1, FP, WP 2/19, TP–3, MP–1, 111225.
145. Mark 4:24; Luke 8:18a, A1/AD, H2, S1, FS, WP 1/6, TP–3, PP–1, 111235.
146. Matt. 13:12; Mark 4:25; Luke 8:18b, AD/A1/AD, H2, S1, FS, WP 0/6, TP–3, 211211.
147. Mark 4:26-29, A1, H2, S1, FP, WP 6/33, TP–1, MP–1.
148. Matt. 13:24-30, A1, H2, S3, FP, WP 24/68, TP–3, PP–1, MP–1.
149. Matt. 13:31-32; Mark 4:30-32; Luke 13:18-19, A1/A1/AGO, H2/H3, S1, FP, WP 7/23, TP–2, PP–1, MP–1, 333327.
150. Matt. 13:33; Luke 13:20-21, A1/AGO, H2/H3, S2, FP, WP 5/14, TP–2, PP–1, 133311.
151. Matt. 13:36-43, AD, H2, S3, FP, WP 26/63, TP–2, PP–1, MP–1.
152. Matt. 13:44, AD, H2, S3, FP, WP 4/18, TP–1, PP–1, MP–1.
153. Matt. 13:45, AD, H2, S3, FP, WP 2/19, TP–1, PP–1, MP–1.
154. Matt. 13:47-50, AD, H2, S3, FP, WP 8/37, TP–2, PP–1.

* 133 subsequently discarded as a separate logion.

155. Matt. 13:52, AD, H2, S3, FN, WP 3/15, TP–1, PP–1.
156. Matt. 14:13-21; Mark 6:30-44; Luke 9:10-17, A1, H2, S1, FM, WP 0/6, PP–1, 111127.
157. Matt. 14:27; Mark 6:50, AD, H2, S1, FM, WP 1/3, 111118.
158. Matt. 14:28-31, AD, H2, S3, FM, WP 1/3, TP–1.
159. Matt. 15:3-8; Mark 7:6-13, AO, H2, S1, FS, WP 6/58, TP–3, 111128.
160. Matt. 15:10-11; Mark 7:14-15, ADG, H2, S1, FP, WP 0/11, TP–3, MP–1, 111128.
161. Matt. 15:13, AD, H2, S3, FP, WP 0/6, TP–1, PP–1, MP–1.
162. Matt. 15:14, AD, H2, S3, FP, WP 0/12, TP–1, MP–1.
163. Matt. 15:16-20; Mark 7:17-23, AD, H2, S1, FP, WP 2/44, MP–1, 111128.
164. Matt. 15:24, AD, H2, S3, FM, WP 2/5, AP–1.
165. Matt. 15:26, 28; Mark 7:27, 29, ADG, H2, S1, FM, WP 1/10, TP–1 (AP–1), 111128.
166. Mark 7:34, ADG, H2, S1, FM, WP 0/1.
167. Matt. 15:32-39; Mark 8:1-10, A1, H2, S1, FM, WP 0/18, 111128.
168. Matt. 16:2-3, AO, H2, S3, FA, WP 1/19, TP–3.
169. Luke 12:54-56, AGO, H3, S4, FA, WP 3/24, TP–3.
170. Matt. 16:4; 12:39; Mark 8:12; Luke 11:29, AO/AO/AO/AGO, H2/H3, S5, FA, WP 6/8, TP–3, PP–1, MP–1, 333227.
171. Matt. 16:5-12; Mark 8:14-21; Luke 12:1, AD, H2/H3, S1, FA, WP 9/36, TP–3, PP–1, 333222.
172. Mark 8:22-26, ADG, H2, S1, FM, WP 1/3, PP–1.
173. Matt. 16:13-16; Mark 8:27-29; Luke 9:18-20, AD, H2, S1, FL, WP 2/6, TP–2, PP–1, 111127.
174. Matt. 16:17-19, AD, H2, S3, FL, WP 6/30, TP–3.
175. Matt. 16:22-23; Mark 8:33, AD, H2, S1, FS, WP 0/8, TP–2, 111118.
176. Matt. 16:24-26; Mark 8:34-37; Luke 9:23-25, AD/A1/AA, H2, S7, FS, WP 13/24, TP–4, PP–2, 111227.
177. Matt. 16:27; Mark 8:38; Luke 9:26, AD/A1/AA, H2, S6/S7, FS, WP 3/12, TP–3, 111233.
178. Matt. 16:28; Mark 9:1; Luke 9:27, AD/A1/AA, H2, S7, FS, WP 4/9, TP–1, PP–1, 111227.
179. Matt. 17:9-13; Mark 9:9-13, AD, H2, S1, FA, WP 2/16, TP–2, 111128.

180. Matt. 17:14-21; Mark 9:14-29; Luke 9:37-43a, A1, H2, S1, FM, WP 4/20, TP–3, 111127.
181. Matt. 17:20; Luke 17:6, AD, H2/H3, S2, FS, WP 3/14, TP–2, PP–1, 333121.
182. Mark 9:29, AD, H2, S1, FS, WP 1/5, TP–1, PP–1.
183. Matt. 17:22-23; Mark 9:31; Luke 9:44, AD, H2, S1, FS, WP 2/10, TP–1, 111127.
184. Matt. 17:24-27, AD, H2, S3, FA, WP 2/30, TP–1.
185. Mark 9:35, AD, H2, S1, FS, WP 2/8, TP–1, PP–1.
186. Matt. 18:4, AD, H2, S3, FS, WP 1/8, TP–2.
187. Matt. 18:5; Mark 9:37; Luke 9:48, AD, H2, S1, FS, WP 3/8, TP–2, 111117.
188. Mark 9:39; Luke 9:50, AD, H2, S1, FS, WP 1/8, TP–2, PP–1, 111135.
189. Mark 9:40; Luke 9:50, SD, H2, S1, FS, WP 0/5, TP–1, 111115.
190. Mark 9:41, AD, H2, S1, FS, WP 1/10, TP–3, PP–1.
191. Matt. 18:6; Mark 9:42; Luke 17:2, AD, H2, S1, FS, WP 3/13, TP–2, 333127.
192. Matt. 18:7; Luke 17:1, AD, H2, S2, FS, WP 6/11, TP–1, 211121.
193. Matt. 18:8; Mark 9:43-48, AD, H2, S1, FP, WP 9/47, TP–2, PP–1, 111128.
194. Mark 9:49, AD, H2, S1, FP, WP 2/5, TP–2, MP–1.
195. Mark 9:50b, AD, H2, S1, FP, WP 2/5, TP–1, MP–2.
196. Matt. 18:10, AD, H2, S3, FS, WP 1/12, TP–2.
197. Matt. 18:12-13; Luke 15:3-7, AD/AO, H2/H3, S2, FP, WP 4/36, TP–3, PP–2, 333331.
198. Matt. 18:14, AD, H2, S3, FS, WP 2/6, TP–2.
199. Matt. 18:15-17; Luke 17:3, AD, H2/H3, S8, FS, WP 2/28, TP–1 (AP–1), 333131.
200. Matt. 18:18, AD, H2, S3, FS, WP 2/13, TP–2 (AP–1).
201. Matt. 18:19, AD, H2, S3, FS, WP 1/13, TP–2 (AP–1).
202. Matt. 18:20, AD, H2, S3, FS, WP 0/6, TP–2 (AP–1), PP–1.
203. Matt. 18:22; Luke 17:4, AD, H2/H3, S2, FS, WP 1/9, TP–1, 233131.
204. Matt. 18:23-35, AD, H2, S3, FP, WP 5/103, TP–3, PP–3, MP–2.
205. Luke 9:61-62, ADG, H3, S4, FS, WP 1/10, TP–1.
206. Luke 10:7-9, ADG, H3, S9, FS, WP 5/21, TP–3.
207. Luke 10:10-11, ADG, H3, S9, FS, WP 3/16, TP–3.

208. Luke 10:16, ADG, H3, S4, FS, WP 1/7, TP–3.
209. Luke 10:17-20, ADG, H3, S4, FS, WP 2/25, TP–3.
210. Matt. 22:34-40; Mark 12:28-31; Luke 10:25-28, AO, H5/H5/H3, S1, FA, WP 3/18, TP–2, 333137.
211. Luke 10:29-37, AO, H3, S4, FP, WP 3/58, TP–2, PP–1.
212. Luke 10:38-42, ADG, H3, S4, FA, WP 4/14, TP–2.
213. Luke 11:5-8, AD, H3, S4, FP, WP 0/40, TP–2.
214. Luke 11:27-28, ADG, H3, S4, FA, WP 1/6, TP–2.
215. Matt. 23:25-26; Luke 11:37-41, A5/AO, H5/H3, S2, FS, WP 4/20, TP–3, 333231.
216. Matt. 23:4; Luke 11:45-46, A5/AO, H5/H3, S2, FS, WP 2/9, TP–3, 333221.
217. Luke 12:13-15, ADG, H3, S4, FA, WP 1/12, TP–2, PP–1, MP–1.
218. Luke 12:16-21, ADG, H3, S4, FP, WP 11/40, TP–2, MP–1.
219. Luke 12:35-38, AD, H3, S4, FP, WP 5/37, TP–2, PP–1, MP–1.
220. Matt. 24:43-44; Luke 12:39-40, AD, H6/H3, S2, FP, WP 3/17, MP–2, 333111.
221. Matt. 24:45-51; Luke 12:41-46, AD, H6/H3, S2, FP, WP 3/47, TP–3, PP–1, MP–1, 133111.
222. Luke 12:47-48, AD, H3, S4, FP, WP 5/24, TP–3, MP–1.
223. Luke 12:49-50, AD, H3, S4, FP, WP 2/14, TP–2.
224. Luke 13:1-5, AGO, H3, S4, FS, WP 4/27, TP–2, PP–2.
225. Luke 13:6-9, AGO, H3, S4, FP, WP 5/34, TP–3, MP–1.
226. Luke 13:10-17, A9, H3, S4, FM, WP 5/20, TP–1.
227. Luke 13:25-27, AA, H3, S4, FP, WP 4/32, TP–3, MP–1.
228. Luke 13:31-33, AO, H3, S4, FS, WP 1/21, TP–2.
229. Matt. 23:37-39; Luke 13:34-35, A5/AO, H5/H3, S2, FS, WP 2/25, TP–4, PP–1, 333211.
230. Matt. 12:11-12; Luke 14:1-6, AO, H2/H3, S9, FM, WP 3/11, TP–1, 333133.
231. Luke 14:7-11, AO, H3, S4, FS, WP 0/36, TP–2.
232. Luke 14:12-14, AO, H3, S4, FS, WP 0/24, TP–1.
233. Luke 14:15-24, AO, H3, S4, FP, WP 10/88, TP–4, PP–1, MP–1.
234. Luke 14:28-33, ADG, H3, S4, FP, WP 3/49, TP–1.
235. Luke 15:8-10, AO, H3, S4, FP, WP 2/31, TP–2, PP–1, MP–1.
236. Luke 15:11-32, AO, H3, S4, FP, WP 7/177, TP–3, PP–1, MP–1.
237. Luke 16:1-8, AD, H3, S4, FP, WP 1/80, TP–1, PP–1, MP–1.
238. Luke 16:9, AD, H3, S4, FS, WP 1/7.

239. Luke 16:10-13, AD, H3, S4, FS, WP 7/16, TP–4, MP–1.
240. Luke 16:14-15, AO, H3, S4, FS, WP 1/11, TP–4.
241. Luke 16:19-31, AO, H3, S4, FP, WP 9/112, AP–5, MP–1.
242. Luke 17:7-10, AD, H3, S4, FP, WP 6/35, TP–2, PP–1, MP–2.
243. Luke 17:11-19, ADG, H3, S4, FM, WP 3/16, TP–1.
244. Luke 17:20-21, AO, H3, S4, FS, WP 2/10, TP–3, PP–1.
245. Luke 17:22, AD, H3, S2, FS, WP 2/9, TP–2.
246. Matt. 24:37-41; Luke 17:26-27, AD, H6/H3, S2, FS, WP 2/21, TP–3, 333131.
247. Luke 17:28-30, AD, H3, S2, FS, WP 5/26, TP–3.
248. Luke 17:31-32, AD, H3, S2, FS, WP 1/15, TP–1.
249. Luke 17:34, AD, H3, S2, FS, WP 1/11, TP–1.
250. Matt. 24:41; Luke 17:35, AD, H6/H3, S2, FS, WP 0/8, TP–1, 333121.
251. Matt. 24:28; Luke 17:37, AD, H6/H3, S2, FS, WP 1/5, TP–1, 333121.
252. Luke 18:1-8, AD, H3, S4, FP, WP 10/49, TP–4, PP–1, MP–1.
253. Luke 18:9-14, AGO, H3, S4, FP, WP 6/47, TP–2, PP–2.
254. Matt. 19:1-8; Mark 10:1-9, AO, H4, S1, FA, WP 3/22, TP–1, 111118.
255. Matt. 19:9; Mark 10:10-12, AO/AD, H4, S1, FS, WP 3/9, TP–1, PP–1, 111338.
256. Matt. 19:10-12, AD, H4, S3, FS, WP 1/22, TP–2.
257. Matt. 19:13-14; Mark 10:13-14; Luke 18:15-16, AD, H4, S1, FA, WP 3/8, TP–2, 111117.
258. Matt. 18:3; Mark 10:15; Luke 18:17, AD, H2/H4, S1, FA, WP 4/7, TP–2, 333136.
259. Matt. 19:16-22; Mark 10:17-22; Luke 18:18-23, ADG, H4, S1, FA, WP 4/27, TP–2, 111117.
260. Matt. 19:23-26; Mark 10:23-27; Luke 18:24-27, AD, H4, S1, FA, WP 4/29, TP–2, 111117.
261. Matt. 19:27-28, AD, H4, S3, FA, WP 7/16, TP–3, PP–1, MP–1.
262. Matt. 19:29-30; Mark 10:28-31; Luke 18:29-30, AD, H4, S1, FA, WP 8/20, TP–4, PP–1, 111127.
263. Matt. 20:1-16, AD, H4, S3, FP, WP 7/120, TP–3, PP–1, MP–2.
264. Matt. 20:17-19; Mark 10:32-34; Luke 18:31-34, AD, H4, S1, FS, WP 7/19, TP–1, PP–1.
265. Matt. 20:20-23; Mark 10:35-40, AD, H4, S1, FA, WP 4/23, TP–5, 111118.

266. Matt. 20:24-28; Mark 10:41-45; Luke 22:24-27, AD, H4/H4/H7, S1, FA, WP 7/28, TP–3, 333122.

267. Matt. 20:29-34; Mark 10:46-52; Luke 18:35-43, ADG, H4, S1, FM, WP 3/6, TP–1, 111117.

268. Luke 19:1-10, ADG, H4, S4, FA, WP 3/21, TP–2 (AP–1), PP–1.

269. Matt. 25:14-30; Luke 19:11-27, AD/A1, H4, S2, FP, WP 18/124, TP–5, PP–1, MP–2, 333221.

270. Matt. 21:1-9; Mark 11:1-10; Luke 19:28-38, A1, H5, S1, FL, WP 3/22, 111127.

271. Luke 19:39-44, A6, H5, S4, FA, WP 3/21, TP–3, PP–1.

272. Matt. 21:10-13; Mark 11:15-18; Luke 19:45-48, AO, H5, S1, FA, WP 1/10, TP–2, 221127.

273. Matt. 21:14-17, AO, H5, S3, FA, WP 0/7.

274. Matt. 21:18-19; Mark 11:12-19, AD, H5, S1, FA, WP 2/4, TP–2, 111128.

275. Matt. 21:20-21; Mark 11:20-23, AD, H5, S1, FA, WP 5/15, TP–1, 111128.

276. Matt. 21:22; Mark 11:24, AD, H5, S1, FA, WP 3/7, TP–2, 111128.

277. Mark 11:25, AD, H5, S1, FA, WP 1/12, TP–3.

278. Matt. 21:23-27; Mark 11:27-33, AO, H5, S1, FA, WP 1/15, TP–1, 111114.

279. Matt. 21:28-32, AO, H5, S3, FP, WP 9/45, TP–3, PP–1, MP–2.

280. Matt. 21:33-46; Mark 12:1-12; Luke 20:9-19, AO, H5, S1, FP, WP 14/80, TP–6, MP–2, 111127.

281. Matt. 22:1-10, AO, H5, S3, FP, WP 8/75, TP–4, PP–1, MP–2.

282. Matt. 22:11-14, AO, H5, S3, FP, WP 0/31, TP–4, PP–1, MP–2.

283. Matt. 22:15-22; Mark 12:13-17; Luke 20:20-26, AO, H5, S1, FA, WP 0/11, TP–1, 111122.

284. Matt. 22:23-33; Mark 12:18-27; Luke 20:27-40, AO, H5, S1, FA, WP 3/31, TP–3, 111122.

285. Mark 12:32-34, AO, H5, S1, FA, WP 1/3, TP–1.

286. Matt. 22:41-46; Mark 12:35-37a; Luke 20:41-44, AO, H5, S1, FS, WP 3/22, TP–1, 111127.

287. Matt. 23:1-13, A1, H5, S8, FS, WP 1/13, TP–1.

288. Matt. 23:5, A1, H5, S8, FS, WP 1/9, PP–1.

289. Matt. 23:6-7; Mark 12:37b-40; Luke 20:46-47, A1/ADG/A1, H5, S1, FS, WP 3/11, TP–1, PP–1, 111113.

290. Matt. 23:8-10, A1, H5, S3, FS, WP 1/15, TP–1 (AP–1).
291. Matt. 23:11, A1, H5, S8, FS, WP 1/2, TP–1.
292. Matt. 23:12, A1, H5, S8, FS, WP 0/4, TP–1.
293. Matt. 23:13; Luke 11:52, A5/AO, H5, S8/S2, FS, WP 1/8, TP–4, 333231.
294. Matt. 23:15-22, A5, H5, S8, FS, WP 13/57, TP–3, PP–1.
295. Matt. 23:23; Luke 11:42, A5/AO, H5/H3, S8/S2, FS, WP 3/17, TP–2, 333221.
296. Matt. 23:24, A5, H5, S8, FS, WP 0/6, TP–1.
297. Matt. 23:27-28, A5, H5, S8, FS, WP 3/23, TP–4.
298. Luke 11:44, AO, H5, S2, FS, WP 0/7, TP–2.
299. Matt. 23:29-31; Luke 11:47-48, A5/AO, H5/H3, S8/S2, FS, WP 2/21, TP–3, 133231.
300. Matt. 23:32-33, A5, H5, S8, FS, WP 1/9, TP–2.
301. Matt. 23:34-36; Luke 11:49-51, A5/AO, H5/H3, S8/S2, FS, WP 4/27, TP–3, PP–2, 133221.
302. Mark 12:41-44; Luke 21:1-4, AD, H5, S1, FA, WP 3/17, TP–2, PP–1, 111123.
303. Matt. 24:1-3; Mark 13:1-4; Luke 21:5-7, AD, H5, S1, FA, WP 0/7, TP–1, 111127.
304. Matt. 24:4-8; Mark 13:5-8; Luke 21:8-11, AD, H6, S1, FS, WP 5/29, TP–3, PP–1, 111117.
305. Luke 21:18, AD, H6, S7, FS, WP 0/3, TP–1.
306. Matt. 24:10-13; Mark 13:13b; Luke 21:19, AD, H6, S6, FS, WP 3/19, TP–2, 111136.
307. Matt. 24:14, AD, H6, S6, FS, WP 4/10, TP–3.
308. Matt. 24:15-16; Mark 13:14; Luke 21:20-22, AD, H6 S1, FS, WP 1/11, TP–1 (AP–1), 111127.
309. Matt. 24:19-21; Mark 13:17-18; Luke 21:23a, AD, H6, S1, FS, WP 2/18, 111118.
310. Mark 13:19; Luke 21:23b, AD, H6, S1, FS, WP 2/12, TP–1, 111133.
311. Matt. 24:22; Mark 13:20, AD, H6, S1, FS, WP 2/9, TP–2 (AP–1), 111128.
312. Luke 21:24, AD, H6, S4, FS, WP 3/13, TP–1.
313. Matt. 24:23-25; Mark 13:21-23, AD, H6, S1, FS, WP 4/4, TP–1, 111128.
314. Matt. 24:26-28; Luke 17:23-24, 27, AD, H6, S2, FS, WP 3/20, TP–4, 333121.

315. Matt. 24:29-31; Mark 13:24-27; Luke 21:25-28, AD, H6, S1, FS, WP 3/37, TP–2 (AP–1), 111116.
316. Luke 21:28, AD, H6, S4, FS, WP 0/9, TP–1 (AP–1).
317. Matt. 24:32-33; Mark 13:28-29; Luke 21:29-31, AD, H6, S1, FP, WP 2/19, TP–1, 111117.
318. Matt. 24:34; Mark 13:30; Luke 21:32, AD, H6, S1, FS, WP 2/7, TP–1, PP–1, 111117.
319. Matt. 24:35-36; Mark 13:31-32; Luke 21:33, AD, H6, S1, FS, WP 2/12, TP–2, 111127.
320. Mark 13:33-34, AD, H6, S1, FS, WP 2/18, TP–2, PP–1.
321. Matt. 24:40, AD, H6, S8, FS, WP 1/5, TP–1.
322. Matt. 24:42; Mark 13:35-37, AD, H6, S5, FS, WP 3/7, TP–3, PP–1, 311128.
323. Luke 21:34-36, AD, H6, S4, FS, WP 3/31, TP–3, PP–1.
324. Matt. 25:1-13, AD, H6, S3, FP, WP 10/84, TP–4, PP–1, MP–3.
325. Matt. 25:31-46, AD, H6, S3, FP, WP 16/125, TP–5, PP–1, MP–1.
326. Matt. 26:1-5, AD, H7, S6, FS, WP 2/10, TP–1.
327. Matt. 26:6-13; Mark 14:3-9, AD/A1, H7, S1, FL, WP 9/29, TP–3, PP–1, 111218.
328. Matt. 26:17-19; Mark 14:12-16; Luke 22:7-13, AD, H7, S1, FL, WP 0/25, TP–1, 111117.
329. Matt. 26:20-21; Mark 14:17-18, AD, H7, S1, FL, WP 3/5, TP–1, PP–1, 111128.
330. Matt. 26:22-24; Mark 14:19-21; Luke 22:21-22, AD, H7, S1, FL, WP 3/20, TP–1, PP–1, 211122.
331. Matt. 26:25, AD, H7, S6, FL, WP 0/1.
332. Luke 22:15-16, AD, H7, S4, FL, WP 2/11, TP–2, PP–1.
333. Matt. 26:29; Mark 14:25; Luke 22:17-18, AD, H7, S1, FL, WP 2/9, TP–1, PP–1, 111122.
334. Matt. 26:26-28; Mark 14:22-24; Luke 22:19-20, AD, H7, S1, FL, WP 0/5, TP–2, 111127.
335. Luke 22:28-30, AD, H7, S4, FS, WP 6/16, TP–2 (AP–1), MP–1.
336. Luke 22:31-34, AD, H7, S4, FS, WP 4/13, TP–1, PP–1.
337. Luke 22:35-38, AD, H7, S4, FS, WP 1/18, TP–2, PP–1 (AP–1).
338. Matt. 26:30-35; Mark 14:26-31, AD, H7, S1, FL/FS, WP 3/10, TP–2, 111118.
339. Matt. 26:36-46; Mark 14:32-42; Luke 22:40-45, AD, H7, S1,

FL/FS, WP 15/28, TP–2, 111127.

340. Matt. 26:47-54; Luke 22:47-51, AD, H7, S3/S4, FL, WP 2/21, 111137.

341. Matt. 26:55-56; Mark 14:48-49; Luke 22:52-53, AO, H7, S1, FL, WP 2/11, 111127 .

342. Matt. 26:64; Mark 14:62; Luke 22:67-70, AO, H7, S1, FL, WP 1/9, TP–2, PP–1, 111127.

343. Matt. 27:11-14; Mark 15:2-5; Luke 23:2-5, AO, H7, S1, FL, WP 0/1, 111117.

344. Luke 23:28-31, ADG, H7, S4, FL, WP 4/27, TP–1, PP–1.

345. Luke 23:34, AGO, H7, S4, FL, WP 0/4, TP–1.

346. Luke 23:43, ADG, H7, S4, FL, WP 2/6, TP–3, PP–1.

347. Matt. 27:46; Mark 15:34, AGO, H7, S1, FL, WP 0/4, 111128.

348. Luke 23:46, AGO, H7, S4, FL, WP 0/4.

349. Matt. 28:9-10, ADG, H7, S3, FL, WP 3/9.

350. Matt. 28:16-20, AD, H8, S3, FL, WP 2/25, TP–2 (AP–2), PP–1.

351. Luke 24:13-53, AD, H8, S4, FL, WP 2/17, TP–3.

352. Luke 24:36-49, AD, H8, S4, FL, WP 2/55, TP–5 (AP–1), PP (AP–1).

353. Mark 16:9-20, AD, H8, S1, FL, WP 6/32, TP–2 (AP–5).

Appendix B
PATTERN WORDS (A)

The following is the listing of all logia pattern words and phrases (cf. Chapter V). The capital letters indicate the pattern orientation of the word; the small letters give the pattern quality category. The simple A designation indicates that the word is characteristic of Jesus without showing a pattern of usage to any particular audience. " (Etc.) " means other forms of the same root.

halas, halizo (A–a)
Abraam (AO–a)
amen (AD–a)
adelphos (AD/A1–a)
agathos (AD/ADG–b)
agros (AD–b)
hades (A–c)
aionios (AD–a)
agrupneo (AD–c)
aiteo (AD–a)
akanthas (AD/ADG/AGO–b)
akolutheo (AD/ADG–a)

achreios (AD–c)
adikias (AD/AGO–a)
adunaton (AD–b)
anabaino (AD–b)
ampelon (AO–b)
anablepousin (AD/ADG–b)
anegnote (A–a)
anektoteros (A–c)
anoigo (AD/A1–b)
anomian (AD/A1–b)
ho huios tou anthropou (A–a, AD–b)

apaggello (ADG–b)

aparneomai (AD–a)

apodidomi (A–b)

apokteino (AO–a)

aphistemi (AD–b)

aphorizon (AD–b)

apokalupto (AD/ADG–b)

apostello (AD/ADG–b)

argos (AD–c)

argurion (AD–b)

arneomai (AG/ADG–b)

askos (AO–b)

astheneo (AD/ADG–a)

axios (AD–b)

akuroo (AO–c)

anaitios (AO–c)

apodekatoo (AO/AGO–b)

basileia tou theou (A–a)

bastazo (AD/ADG–b)

blepo (AD/ADG–a)

ballantion (AD/ADG–b)

broche (A1–c)

brugmos (AD/ADG–b)

genea (A–b)

geenna (AD/A1–b)

gemizo (AO/AY–b)

geiton (AO–c)

ginosko (AD/ADG–b)

georgos (AO–c)

gregoreo (AD–a)

daktulo (AO–b)

danizo (AD/ADG–b)

dero (AD/AO–b)

David (AO–a)

dechomai (A–a, AD–a)

dedemenos (AD–a)

didomi (AD/ADG–b)

dei (AD–b)

diablepo (A–c)

diabolos (AD–b)

deipnon (A–c)

deiknumi (AD/ADG–b)

dendron (A–c)

diakonos (AD–a)

diakoneo (AD–a)

diakrino (AD–c)

diamerizo (AD–c)

dianoia (AO–b)

diarpazo (A–b)

diaskorpizo (AD–c)

diatasso (AD–c)

diatheke (AD–c)

diastellomai (ADG–c)

dikaiosune (A1–b)

doulos (TP–a)

dodeka (AD–b)

doxa, doxazo (AD/ADG–c)

diaphero (AD–c)

dikaioo (AD/AGO–b)

echete (AD–a)

echonta (AD–a)

eggizo (AD/ADG–b)

eggus (AD–a)

ginosko (AD/ADG–a)

eirene (AD/ADG–b)

eisporeuomai (AD–b)

ekdikeo (AD–a)

ekklesia (AD–c)

ekkopto (AD/AGO–b)

eklektos (AD–a)

ekleipo (AD–c)

elachistos (AD/A1–b)

emos (AD–1)

emprosthen (AD/A1–b)

epanistemi (AD–c)

epiblema (AO–b)

epigraphe (AO–b)

epistrepho (AD–b)

ergates (AD/ADG–a)
ethnikos (AD–c)
ethnos (AD–a)
hetoimazo (AD–a)
echthros (A–b)
euaggelion (AD–b)
eukopoteros (AD/AO–a)
euonumos (AD–a)
euphraino (AO–b)
exestin (AO–a)
exothen (A–a)
egeiro (AD–a) (Son of Man)
eiserchomai (AD–c)
heneka (AD–c)
ekdidomi (AO–c)
entole (AO–c)
epithumeo (AD/AO–b)
ergon (A–b)
zao (AD/AO–b)
zoe (AD–b)
hegemon (AD–a)
hekastos (AD–b)
etairos (AD–c)
thanatos (AD–b)
tharseo (AD/ADG–a)
thelo, thelema (AD/ADG–b)
therismos (AD/ADG–a)
therizo (AD–c)
thesaurizo, etc. (AD/A1–b)
thlipsis (AD/ADG–b)
thrix (AD–c)
thronos (AD–b)
thugater (AD/ADG–a)
thusian, thusiasterion
    (AO/AY/A1–b)
threneo (AGO–c)
eggiken (*he basileia*)
    (AD/ADG–a)
Ioannen (AO/AGO–a)

Iona (AO/AGO–a)
Israel (AD/ADG–a)
hieron (AO/AX–a)
Kaisar (AO–a)
kakos (AO–a)
kalos (AD/ADG–a)
karpos (A–b)
katakrino (A–a)
kataleipo (AO–b)
katanoeo (AD–b)
kataphroneo (A–c)
kataskenoo (A–b)
kathistemi (AD–b)
katenanti (AD–c)
katharizo (ADG–b)
katheudo (AD/ADG–a)
katischuo (AD–c)
klaio (ADG–a)
klauthmos (AD/ADG–b)
klepto (AD/ADG/A1–b)
koluo (AD–b)
koniortos (AD/ADG–b)
kopos (AD–b)
krino, krima, krisis
    (AD/ADG–b)
kosmos (AD–b)
kleronomos (AO–b)
krupto, (AD/A1–b)
krouo (AD/AGO–a)
krateo (AO/AX–b)
kremmannumi (AO/AD–c)
laleo (AD–a)
lampo (AD–c)
lambano (AD–c)
lego (A–b)
lestai (AO–b)
luchnos (AD/A1–b)
luo (AD–c)
makarios (AD/ADG–a)

makrothumeo (AO–c)
malakois (AGO–c)
moichalis, etc. (A–a)
mallon (AD–b)
martureo (AD/ADG–b)
mastigoo (AD–b)
medeis (AD/ADG–a)
meno (AD/ADG–b)
merimnao, etc. (AD/ADG–a)
mesoo, etc. (AD/ADG–b)
mesonuktian (A–c)
metabaino (AD/ADG–c)
mikros (AD–a)
misthos (AD/A1–a)
moros (A–a)
mamonas (AD–c)
Mouses (AO/ADG–b)
naos (AY–b)
neos, etc. (AO–a)
nesteuo (AO–a)
nepios (A–c)
nomos (AO/A1–b)
numphios (A–a)
Noe (AD–c)
noeo (AD–a)
nomizo (AD/A1–c)
oikodespotes (A–a)
oikonomeo (AD–b)
oinos (AO/AGO–a)
oligoi (AD/ADG–b)
oligopistos (AD–a)
onoma, etc. (AD–b)
opheilo (AD–b)
opiso (AD–c)
ouai (A–a)
oudepote (AO–b)
oikiakos (AD–c)
homologeo (AD–b)
oupo (AD–a)

homoioo (AD/AGO–b)
ous (AD/AGO–b)
omnuo (AY–c)
hora, etc. (AD–c)
ophthalmos (AD/A1–b)
paidion (AD–b)
palaio, etc. (AO–b)
paradidomi (AD–b)
paradosis (AO–b)
parerchomai (AD–b)
paraptomata (AD/A1–c)
pascha (AD–a)
pascho, etc. (AD–a)
pater (A–c)
peirasmos (AD–a)
pempo (AO/AGO–a)
penthera (AD–c)
peran (AD–b)
periballo (AD/A1–b)
peteinon (AD/AGO–c)
perizonnumai (AD–c)
pera (AD/ADG–a)
poso mallon (AD–b)
poterion (AD–c)
potizo (AD–b)
protos (AD–c)
pino (AD–b)
pisteuo (AD/ADG–b)
pistis (AD/ADG–a)
poneros (A–b)
pous (AD/ADG–b)
poimaino, etc. (AD–b)
polloi (AD–c)
porneo (AO–b)
probaton (AO/AD–a)
prosecho (AD–b)
prothesis (A–c)
proseuchomai (AD–b)
pur (AD–b)

plen (A–b)
hrabdos (AD–c)
hriza (AD–c)
sabbaton (AO–a)
satan (A–a)
sapron (A–a)
sarx (A–b)
semeion (A–b)
sozo (AD/ADG–b)
speiro (AD/A1–a)
sperma (AD/A1–b)
sunagogon (A–c)
sundoulos (AD–a)
sunteleo (AD–a)
pule (AD–b)
skandalon (AD–a)
skandalizo (AD/ADG–b)
sunairo logon (AD–c)
sitos (AD/AGO–b)
skoteinos (AGO/ADG–c)
suniemi (AD–b)
soma (AD/AGO–a)
telos (AD–b)
telones, etc. (AO/AGO–a)
toioutos (AD–a)
trepho (AD–c)
talanton (AD–c, A–a)

hupokrites (A–a)
phobeomai, etc. (AD–b)
phragmos (AO–c)
phronimos (AO–a)
phulake (AD–b)
photeinos (AGO–c)
phortizo, etc. (AO–c)
phos (A–c)
chalkos (AD–c)
charin (AD/ADG–a)
cheilos (AO–c)
chiton (AD/ADG–c)
chreiopheiletes (AD/ADG–c)
pseudoprophetes (AD/A1–c)
psuche (A–b)
hora (AD–c)
hoste (AO–c)
huioi . . . ktl
    (A–a, AD/ADG–b)
homoia estin, etc.
    (A–a, AD/A1–b)
*ho klauthmos ho brugmos ton
    odonton* (AD–c, A–a)
skotos to exoteros (A–c)
protos . . . eschatos (AD–b)
blepontes . . . blepousin (AD–b)
amen lego humin (A–a)

Appendix C

PATTERN WORDS (E)

The following is a listing of all pattern words in the E or nonlogia tradition (cf. Chapter IV). The capital letters represent the speaker, the smaller letters the pattern quality category (cf. Chapter IV, note 1). The single E designation indicates a word typical of the nonlogia tradition generally, but not of any one editorial stratum particularly.

agele (E–a)
aitia (E–a)
akatharton (E–b)
akolutheo (E–a)
alabastron (E–a)
aigupton (ET–a)
aletheia (EO–b)
anechoresen (ET–a)
anekraxen (E–b)
anepempsen (EK–c)
anepesan (EK–c)
aner (EK–a)

apegagon (E–b)
apeggeilan (E–a)
apethanen (E–c)
apodokimazo (E–c)
apographe (EK–b)
exestin (EO–b)
apostasion (EO–c)
apostolos (EK–c)
archisunagogos (E–b)
arrostos (E–c)
aule (E–b)
azor (ET–c)

azumos (E–b)
aganakteo (EO–b)
akolutheo (E–a)
arneomai (E–a)
archontai (E–b)
aiteo (E–b)
babulonos (ET–b)
Barabban (E–a)
bebaremenoi (E–c)
Bethania (E–b)
Bethleem (E–b)
Bethphage (E–c)
Bethsaida (E–c)
biblion (E, AO–c)
boetheo (E–c)
brephe (EK–b)
David (E, AO–c)
daimonia (E–c)
de (EK–c)
dekapolis (E–c)
deomai (E–b)
diaperao (E, AO–c)
diaphulaxai (EK–c)
diarrexas (ER–c)
diasaphisan (ED–c)
diasozo (EK–c)
diastriphonta (EO–c)
didache (E–a)
didaskale (EO–a)
diegeiro (E–b)
diegeomai (E–b)
dialaleo (E–c)
dierchomai (E, AO–b)
didasko (EO, AD–b)
doxazo (E–b)
dunamai (E–a)
agomen (E–a, EK–b)
egeneto (E–a, EK–b)
eie (EK–b)

eginosko (E–a)
ekatheto (E–a)
ekthambeomai (ER–c)
enantios (E–a)
enteuthen (EO–c)
enthumeomai (ET–b)
eperotao (E–a)
epitimao (E–a)
epilambano (EK–b)
epistates (ED–a)
ethos (EK–c)
eukairos (E–b)
euphraino (S4–a)
eutheos (ET–b)
euthus (ER–b)
heorte (E–b)
euaggelion (ER, S1–b)
thambeo (ER–c)
thaumazo (E–a)
therapeuo (E–a)
hieron (E–a)
krazo (E–a)
kategoreo (E–a)
kremnou (E–c)
Kaisar (EO–a)
laleo (E–b)
laos (E–a)
lian (E–a)
monogenes (E–c)
horion (E–a)
ochlos (E–a)
onar (ET–a)
ophthe (E–a)
pimplemi (EK–a)
poreuomai (E–a)
parachrema (E–a)
paraggeilo (E–c)
periblepo (ER–b)
perichoros (E–b)

peristeran (E–b)
plethos (E–a)
ploion (E–a)
potapos (ED–c)
presbuteron (E–a)
Petros (E–a)
siopao (E–a)
sphodra (ET–b)

stratiotes (E–b)
sumboulion (E–b)
tarasso (E–c)
tote (ET–b)
phobeomai (E–b)
pheugo (E–a)
pais (E–b)

NOTES

Chapter I. A NEW PROBLEM OF SYNOPTIC CRITICISM

1. K. L. Schmidt, *Der Rahmen der Geschichte Jesu* (Berlin, 1919).

2. J. Jeremias, *Die Gleichnisse Jesu* (Zurich, 1947), pp. 15 ff.

3. Cf. J. Arthur Baird, "A Pragmatic Approach to Parable Exegesis: Some New Evidence on Mark 4:11, 33-34," *Journal of Biblical Literature*, Vol. LXXVI, Part III (1957), pp. 201–207. Cf. T. W. Manson, *The Teaching of Jesus* (London: Cambridge University Press, 1945), p. 16.

4. Schmidt, *op. cit.*, p. 258.

5. *Ibid.*, p. 26.

6. Rudolf Bultmann, *The History of the Synoptic Tradition* (Harper & Row, Publishers, Inc., 1963), p. 344.

7. Manson, *op. cit.*, pp. 19–21.

8. *Ibid.*, pp. 98, 113, 120.

9. Jeremias, *op. cit.*, pp. 29, 95.

10. John Wick Bowman, *The Intention of Jesus* (The Westminster Press, 1943); *The Religion of Maturity* (Abingdon Press, 1948).

11. Oscar Cullmann, *Christ and Time*, tr. by Floyd V. Filson (The

Westminster Press, 1950); *The Christology of the New Testament*, tr. by Shirley C. Guthrie and Charles A. M. Hall (The Westminster Press, 1959).

12. Wilhelm Wrede, *Das Messiasgeheimnis in den Evangelien* (Göttingen, 1901), p. 3. Robert W. Funk seems to point to such a non-scientific spirit in German existential hermeneutics in the anti-Cartesian nature of those who use Heidegger as justification for rescuing language from " the tyranny of the subject — Thinker " (*Language, Hermeneutic, and Word of God*, p. 43; Harper & Row, Publishers, Inc., 1966).

13. James B. Conant, *Modern Science and Modern Man* (Doubleday & Company, Inc., 1959).

14. For this phrase I am indebted to Prof. William Kieffer, Department of Chemistry, The College of Wooster.

15. Conant, *Modern Science and Modern Man*, p. 44.

16. James B. Conant, *On Understanding Science* (Mentor, 1951), p. 37.

17. Wrede, *op. cit.*, p. 3.

18. Robert W. Funk, "The Hermeneutical Problem and Historical Criticism," in James M. Robinson and John B. Cobb, Jr. (eds.), *The New Hermeneutic* (Harper & Row, Publishers, Inc., 1964), p. 192.

19. Rudolf Bultmann, *Die Geschichte der synoptischen Tradition* (Göttingen: Vandenhoeck & Ruprecht, 1957), pp. 36–37.

20. Van A. Harvey, *The Historian and the Believer* (The Macmillan Company, 1966), p. 277.

21. *Ibid.*, p. 49.

22. The work of John W. Ellison in preparing the Concordance to the RSV is well known, but this is not content analysis. Other than this, the only work done has been on the question of the authorship of the Pauline corpus and John. Cf. Grayston and Herdan, *New Testament Studies*, Vol. 6, No. 1 (October, 1959); G. H. C. MacGregor and Andrew Q. Morton, *The Structure of the Fourth Gospel* (Edinburgh: Oliver & Boyd, Ltd., 1961); Cameron Dinwoodie, "Notes on the Use of Computing Machines in New Testament Literary Research," *University of Edinburgh, New College Bulletin*, Vol. 1, No. 2 (1964). Other work is in progress, and the future of this type of study seems bright.

23. Andrew Q. Morton and James McLeman, *Christianity in the Computer Age* (Harper & Row, Publishers, Inc., 1964); see also Mor-

ton's article in the symposium entitled *The Authorship and Integrity of the New Testament* (London: S.P.C.K., 1965).

24. Morton and McLeman, *op. cit.,* p. 14.

25. The details of this will be seen in a forthcoming article, and the basic print-outs will be published in a form that can be used for many types of Synoptic research.

26. Harvey, *op. cit.,* p. 62. Cf. Andrew Q. Morton, "Statistical Analysis and New Testament Problems," Kurt Aland *et al., The Authority and Integrity of the New Testament* (Allenson, 1965).

27. Cf. J. Venn, *The Logic of Chance,* 1866; "The Foundations of Chance," *Princeton Review,* Vol. 2 (1872), pp. 471–510; "On the Nature and Uses of Averages," *Statistical Journal,* Vol. 54 (1891), pp. 429–448; cf. John Maynard Keynes, *A Treatise on Probability* (Harper & Row, Publishers, Inc., 1962), p. 99.

28. Keynes, *op. cit.,* p. v.

Chapter II. THE IDENTIFICATION OF JESUS' AUDIENCE

1. This includes narratives and sayings, and counts each section in each Gospel.

2. Cf. Appendix A.

3. So also Bultmann, *History of the Synoptic Tradition,* pp. 343 ff.

4. I am using a modification of Manson's D, G, and P categories.

5. The latest phase of this discussion is seen in the opposing views of Beda Rigaux, who considers it necessary "*die Einsetzung eines Zwölferkreises durch Jesus selbst als eine Tatsache zu betrachten,*" and Günter Klein, who insists that the Twelve as an institution do not belong to the life of Jesus (Beda Rigaux, "*Die Zwölf in Geschichte und Kerygma,*" *Der historische Jesus und der kerygmatische Christus,* p. 482; Berlin: Helmut Ristow und Kark Matthiae, 1962; G. Klein, *Die Zwölf Apostel;* Göttingen, 1961). Emil Kraeling feels that the term "apostle" was superimposed upon the Synoptics at a later period because there is no pre-Christian Hebrew equivalent. (Emil Kraeling, *The Disciples,* p. 19; Rand McNally & Company, Inc., 1966.) T. W. Manson assumes that Jesus did use *apostolos* as a designation for certain of his followers, not in the exclusivist sense given it in the later church, but in the missionary sense implied by *apostello* in Mark 3:14 (*op. cit.,* p. 240).

6. Cf. also Matt. 15:15-20; 17:1-8, 24-27; 18:21-22; 20:20-28; 26:36-46; Mark 1:35-38; 9:2-8, 38-41; 10:35-45; 13:1-4; 14:32-42;

Luke 9:28-36; 9:49-50, 54; 11:20-25; 12:41; 22:7-13, 31-34, 45.
No attempt will be made here to resolve the differences between these
names. Cf. Rendel Harris, *The Twelve Apostles* (Cambridge, 1927);
whether there were twelve or some other number is a question that is
irrelevant here. The point is that a select number formed an inner circle, and the Evangelists referred to them as "twelve."

7. For a demonstration of the interchangeable use of *dodeka* and
mathetai, cf. Rigaux, *op. cit.,* p. 471.

8. Luke 5:1-11; 13:23-24; 9:51-58; 11:1-4; 17:4; 24:13-53;
Matt. 13:10, 36; 15:15; Mark 6:30-44, 45-52; 8:27-33; 9:9-13, 30-32,
33-37; 10:23-27, 28-29; 13:1-4; 14:3-9.

9. Mark 4:38 to 5:4; 9:2-8, 30-32; 11:20-25; Luke 5:1-11; 24:13-
53.

10. Matt. 15:33; Mark 6:30-44; 8:27-33; 11:20-25; Luke 17:5-6;
24:13-53.

11. Matt. 15:23, 33; Mark 6:30-44; 7:10-22; 8:27-33; 9:38-41;
10:35-45; 13:1-4; 14:26-31, 39; Luke 9:51-58; 22:31-34.

12. Matthew Black finds many examples of Aramaic idiom in the
dialogue material which for him " clearly suggests that besides an oral
tradition of the sayings of Jesus, the Evangelists and especially Mark
may have possessed an Aramaic tradition of the dialogue and speeches
of Jesus' many interlocutors " (*An Aramaic Approach to the Gospels
and Acts,* p. 66; Oxford University Press, 1954).

13. Cf. Samuel Umen, *Pharisaism and Jesus* (Philosophical Library,
Inc., 1963).

14. Lawler and Oulton, *Ecclesiastical History,* 2 vols. (London,
1954), Vol. 1, pp. 12 ff.

15. Manson, *op. cit.,* p. 19.

16. E.g., Umen, *op. cit.*

17. Cf. Mark 3:22, *grammateis,* Matt. 12:23, *Pharisaioi,* Luke
11:15, *tines;* Mark 3:6, *Pharisaioi,* Matt. 12:14, *Pharisaioi,* Luke 6:7,
hoi grammateis kai hoi Pharisaioi; Luke 5:17, *Pharisaioi kai nomodidaskaloi,* Mark 2:2, *polloi,* Matt. 9:1, no indication; Mark 12:28,
grammateon, Luke 10:25, *nomikos,* Matt. 22:34, 35, *Pharisaioi,
nomikos.*

18. Matt. 11:20-29 is AA. Cf. Appendix A.

Chapter III. THE CORRELATION OF AUDIENCE

1. This number must remain approximate, for, as Form Criticism
has made clear, it is at times extremely difficult to be certain whether

or not some of these units should stand alone.

2. Cf. Key to Abbreviations. As will be seen from Appendix A, certain possible combinations which had to be anticipated in the computer study did not yield any examples, namely A2, A3, AX, AY.

3. Cf. Key to Abbreviations.

4. Some situations of both S and A occur so infrequently that there is no need to work out percentages.

5. Cf. Key to Abbreviations.

6. These dual audience symbols represent Q situations where Matthew directs the logion to the one audience and Luke to another. Some fall in category #2 and some in #3.

7. Joachim Jeremias, *The Parables of Jesus* (Charles Scribner's Sons, 1962), pp. 33 ff.

8. Cf. Jeremias, English edition, *op. cit.*, pp. 33–42. Jeremias is the only scholar known to me who goes into this matter in any depth. Ignoring the agreements, he lists approximately thirty-one examples of audience disagreement, especially where parables addressed to the crowd are changed into parables addressed to the disciples. The impression he gives is one of general, widespread audience disagreement. Two of his illustrations I can agree with (Matt. 18:12-14; Luke 8:16). The rest do not in my opinion constitute valid examples of what I am calling hard-core disagreement. Basically Jeremias errs in four ways. (1) Some of these logia do not disagree. Jeremias has wrongly identified the audience (Mark 13:33 f.; Luke 12:39, 41; Matt. 24:43, 45; 25:1 ff. See Appendix A. (2) Some of these are cases where the similarity between two logia does not in my opinion mean they are identical (Luke 13:23 f., 35 f.; 8:16; Matt. 7:16-20; 25:1 f.). See *JGTJ* for my detailed exegesis of these passages. (3) Some of these passages represent the M source (Matt. 13:47; 20:1 f.) and the L source (Luke 16:1 f.; 17:7 f.), and his judgment on the shifting of audience is based on his own conjectural argument, which is tenuous at best. (4) Mostly his illustrations involve situations where one source is what I have called A1, and the other AD (Matt., chs. 5 to 7; 15:14; Mark 9:50; 4:10; Luke 11:11-13; 12:25). His error here lies in not realizing that *ochlos* can, and indeed most often does, identify a *sympathetic* crowd (DG), or in not distinguishing carefully between hard-core disagreements, and those which I have classed as being in general agreement. The problem is that Jeremias' work is based on Manson's audience categories, which did not include the DG, and where " agreement " was not carefully enough defined. Actually Jeremias has missed most of

the really important disagreements, and more significantly he has made some generalizations about the untrustworthy nature of the audience on the basis of the most inadequate treatment of the evidence.

9. Cf. B. P. W. Stather Hunt, *Primitive Gospel Sources* (Philosophical Library, Inc., 1951), p. 84.

Chapter IV. SYNOPTIC DISCONTINUITY

1. Category (a) will include those words attributed exclusively to the E stratum (editor or someone in the audience) or exclusively to Jesus in the logia. This will also indicate A words (logia) given always to a particular audience with approximately six or more examples, or with two or three exceptions where there are at least ten or more examples. In all cases there must be at least three sources represented in the pattern. Category (b) includes those words attributed only to the A or E strata where there are three or more examples, or with some exceptions where there are more than ten examples. It also designates A words exclusively to one or another audience, where there are not more than two or three exceptions, or where there are no exceptions, but not enough examples to be in category (a). All cases must cut across at least two sources. Category (c) refers to words included only in the E or A material with two or more examples where there is more than one source, or with one source, but with many examples. With the A words, this category designates cases where a word is always given to a particular audience, but where there are only a few examples, or where the examples, no matter how many, are only from one source, or where a word is used as often or more often by the E than by Jesus, but still contains an audience pattern. All of these situations will identify patterns; and in this somewhat arbitrary way we shall attempt to evaluate the quality of the patterns.

2. Cf. Appendix C. My list differs from that of Hawkins' because I do not include the *hapax legomena,* or those used only twice which make up most of Hawkins' list of characteristic words. For our purposes they must occur more often to be called " characteristic." Cf. John Hawkins, *Horae Synopticae* (Oxford, 1899).

3. *Shelihah, abar, shamah, shub.* Cf. Ch. II for *apostolos* problem.

4. Black, *op. cit.*

5. *Ibid.,* p. 206 (italics mine).

6. *Ibid.,* p. 43.

7. *Ibid.,* p. 93.

8. Cf. Mark 10:35-40; Matt. 4:8; Luke 17:21; etc. Cf. *JGTJ*, 169 ff.

9. Matt. 4:6, 11; 28:2; Mark 1:13; Luke 1:11 f.; 2:9 f.; 22:43.

10. Luke 12:1-9; 15:10; Mark 8:38; 13:26; 13:27; Matt. 25:31. Cf. *JGTJ*, 90.

11. Mark 6:11; 9:37; 10:15; Matt. 10:40, 41; 11:14; Luke 10:8; 16:9; etc.

12. Mark 15:8; Luke 1:63; 23:23, 24; Matt. 20:20; 27:20.

13. Cf. Stephen C. Neill, *The Interpretation of the New Testament, 1861–1961* (Oxford University Press, 1966), p. 241.

Chapter V. AUDIENCE CONTINUITY: WORD AND PRAXIS

1. Cf. Ch. IV, note 1, for definition of pattern categories.

2. *Ampelon* occurs once in I Cor. 9:7.

3. There are two exceptions, where Jesus uses *sunagagon* and *Israel* regularly to the D.

4. These are only those words in pattern quality category (a) or those in category (b) found in the audience situation for which they are characteristic. Parentheses indicate percentages derived from so few words as to be of doubtful value.

5. This will appear in a forthcoming sequel to the present book, tentatively entitled "The Synoptic Mode and Its Formation."

6. AD, ADG, A1 (37 logia); AO, AGO (5 logia).

7. Luke 9:58; 6:22; 22:22, 48; 24:7; Matt. 17:12; 26:2; Mark 9:31; 10:33, 45; 14:21, 41, 62; 8:31; 9:12.

8. Matt. 21:25; 23:22; Mark 14:62; Luke 15:7, 18, 21; 19:38.

9. A word must be added here about a possible challenge to this method from James Barr in his book *The Semantics of Biblical Language* (Oxford University Press, 1961). This book is a technical critique of linguistic and lexicographic methodology, and turns out to be a running battle with Thorleif Boman and Kittel's *Wörterbuch*. He objects to such things as an atomized, one-word approach to theological concepts based on etymology and root ideas divorced from the total sentence and passage context. He argues for a Biblical theology based on the larger sentence or passage unit rather than on the single word. He comes close to a critique of what I am doing when he warns against what he calls "totality transfer" when the meaning of a word derived from a total survey of the literature is read into a particular case (p. 218). Actually I find little to criticize in Barr's presentation. As an

Old Testament scholar, his thesis serves primarily as a warning against deriving word meanings from a cross survey of word usages covering many centuries, and including many types of literature. I would agree. For this reason, one must be very cautious about using Pauline language to interpret a particular Synoptic word. For this reason one should also be very careful about employing a redactor's usage to interpret a word as found in the logia. For this reason one should also be careful about using an AO word usage to interpret an AD logion. This is exactly the kind of carefulness for which we are pleading. But in the Synoptics, we are possibly dealing with the words of one particular individual, Jesus of Nazareth, and if so, this makes all the difference; for the logia words would then not only permit, but demand, the application of meaning at one point to word usage at another. One must not allow Barr's thesis to beg this historical question.

10. Cf. Baird, " A Pragmatic Approach to Parable Exegesis," *Journal of Biblical Literature,* Vol. LXXVI, Part III (1957), p. 201.

11. *The Interpreter's Bible,* Vol. VII (Abingdon Press, 1951), p. 636.

12. Charles G. Montefiore, *The Synoptic Gospels* (London: Macmillan & Co., Ltd., 1909), Vol. I, p. 123.

13. Adolf Jülicher, *Die Gleichnisreden Jesu,* 2 vols. (Freiburg, 1899). For the most thorough recent defense of this thesis, cf. Jeremias, *The Parables of Jesus.* He advances a rather unusual suggestion that *tois exo en parabolais* " has no reference whatever to the parables of Jesus " (p. 16). For my refutation of the rather basic error in this logic, cf. " A Pragmatic Approach to Parable Exegesis," *Journal of Biblical Literature,* p. 202.

14. It has often been pointed out that Matt. 22:11-13 is a different parable from Matt. 22:1-10. Since v. 14 refers to those " called " and there is no mention of a calling in vs. 11-13, then v. 14 would seem to refer back to the first parable in vs. 1-10 rather than vs. 11-13.

15. Jeremias, *The Parables of Jesus,* p. 67.

16. Vincent Taylor, *The Gospel According to St. Mark* (London: Macmillan & Co., Ltd., 1952), p. 124.

Chapter VI. AUDIENCE CONTINUITY: THEOLOGY

1. Joachim Jeremias, *Jesus' Promise to the Nations* (Alec R. Allenson, Inc., 1958), p. 73.

2. I shall use " hermeneutic " here in its narrower sense as the

theory of Biblical interpretation, recognizing, as Robinson and Cobb have recently pointed out (*op. cit.*), that the term more properly must be expanded to cover religious " understanding " in general. Any more complicated discussion of hermeneutics would cloud our presentation in this book.

3. For a similar view of *mikros* as a reference to the Twelve, cf. Günther Bornkamm *et al., Tradition and Interpretation in Matthew,* tr. by Percy Scott (The Westminster Press, 1963), p. 121. Werner G. Kümmel refers to the development of this thesis by O. Michel and Kittel's *Wörterbuch,* and then rejects the thesis (*Promise and Fulfillment: The Eschatological Message of Jesus,* p. 93; Allenson, 1957).

4. Only two logia deal exclusively with eschatology (log. 282, 342), and six stress both present and eschatological crises (log. 134, 136, 137, 232, 241, 300).

5. Some of these are addressed to the D, but their *message* is against the O.

Chapter VII. EXPLAINING THE PHENOMENA

1. Cf. Bultmann, *The History of the Synoptic Tradition,* pp. 52 ff., 343.

2. Wrede's influence still hangs heavily over Bultmann and the entire post-Bultmannian school. Cf. Hans Conzelmann, *The Theology of St. Luke,* tr. by Geoffrey Buswell (Harper & Brothers, 1960). Even James Robinson is unable to break out of this mold and takes the work of Wrede as axiomatic, *A New Quest of the Historical Jesus* (London: SCM Press, Ltd., 1959), pp. 35–36.

3. *Petros* occurs fifty times, of which forty-nine are E: 13 S7, 30 S1, 2 S2, 1 S4, 3 S3.

4. For other indications of verbal source characteristics, see Pierson Parker, *The Gospel Before Mark* (The University of Chicago Press, 1953), pp. 239 ff. His list is much more optimistic than mine for several reasons. He has a very loose definition of what is characteristic. He doesn't distinguish between what is characteristic of Q, M, and L. He doesn't distinguish between logia and narration words. We are talking at this point only about the logia.

5. Perhaps the most complete treatment of this approach is still that of W. L. Knox, *The Sources of the Synoptic Gospels* (London: Cambridge University Press, 1953), 2 vols. See also G. H. C. Mac-Gregor and Andrew Q. Morton, *The Structure of Luke and Acts* (Har-

206   NOTES

per & Row, Publishers, Inc., 1964).

6. Bultmann, *Die Geschichte der synoptischen Tradition*, p. 33.

7. Bultmann shows his refusal to separate the E and the A material when he insists that the needs of the church gave rise to both the words of Jesus and the history of him, and it is not a debatable matter as to which arrived earlier at a stable form (*The History of the Synoptic Tradition*, p. 11).

Chapter VIII. BREAKING THE *GESCHICHTE* BARRIER

1. Rudolf Bultmann, *Glauben und Verstehen*, Vol. 1, 2d ed. (1954), p. 20; *The History of the Synoptic Tradition*, p. 372.

2. Perhaps the strongest expression of this point of view in English is still John Knox, *Criticism and Faith* (Abingdon Press, 1952).

3. Carl E. Braaten, "Martin Kähler on the Historic Biblical Christ," *The Historical Jesus and the Kerygmatic Christ: Essays on the New Quest of the Historical Jesus,* ed. by Carl E. Braaten and Roy A. Harrisville (Abingdon Press, 1964). Cf. Ernst Fuchs, *Studies of the Historical Jesus* (Alec R. Allenson, 1964). See also Conzelmann, "The Method of the Life-of-Jesus Research," Braaten and Harrisville (eds.), *op. cit.*

4. It is also philosophically illegitimate as Brunner made quite clear in his insistence that revelation must be informed by reason. (*Revelation and Reason: The Christian Doctrine of Faith and Knowledge;* The Westminster Press, 1946.)

5. Donald Baillie, *God Was in Christ* (Charles Scribner's Sons, 1955), p. 26.

6. Cf. G. Ebeling, "Who shall forbid us to ask the question concerning the historic Jesus?" (*Zeitschrift für Theologie und Kirche,* p. 20; 1959). See also Neill, *op. cit.*, p. 271.

7. This is too common to need much documentation. Cf., for example, the conclusion to the essay by Van Harvey and Schubert Ogden, "How New Is the New Quest?" in Braaten and Harrisville (eds.), *op. cit.*, pp. 239–241. They point to the scant historical evidence for the life and teachings of Jesus and conclude, "There is ample reason for asking whether it is either possible or legitimate as Robinson would have us believe."

8. Conant, *Modern Science and Modern Man*, p. 86.

9. Ludwig Wittgenstein, *Tractatus Logico Philosophicus* (London: Routledge & Kegan Paul, Ltd., 1960).

10. A discovery made by the pre-Socratic Sophists, as by the Old Testament, as by Jesus and Paul and Augustine and Schleiermacher and Kant and the Logical Positivists.

11. Braaten and Harrisville (eds.), *op. cit.*, p. 205. What Harvey and Ogden say is, no doubt, true. But they omit one important quotation from the same book, *Jesus*, which they use to show Bultmann's attention to *Historie:* "We can sum up what can be known of the life and personality of Jesus as simply nothing" (p. 12). It is, no doubt, true that one can distinguish between the meaning of "person" and "personality" in Bultmann's thought, but one wonders if they are not straining too hard to defend Bultmann's inerrancy. It would seem truer to the man to allow him the luxury of a divided mind at this point (cf. pp. 159–160).

12. Rudolf Bultmann, *History and Eschatology* (Harper & Row, 1962), surprisingly not mentioned by Harvey and Ogden.

13. Bultmann, *Die Geschichte der synoptischen Tradition*, again, a book that Schubert Ogden seems to prefer to ignore in his many assessments of Bultmann.

14. Rudolf Bultmann, *Form Criticism: A New Method of New Testament Research*, ed. and tr. by Frederick Grant (Willett, Clark & Company, 1934), p. 61.

15. Witness the two conclusions of this otherwise brilliant article by Harvey and Ogden: "We have such scant historical evidence . . . we can't get at the inner life of a figure of history" (Braaten and Harrisville [eds.], (*op. cit.*, pp. 239–242).

16. Braaten and Harrisville (eds.), *op. cit.*

17. Günther Bornkamm as translated by Neill, *op. cit.*, p. 271.

18. Robinson, *op. cit.*, pp. 100, 104.

19. *Ibid.*, pp. 96, 122.

20. Ernst Fuchs shows his thorough dependence on Bultmann's existential philosophy of history when he redefines the quest in existential terms: "The quest of the historical Jesus is now essentially transformed into the quest of the reality of the encounter with God in preaching" (*op. cit.*, p. 31). Fuchs's impatience with *Historie* is evident in the ways in which he dismisses Synoptic material as "due to dogmatic considerations" that "reveal to us not more but less than Jesus' own conduct" (p. 21). The entire redactional emphasis of Conzelmann, Käsemann, Bartsch, and others in this tradition testifies to the fact that they have not really gone beyond the *kerygma*, beyond

the redactional interpretation of the early church, in their attempts to penetrate to the historical Jesus.

21. Cf. Neill, *op. cit.,* p. 283.

22. Bultmann consciously goes beyond Dibelius in using Form Criticism as a tool for making *sachkritischen* decisions: i.e.," *über Echtheit eines wortes, Geschichtlichkeit eines Berichtes und vgl"* (*Die Geschichte der synoptischen Tradition,* p. 6).

23. E. F. Scott, *The Validity of the Gospel Record* (London: Ivor Nicholson & Watson, Ltd., 1938), p. 2.

24. Martin Dibelius, *From Tradition to Gospel,* tr. by Bertram Lee Woolf (London: Ivor Nicholson & Watson, Ltd., 1934), p. 9.

25. For two of the most recent expressions of this argument, cf. Morton Smith, *Journal of Biblical Literature,* Vol. LXXXII (1963), p. 172. See also Frederick C. Grant, *The Gospels: Their Origin and Their Growth* (Harper & Brothers, 1957).

26. Emil Fascher, *The Form Historical Method* (1924); B. S. Easton, *The Gospel Before the Gospels* (1928); Taylor, *The Gospel According to St. Mark;* Scott, *op. cit.;* etc.

27. *Ab. R.N.,* Verse II, XXXIII, 36b; *Aboth* III, 18: *P.B.,* pp. 193–194, in C. G. Montefiore and H. Loewe, *A Rabbinic Anthology* (Meridian Books, 1963).

28. Vincent Taylor, *Formation of the Gospel Tradition* (The Macmillan Company, 1953), pp. 202–209.

29. Those parables which are shorter in Thomas are G.T. 57 (Matt. 13:24-30); G.T. 9 (Mark 4:3-9); G.T. 8 (Matt. 13:47-50); G.T. 65 (Mark 12:1-9); G.T. 63 (Luke 12:16-21); G.T. 107 (Matt. 18:12-14); G.T. 75 (Matt. 25:1-13); G.T. 98 (Luke 14:31-33); G.T. 110 (Mark 10:17-23). Those longer in Thomas are G.T. 109 (Matt. 13:44); G.T. 64 (Luke 14:16-24).

30. Cf. Stith Thompson (ed.), *Four Symposia on Folklore* (Indiana University, 1953), p. 314; C. W. von Sydow, *Selected Papers on Folklore* (Copenhagen: Rosenkilde and Bagger, 1948).

31. Cf. the Preface to Bultmann, *Die Geschichte der synoptischen Tradition.*

32. What is needed now is a description of the formation process that will permit such a result. This is beyond the scope of the present study but will form the substance of another volume.